# Fundamentals of
Physical Surveillance

Plate 1. Camouflage clothing and skin toning is effective for blending with vegetation. Study this illustration from a distance of 2 - 3 feet to get a better idea of how a subject would likely view the surveillant.

# Fundamentals of Physical Surveillance

## A GUIDE FOR UNIFORMED AND PLAINCLOTHES PERSONNEL

*By*

**RAYMOND P. SILJANDER, B.A.**

*Police Officer*
*Marshall, Minnesota*

*With a Foreword by*

**LIEUTENANT DRAKE POWERS**

*Police Department*
*Minneapolis, Minnesota*

CHARLES C THOMAS · PUBLISHER
Springfield · Illinois · U.S.A.

*Published and Distributed Throughout the World by*
CHARLES C THOMAS • PUBLISHER
Bannerstone House
301-327 East Lawrence Avenue, Springfield, Illinois, U.S.A.

This book is protected by copyright. No part of it may be reproduced in any manner without written permission from the publisher.

© *1977, by* CHARLES C THOMAS • PUBLISHER

ISBN 0-398-03660-8

Library of Congress Catalog Card Number: 77-2185

*With THOMAS BOOKS careful attention is given to all details of manufacturing and design. It is the Publisher's desire to present books that are satisfactory as to their physical qualities and artistic possibilities and appropriate for their particular use. THOMAS BOOKS will be true to those laws of quality that assure a good name and good will.*

**Library of Congress Cataloging in Publication Data**

Siljander, Raymond P.
   Fundamentals of physical surveillance.

   Includes index.
   1. Police patrol—Surveillance operations. I. Title.
HV8080.P2S57     363.2'32     77-2185
ISBN 0-398-03660-8

*Printed in the United States of America*
*C-1*

**TO THE MEMORY OF
LEO JOHNSON**

# Foreword

PUBLICATIONS ON PHYSICAL SURVEILLANCE, a subject so important to today's investigator, have in the past been inadequate in scope and have consisted largely of scattered articles appearing in the various peace officer's journals, each article dealing with only a limited phase of the topic.

Mr. Siljander has been able to produce a broad and accurate treatise on this topic; he is recognized as a capable and scholarly officer.

Mr. Siljander has presented surveillance photography instruction to personnel within the Minneapolis Police Department. The way his instruction was grasped indicates he can present his ideas well and that he knows his subject matter thoroughly.

Although indisputably basic, this book makes tremendously interesting and informative reading and will be a valuable asset to the experienced investigator and the judicial student as well.

LT. DRAKE POWERS

# Introduction

PHYSICAL SURVEILLANCE, in the context in which it is treated in this writing, is the direct visual observation of persons, vehicles, or activity taking place at some given location for the purpose of obtaining information regarding the identity and activities of persons. Furthermore, physical surveillance as it is treated herein deals with its surreptitious aspects. Hence, this book presents a discussion of the fundamentals and techniques of *the covert observation of persons, vehicles, and premises*. The investigator conducting the surveillance is often referred to as the *surveillant* while the person being surveilled is referred to as the *subject*.

Because of the complexity of physical surveillance operations, it must be emphasized that this book is intended to serve only as a *general guide* offering the *fundamentals* of this art. The reader, therefore, must understand that the techniques set forth herein will generally prove to be most successful if an attempt is made to use variations which are in keeping with ever changing conditions, rather than attempting to employ them exactly as presented. Flexibility is necessary because of the complexity and uncertainty of man's nature and because of the varying circumstances and topographical conditions under which physical surveillance is conducted.

With the exception of certain specialized areas of investigation, physical surveillance is most often used when other investigative methods have failed to produce the desired information. It is usually after an investigator has exhausted all reasonable efforts at questioning and interviewing people, examining records, and working with physical evidence that this investigative technique is employed. When all these avenues have been tried to no avail, the investigator will often seek to obtain the desired information by means of a physical surveillance. Physical surveillance, however, is not normally a complete or absolute means to an end, but simply *aids* one in achieving an end. In some exceptional cases an investigator may engage in this activity early in the investigation if it is apparent for some reason that conducting a surveillance will provide quick results. However, this is the exception, not the rule. Because physical surveillance is so often used as a last resort effort, one should view this art as a most important skill.

This book has been written and is intended to benefit the reader in a number of ways, the foremost of which is offering within one source a variety of information applicable to physical surveillance that was previously available only through a wide variety of sources. Additionally, some of the material provided in this book was formerly available only to law enforcement personnel attending specialized in-service schools offered by state and federal law enforcement agencies. Obviously, the opportunity for the majority of law enforcement personnel and civil investigators to attend such schools does not exist. It is hoped, therefore, that this book will fill the needs of law enforcement officers and investigators unable for various reasons to attend such schools.

While this book does not attempt to go into extreme depth in any one aspect of physical surveillance, each area is treated in a manner sufficient to provide the reader with the degree of knowledge necessary to make him comfortable with each area. For example, the section in which *bumper beepers* (electronic locating and tracking systems) are discussed does not endeavor to illustrate and discuss each model presently on the market with strict attention given to operational detail, but discusses such systems in general terms, their general methods of operation, and what one can realistically expect to be accomplished through their use.

The various types of physical surveillance will be discussed so that the reader will have an understanding of the merits of each and under what conditions the various techniques and methods are applicable. Stake-outs (fixed or stationary surveillance) will be discussed with attention being given to when and for what reason such investigative techniques are employed, and some of the more common vantage points that have proven to be effective. Attention is given to conducting stake-outs in both urban and rural settings. The use of pretexts is also discussed as a means to justify being in a given area for brief or extended periods of time. Pretexts are useful when one cannot, for any number of reasons, secure a position that conceals him from view and, therefore, must remain in the open while making his observations.

Of special interest to investigators having occasion to engage in surveillance activity are the many aids and extensions to one's vision that are illustrated and discussed in terms of what purpose each can be expected to serve. Such aids include telescopes, binoculars, infrared viewers, and electronic light intensifiers. Included also is a chapter that discusses and illustrates the use of various types of photographic equipment for surveillance applications.

In regard to moving surveillance, the reader is introduced to methods and techniques which lend themselves to both foot and vehicle surveillance, employing one or more operatives. Common pitfalls characteristic of inexperienced investigators are discussed, as well as a number of evasive tactics a subject may employ when he fears or suspects he is the subject of a surveillance. Possible counter measures for common evasive tactics are also discussed.

There are ways in which investigators can often reestablish a broken surveillance, or, in other words, relocate a subject once he has, by chance or by design, managed to elude the surveillant. For the most part, this is accomplished by knowing as much as possible about the subject and the area before the surveillance is begun. This consideration is discussed in sufficient depth so that the reader, when preparing for a moving surveillance, can take reasonable safeguards against such misfortunes. Nothing, however, is foolproof, and the best investigator will occasionally lose his subject.

A common misconception shared by people not employed in the investigative field is the belief that keeping a subject in sight while he goes about his daily activities is an easily accomplished task requiring little qualification on the part of the investigator. However, the contrary is true. To keep a subject under constant surveillance is one thing, but to keep him under surveillance without his becoming aware of the fact is quite another. Any experienced investigator will readily attest to the fact that conducting a physical surveillance of a moving subject for an extended period of time is at best a most difficult task requiring a high degree of perseverance, patience, and skill.

In any phase of investigative work, accurate and concise reporting is essential, with physical surveillance being no exception. There are a number of reporting methods employed by investigators, depending upon the type of investigation and for whom it is being conducted, but, regardless, it will be found that surveillance reports are almost always *time caption* reports.

Undercover investigation, often not thought of as being a form of surveillance, most assuredly is. Such an operation is often referred to as *undercover surveillance*. This type of an operation consists of an operative using a *pretext* to conceal his true purpose and to justify his being in a certain area, and establishing a rapport with a subject so that he may observe his actions directly.

The laws by which an investigator must abide when engaging in surveillance activity will be influenced to some degree by whether one is a civil or a criminal investigator and also to some degree upon the state within which he operates. Generally speaking, both must concern themselves with the laws as they address themselves to invasion of privacy, trespassing, and, in the case of undercover surveillance, entrapment. In addition, law enforcement investigators must abide by search and seizure laws.

The reader should be aware of the fact that there exists a distinct difference between physical surveillance and technical surveillance. The former refers to the following and/or observing of an individual, a vehicle, or a premises. The latter most commonly refers to electronic eavesdropping, often referred to as *bugging* and *wiretapping*. The laws that address themselves to each are quite different and to engage improperly in the former is not as serious an offense or violation as the latter would be. The reader will find that the federal laws pertaining to electronic eavesdropping are quite strict and the penalties severe should one be found to be in violation and subsequently convicted. Although, technically, photographic surveillance techniques fall into the technical surveillance classification, the eavesdropping laws do not curtail its use as they do equipment intended to intercept and/or record wire and oral communications. If photographic equipment is used while conducting a physical surveillance in a lawful manner, there will be no problem.

When considering the many reasons for conducting a physical surveillance, one should endeavor to first identify who has reason to engage in such activity and their objectives. Generally speaking, investigators engaging in such activity will be either law enforcement or civil. The latter includes quite a large group if one is to consider the number of governmental concerns that utilize investigators who possess no police powers, private investigators who market their service to those who have a legitimate and lawful need, and also the many investigators employed by industrial concerns, insurance companies, and law firms. When considering these factors, one begins to realize that there are many investigators whose efforts are geared towards the fulfillment of a wide range of needs, not only within the law enforcement field, but outside the realm of law enforcement as well.

Naturally, there are a variety of objectives for conducting a physical surveillance, but all the various reasons, in the final analysis, consistently lead back to one basic objective: the gathering of information. The type of information desired will, of course, depend entirely upon the specific circumstances and the needs in question. This fact exists whether the case is civil or criminal in nature. The following list is by no means all-inclusive, but it should prove to illuminate some typical objectives for conducting a physical surveillance of a person, a vehicle, or a premises.

1. To obtain information or develop leads.
2. To obtain evidence of a crime that has been committed or to observe a crime actually being committed.
3. To check the reliability of informants.
4. To check the loyalty of employees.
5. As preliminary to a raid for planning purposes.
6. To monitor the movements and activities of subversives.

7. To determine if a subject is frequenting a certain establishment or location.
8. To establish a subject's habits, such as his hangouts, associates, or place of employment.
9. To provide the basis for obtaining a search or arrest warrant.
10. To confirm a subject's whereabouts.
11. To put pressure on an individual to force him to alter his life style by changing meeting places, hangouts, and sometimes place of employment.
12. To curtail criminal activity.
13. To observe meetings and transactions.
14. To determine when and where an individual will be available for the serving of papers.
15. To determine an individual's availability for an interview, interrogation, or apprehension.
16. To obtain photographs. Useful in many cases such as sales of contraband or in fraudulent disability claims.
17. To establish and/or verify the identity of a subject and/or his associates or contacts.

Finally, because the investigator conducting a physical surveillance observes activity actually taking place, he often is in a position to testify in court as a witness.

R.P.S.

# Acknowledgments

IT WOULD BE PRESUMPTUOUS to assume that the authoring of a book of this nature would be possible without the generous cooperation and assistance of many people in a number of areas. The author would like to acknowledge and thank most sincerely the following people who have contributed so significantly towards this publication both by way of illustrative material and information. The author's heartfelt thanks and appreciation go out to:

Mr. Floyd Ragen, Minnesota Conservation Enforcement Officer; Mr. Ronald Smith, Minnesota Conservation Enforcement Officer; Mr. John D. Tierney, former Special Agent of The Federal Bureau of Investigation, Attorney; Mr. George Harrelson, Attorney at Law, Marshall, Minnesota; Mr. Merrill Hughes, Hennepin County Sheriff's Deputy; Sgt. Dennis Hefti, Lyon County Sheriff's Department; Officer Michael Schoephoerster, Officer, Anoka, Minnesota, former Detective of Marshall Police Department; Officer Gary Johnson, Marshall Police Department; Officer Thomas Thompson, Marshall Police Department; Officer Rich Neisen, Marshall Police Department; Marshall Reserve Officer Dave Van Den Broeke; Mr. Donald A. Rush, Branch Manager of the Phoenix Office of Pinkerton's, Inc.; Dr. Alvin N. Rusk, Chairman, Physics Program, Southwest State University; Mr. David W. Nelson, Manager, Driver Education Department, Automobile Club of Minneapolis; Mr. Wayne A. Ayers, Energy Conservation Consultants, Inc.; Officer Richard Johnson, Minneapolis Police Department's Bureau of Identification; Mr. Leonard O. Johnson, Marshall Public School System; Mr. John E. Warraniemi, former business associate and friend; my sister, Detta, for having typed the manuscript; and to the many companies and agencies who responded to various written requests for information, illustrations, and sample products.

R.P.S.

# Contents

|  | Page |
|---|---|
| *Foreword* | vii |
| *Introduction* | ix |
| *Acknowledgments* | xv |

*Chapter*

1. PERSONAL AND PHYSICAL QUALIFICATIONS OF A SURVEILLANT . . . 3
2. PREPARING FOR A PHYSICAL SURVEILLANCE (URBAN) . . . 9
3. FOOT SURVEILLANCE . . . 15
4. AUTOMOBILE SURVEILLANCE . . . 31
5. STATIONARY SURVEILLANCE (URBAN) . . . 76
6. PHYSICAL SURVEILLANCE BY UNIFORMED OFFICERS USING MARKED SQUAD CARS . . . 83
7. SURVEILLANCE IN RURAL AREAS . . . 93
8. UNDERCOVER SURVEILLANCE . . . 121
9. FACTS ABOUT VISION . . . 129
10. OPTICAL AND RELATED AIDS FOR VISION EXTENSION . . . 136
11. SURVEILLANCE PHOTOGRAPHY . . . 181
12. REPORT WRITING . . . 223
13. LEGAL ASPECTS OF SURVEILLANCE . . . 229

*Index* . . . 265

# Fundamentals of
Physical Surveillance

## CHAPTER 1

# Personal and Physical Qualifications of a Surveillant

### GENERAL CONSIDERATIONS

THERE IS NO ONE KIND of individual who is the *ideal* person for conducting a physical surveillance inasmuch as each investigator will generally possesss certain characteristics that are desirable. It has been found, however, that there are certain qualities, some physical and some personal, that are most favorable for work of this nature. It should be borne in mind that no one person will possess all of the qualities listed but will most likely possess certain ones to varying degrees.

It would be impossible, and also undesirable, to attempt to list these desirable qualities in the order of their importance because the importance of any particular quality in relation to another is relative to the specific needs and circumstances of each case. In one case a certain set of qualities will prove to be more desirable than in another.

Although the various qualities have been broken down and labeled, it will become evident to the reader that there is a considerable degree of overlap among them. For example, how can a person display a high degree of *adaptability* and not be a *resourceful* individual? Thus, although these two qualities have been labeled as two different qualities, they do overlap considerably. Another thing the reader will most likely notice is that the physical and the personal qualities that make a good surveillant are for the most part the same qualities that make a person a good police officer or investigator. This fact holds true especially for personal qualities.

### PERSONAL QUALITIES
#### Competent Police Officer or Investigator

Because the surveillant is engaged in activity that is intended to produce information for a matter that is under investigation, a matter that may very well at some point go to court, the surveillance operation must be conducted in a manner that will not render any information obtained inadmissable as evidence. The surveillant must be knowledgeable of the various laws governing his activities, such as trespass laws, invasion of privacy laws, search and seizure laws, and in the case of undercover investigations, laws regarding entrapment.

## Attitude

An important consideration that has a direct influence on one's suitability for work of this nature is his attitude. It can be presumed that if one is a competent police officer or investigator, he has formed healthy attitudes about himself and his work. It is important that the individual strive to perform his assigned tasks in an efficient and professional manner with a willingness to contribute that little extra time and effort to ensure that a job is done correctly.

## Powers of Observation

A person's powers of observation can be trained by constant practice, by making every effort to be alert to those things that go on around him and by paying attention to detail. For example, one should not just see a person, but should take note of that person's general description, what, if anything, is being carried, its significance, and the significance of his being in the area. If a person makes it a habit to make a mental note of such things, he will develop keen powers of observation in a relatively short period of time and will find that he will begin noticing such details without making a conscious effort. He will find that it will come naturally after a short period of time.

## Memory

When a person makes a point of being alert to detail and events occurring around him, a good memory for what has been observed will quickly be developed. A good memory, which can be improved by constant exercise and practice, is essential for the surveillant because, although he can at times record observations in the form of notes, it is often necessary to rely heavily on one's memory for a period of time before the opportunity to write presents itself. This is especially true when conducting an undercover surveillance.

## Patience and Perseverance

It was stated earlier that it would be impossible to list the various qualities desirable for a surveillant in the order of their priority because each case will have different needs and will make different demands on the investigator. However, one must regard patience and perseverance as being among the most essential qualifications in anyone who will attempt to conduct a physical surveillance of any type. This is especially true in situations calling for a fixed (stationary) surveillance, which often results in long hours of just waiting for something to occur. This quality is essential if one's attention is to remain sharp even after long hours of waiting and watching.

## Resourcefulness and Adaptability

The investigator assigned to a surveillance operation should possess a reasonable amount of resourcefulness and adaptability so that he can effectively blend with the environment, both in appearance and conduct. If he is able to do this, others in the area will most likely not become either suspicious or curious about him. In this respect, a role-playing type of ability is a great asset. The investigator when engaging in physical surveillance activity will find that he will surveil a wide variety of personality types under ever-changing circumstances and conditions. It is for this reason that this quality is so desirable. A surveillant must be able to *think on his feet,* so to speak, so that he can react quickly and decisively to situations as they arise. It must be remembered also that it is not possible to anticipate fully what will occur, either by way of chance happenings or by deliberate actions on the part of the subject, and for this reason, the investigator must be quick thinking and resourceful. When a situation does arise, and it will from time to time, if the investigator is unable for some reason to react in an appropriate manner without unnecessary time delay, his percentage of success will suffer significantly.

### Self-Confidence

The surveillant must have the necessary self-confidence to react quickly and decisively to ever-changing conditions. By and large, however, it will be found that confidence will come as a result of competence, and herein lies the importance of constant study and practice on the part of the investigator. All persons engaged in the law enforcement and investigative fields would be well advised to engage in frequent outside reading, attend seminars, and associate with others in the same field as a great deal is to be learned by their experiences. One should also practice surveillance techniques frequently even if it means selecting someone arbitrarily and following him.

### Good Judgment

The investigator who utilizes good judgment when engaged in a surveillance will naturally experience a much better percentage of success than one who does not. Being able to make appropriate decisions while in the field will depend to a large degree upon the extent of the surveillant's knowledge of surveillance techniques and the quality of his judgment in appraising a situation and selecting a technique that is most appropriate under the circumstances.

### Report Writing

It has been said that an investigator is only as good as his ability to prepare concise reports that bear the facts pertaining to a case. Unfortunately, it has been found that many otherwise good police officers and investigators working both in the criminal and civil fields experience a considerable degree of difficulty with this most important task. If one does have difficulty in this area, he should seek to improve himself.

### Verbal Communication

The investigator will often be required to testify orally on the witness stand. It is therefore important that he be capable of expressing himself verbally so that he can relate his observations in a manner that is easily understood by others.

## PHYSICAL QUALITIES

### Average Size

The investigator should be within an acceptable range insofar as height and weight are concerned so that he does not become distinctly noticeable. In this same respect, it is important that the investigator not only be within reasonable limits of size, but be of normal proportion as well. An unusually small, large, or strangely proportioned individual will be quickly noticed by other people.

### Good Physical Condition

The investigator must be in good physical condition, for it can happen that he will be called upon to follow a person who is in good shape, a brisk walker, and one who favors stairs over elevators. It can be presumed in this case that the investigator who is in good physical condition will also possess the necessary *endurance* and *coordination* to operate effectively.

### Good Eyesight

Physical surveillance activity involves making *visual* observations, and it is therefore important that the investigator have good eyesight. It is desirable for the investigator to have periodic eye examinations to ensure that his vision is properly corrected (if corrective lenses are needed) so that his eyes are serving him at their maximum efficiency. It is also desirable for the investigator to possess good night vision. It has been found that a diet deficient in vitamin A can cause night blindness. Conversely, a proper diet with an adequate amount of vitamin A will ensure that one's eyes will operate at their full potential under low light conditions.

### Good Hearing

Good hearing is important because the surveillant will sometimes have the opportunity to move in close enough to a subject to overhear what is being said between himself and another person. Consider a restaurant or barroom setting, for example.

### Driving Skill

This skill could appropriately be placed under either *personal* or *physical* qualities inasmuch as skillful driving requires good perception, judgment, self-confidence, good reflexes, good eyesight, and coordination. It is also essential that the driver has had a great deal of driving experience and knows the handling characteristics of the particular vehicle he is driving.

CHAPTER 2

# Preparing for a Physical Surveillance (Urban)

## GENERAL CONSIDERATIONS

As PREVIOUSLY STATED, when an investigator reaches a point in his investigation where nothing more is to be learned through normal investigative methods such as interviewing and interrogating people, checking records and working with physical evidence, it is time to consider the feasibility of obtaining the desired information by conducting a physical surveillance. By so doing, the investigator will attempt to observe directly for himself that which he desires to learn. This may consist of attempting to obtain evidence pertaining to a specific offense, or in some cases, attempting to observe a crime or offense actually being committed. Whatever the case may be, however, the ultimate objective of any physical surveillance operation is that of obtaining information and/or evidence.

The success of any physical surveillance operation will depend largely upon the thoroughness and care with which the preplanning has been conducted. This fact exists whether the case is civil or criminal in nature, whether the circumstances call for a moving surveillance, to be conducted either on foot or by vehicle, or a stationary surveillance (stake-out).

When preparing for a physical surveillance, the investigator must consider the specific needs of the investigation and the circumstances under which the actual surveillance will be conducted. Does the situation address itself to a *loose tail* because of a need to simply develop information of a general nature concerning a subject's habits, associates, and life style in general or does the situation call for what is referred to as a *close tail* because of the sensitive nature of the case and a need to observe the subject's actions at all times? Such factors must be considered if the operation is to be conducted in a manner that will ensure a satisfactory conclusion of the case. To employ one method under circumstances that call for another will result either in an unsuccessful surveillance or in an unnecessary expenditure in both time and monetary expense. The extent of the preplanning, the number of investigators that will be assigned to a case, and the technical equipment employed must all be in keeping with the needs and seriousness of the particular matter in question.

When preparing for a moving surveillance, it is important that the investigator carry a sufficient supply of cash, including ample small change, so that he can conveniently follow wherever the subject may choose to go. It must also be considered whether the investigator will most likely conclude the surveillance by simply writing a report or by making an apprehension, and then be prepared accordingly.

## THE PRELIMINARY SURVEY

During the preplanning stage of any surveillance operation, whether the surveillance will be moving or stationary, it is highly advisable that one make a *preliminary survey* of the area in which the subject will be observed or first sighted. If, for example, moving surveillance will begin when a subject leaves his home in the morning, it is recommended that the investigator conduct a preliminary survey of the subject's neighborhood so that he can make a good vantage point selection: the point from which he will watch and wait for the subject to appear. If the surveillance is to be stationary rather than moving, and will perhaps be conducted over an extended period of time, the care with which the preliminary survey is conducted and a vantage point selected becomes increasingly important.

A preliminary survey will also enable the investigator to select a vehicle, if one is needed, and a mode of dress that will be consistent with the area. In the case of a moving surveillance, it is naturally recommended that a survey be made of the area in which the surveillance is to begin, but it is also desirable to conduct a survey of the area to which the subject will be going, if there is any indication. However, in many cases there will not be.

After conducting a preliminary survey, one will be in a better position to decide what, if any, equipment will be needed, such as binoculars, telescopes, night viewing devices, or cameras.

The importance of the preliminary survey cannot be overemphasized. In fact, one private investigative firm sees it as being so important that it is not uncommon for two investigators to make a preliminary survey, independent of each other, on all of their more sensitive cases. The findings of the two are then examined and used for planning purposes.

When making the preliminary survey, one should accomplish it in a manner that does not serve to alert the subject nor arouse curiosity on the part of others in the area. One should not make repeated trips through the area in a car. If more than one pass is necessary, a switch of vehicles should be made. Note also that a man and a woman in a car will arouse less suspicion than will two men.

## When to Conduct the Surveillance

When preparing for a physical surveillance, one should endeavor to determine when the most appropriate time will be for such activity. If, for example, it is desired to learn where an individual banks, one might establish first where that individual works, what shift he works, when he gets paid, and then follow him when he leaves work after being paid. If the individual gets paid on a Friday, it would seem reasonable that he might stop at the bank on his way home from work, which would, therefore, be a reasonable time to conduct the surveillance. One could, as an alternative, simply begin following the subject at any arbitrarily selected time and, at some point, it would probably be learned where he banks, but the result in most instances would be an unnecessarily high expenditure in both time and cost, and there would be an increased possibility of detection by the subject. In any case, the longer someone is surveilled, the greater will be the possibility of his becoming aware of the fact. Therefore, the two most notable reasons for efficient planning are a decreased chance of detection by the subject and a lower time-cost factor.

Using another example, if it is desired to learn what a person's normal daily activity consists of, it would not be reasonable to begin watching his residence at midnight, but it would be reasonable to watch for him to leave his home in the early morning, perhaps beginning the surveillance at about 5:00 AM.

Basically, one should determine exactly what information is needed, and then attempt to engage in surveillance activity during the times most likely to produce the desired results. To do so can prevent wasting time observing a subject during times when it is highly doubtful that the desired information would be obtained. To do this effectively will in many instances require developing some background information on a subject; however, the time devoted to developing such information will usually be time well spent.

**Subject Identification and Background Information**

Perhaps the most important consideration to be made when planning for a physical surveillance is the identity of the subject. It has happened on occasion that an investigator has begun following the wrong individual, or he has started out following the right individual but has at some point lost the real subject and ended up following someone that closely resembled him. The investigator, when possible, should endeavor to have both a photograph and a complete description of the subject before starting out on such an assignment, and, in cases where it can be arranged, it is desirable to have someone that knows the subject point him out to the investigator. If the subject has any special peculiarity that serves to make him distinguishable, especially when viewing him from the rear, it should be brought to light. The reason that peculiarities noticeable from the rear are important is because that is the angle from which the subject will most often be viewed by the surveillant. Furthermore, one should get into the habit of observing the person, not the clothing, because he may change somewhere along the way. However, changing clothes will not change a person's posture or way of walking, height, or weight. The surveillant must be alert to these things.

In addition to a complete description of the subject, the investigator should know as much as possible about the subject such as his habits, life style, friends, family, and employment. Having such information will enable the investigator to better interpret the significance of things the subject may do, and it may enable him to reestablish contact with the subject in the event he manages to elude the investigator, either by design or by chance. The following is a list of information the investigator should obtain regarding a subject before attempting to follow him. This list is presented here only as a general guide to furnish the reader with ideas, because each case is unique in itself and the information needed will vary depending upon the subject and the nature of the case. Nonetheless, this listing is broad enough in nature that it will serve reasonably well for most situations.

1. Subject's full name.
2. Any nicknames.
3. Correct address of residence.
4. Telephone number (home and work with extension number if any).
5. By whom employed and his capacity.
6. Address of subject's place of employment.
7. Days and hours the subject works.
8. How the subject goes to work: private vehicle, taxi, bus, car pool, etc.
9. Registration number of all cars owned and driven by the subject.
10. Make, model, year, and any peculiarities of vehicles the subject owns or drives.
11. Where the subject generally parks when at work.
12. Manner in which subject drives (cautious or reckless).
13. Particular service station patronized by the subject.
14. Listing of relatives, friends, and associates; their names and addresses.
15. Information about relatives and friends. Type of business in which each is engaged, hobbies, address, etc.
16. The subject's social and/or lodge affiliations, if any.
17. Form of recreation engaged in by the subject.
18. Does subject drink? If so, where and to what extent?
19. What form of tobacco he uses, if any.
20. Complete physical description (age, height, weight, color of hair, color of eyes, complexion, any peculiar marks,

peculiar habits, mode of dress, jewelry, manner or speech, condition of health).
21. Name and location of doctor.
22. Name and location of dentist.
23. Name and location of bank.
24. Name and location of barber.
25. Name of any clubs in which he holds membership.
26. Does he gamble? If so, how and to what extent?
27. Does he make friends easily?
28. Is he easily engaged in conversation?
29. Is he easily persuaded to make contributions to worthy causes?
30. Is he easily persuaded to buy from a strange salesman?
31. Is he easily excited?
32. Is he prone to assaultive behavior?
33. Has anything been done that would lead the subject to suspect that someone may be interested in him or his activities?

The investigator in possession of the answers to these questions will obviously be at a decided advantage when surveilling a subject. Should the subject, for example, stop at a private dwelling, it is to the investigator's advantage to know who resides there and the relationship of that person to the subject. If the subject is lost from view at some point during the surveillance, the investigator has a better chance of reestablishing contact with the subject by examining the list and anticipating his possible destination. The point is simply that the more the investigator knows about a subject and his habits, the easier it will be to follow him successfully. Similarly, if the subject is one who tends to be highly excitable and prone to assaultive behavior, the investigator should be aware of that fact so that he can take appropriate precautions.

In civil cases, the person requesting the surveillance will very often have access to most of the necessary information concerning the subject. Should the person requesting the investigation not possess such information, or if the case is criminal in nature, it will generally be necessary for the investigator to engage in some field work to develop it for himself.

# CHAPTER 3

# Foot Surveillance

## GENERAL CONSIDERATIONS

AN INVESTIGATOR will endeavor to follow a subject on foot when the subject himself travels on foot. When conducting a foot surveillance, one must anticipate the possibility of the subject's using some form of public transportation, such as taxi cabs, buses, street cars, and trains. This form of surveillance can be conducted employing one or more investigators; however, the effectiveness of the operation will be significantly increased when using two or more investigators.

Before engaging in a foot surveillance, as is the case with any form of moving surveillance, the investigator should have a sufficient supply of expense money in his possession so that he can readily go where the subject goes. Should the subject board a bus, for example, it is to the investigator's advantage, and in the best interests of the case, if he has had the foresight to obtain a quantity of small change. Should the subject purchase a bus ticket to another town and it is deemed desirable for the investigator to follow suit, he will need fare money and perhaps money also for meals and lodging.

The two principal risks faced by an investigator when conducting a foot surveillance are those of being discovered by the subject or losing sight of him. The better the investigator knows the subject and his habits and the area in which the surveillance is to be conducted, the less chance there will be of either of these two possibilities becoming a fact. When an investigator is familiar with a subject, his general activities, and the area, he will stand a better chance of reestablishing contact should he lose the subject. The reader may wish to refer back to Chapter 2 and review the list of pertinent information which it is desirable to possess.

Because the investigator will generally be observing the subject from behind, it is desirable that he be familiar with those characteristics that will enable him to distinguish the subject from other people in the area while viewing him from the rear. It happens on occasion that an investigator will start out following the right individual only to have a switch made somewhere along the line and end up following a different person.

**GENERAL TECHNIQUES**

When conducting a foot surveillance, the most appropriate distance to be maintained between the subject and the investigator will be influenced largely by the area in which the surveillance is being conducted, the amount of pedestrian traffic in the area, and the sensitivity of the case. If in a very crowded downtown area, the investigator would naturally remain much closer to the subject to prevent losing sight of him than he would if in a quiet residential district. Similarly, in a crowded setting, the investigator would have a smaller chance of being discovered by the subject even though remaining fairly close to him. This would not hold true, however, in a quiet area relatively free of pedestrian traffic. The proper distance to be maintained, therefore, is dependent upon the conditions and can range from as little as five to ten feet to one-half a city block or more. This is something that a new investigator will pick up rather quickly as it involves little more than good judgment and practice. Logically, then, the investigator must remain close enough to the subject to see what he is doing and to avoid losing him, yet remain far enough from him so that he is not detected.

While following a subject along a city sidewalk, if the subject turns a corner, the investigator must attempt to get to the corner as quickly as possible to avoid losing contact with him should the subject enter a building immediately upon making the turn. However, the investigator must avoid rushing to the corner in a manner that would attract unwanted attention to himself and possibly alert the subject to the surveillance. Should the investigator discover upon turning the corner that the subject has stopped and the two are now face to face, the investigator should casually continue along his way as if nothing were wrong and attempt to discreetly reestablish his position behind the subject when conditions permit. In so doing, the investigator should take advantage of any cover that may be present. In the absence of adequate cover, the investigator should take advantage of distance.

When a subject turns and looks at the investigator, he should not look away, thus making it apparent that he is consciously avoiding eye contact with him. However, the investigator should not look the subject directly in the eye, for such an act will ensure that the subject will remember him. Under such circumstances, the investigator should regard the subject in the same unconcerned manner in which people normally view others on a busy street. Never should the investigator resort to slinking mannerisms, darting in and out of doorways, peeking out while crouched behind parked vehicles and the like. To do so will ensure unsuccessful results.

When one is following a subject, it is both unnecessary and undesirable to look directly at him constantly. It is much more desirable to watch a person by looking in his general vicinity and by taking advantage of such things as reflections in store windows.

Should the subject enter a building at some point, the type of building and the nature of the case will dictate whether the investigator should follow him inside or wait outside for the subject to reappear. If the building in question is a busy department store, the investigator would, under normal circumstances, follow the subject inside and probably remain fairly close to him. If, however, the building is a barber shop, for example, the investigator would perhaps do better to wait until the subject returns to the street and resume the surveillance at that time. In the event that the subject enters a hotel, the investigator should follow him in at a reasonably close distance to avoid losing him inside. Should the subject go to the desk to secure or reserve a room, or perhaps to inquire as to the room number of another person, the investigator should get in line behind him and attempt to overhear what is said. Should the subject be nowhere in sight when the investigator follows him into a hotel and reaches the lobby, a check of the men's room should be made because the subject may have gone directly there.

In the event that the subject enters a bar or night club, it is again important that the investigator enter reasonably close behind him because it will often be difficult to locate him once he has had an opportunity to become seated. This possibility arises because of a number of factors. The subject may remove a hat and coat and consequently appear different. He may sit at a table or booth with several other people, or the establishment may be crowded and the light level fairly low. Exactly where the investigator should position himself relative to the subject is something that must be decided upon at the time because of the specific circumstances involved. In any event, the investigator making this decision must guard against hesitating in a manner that could arouse suspicion or curiosity on the part of the subject or others in the area. In some instances, it may be advantageous for the first investigator, who has entered the bar initially, to appraise the situation and leave, allowing a second investigator, benefiting from what has been learned by the first investigator, to enter the bar and go without hesitation to wherever it has been decided is the best position from which to observe the subject. Although specific circumstances will make each situation different, there are a couple of things that one should bear in mind when following a subject into a bar. If there is a television set which is on, a seating position should be selected that is as far from it as possible. It is also desirable in the majority of cases to attempt to place one's self as far to the rear of the bar as practical, in that such a position generally offers a good area of observation. If the subject enters a building and the investigator follows him inside, the other investigators, if more than one has been assigned to the case, should position themselves so that they can observe the exits. By positioning themselves at the corners of the building, two men can watch all four sides.

In the event that the subject enters a movie theatre, an effort should be made to get in line behind him so that he won't be lost once inside. A seat fairly close behind him should be selected. It should not be assumed, because a subject enters such an establishment alone, that he will remain so once inside or when leaving.

When a subject boards a bus, street car, or some similar public transportation facility, the investigator should get on fairly close behind him and select a seat a short distance behind him. If the subject takes a back seat, the investigator will naturally have no alternative but to sit across from or in front of him. If the subject sits on a seat that is positioned lengthwise, an effort should be made to secure a position on the same side of the vehicle and a few seats away from him.

The investigator, when conducting a foot surveillance, should have some idea in mind as to what he will use for an excuse or justification for being in the area should the subject become suspicious and accuse him of following. The best reaction in some cases is to act indignant at the suggestion that he would be following anyone. In other instances, a well prepared cover story supported by fictitious credentials will be the best solution. Again, this will depend upon the circumstances of the case in question as they will all be different.

## MULTIPLE MAN SURVEILLANCE TEAMS

When the seriousness of a situation justifies the use of more than one investigator to conduct a foot surveillance of a subject, a technique often referred to as the A-B-C method or appropriate variations of this technique may be put to good use. By using a multiple man surveillance technique, the chances of a successful operation are increased many times over those possible were the same task being attempted using one lone investigator. This is a result of being able to frequently rotate the position of the investigators in relation to the subject, and because the subject is flanked he can be observed even after turning a corner.

The A-B-C method, often referred to as the *three man shadow*, is not a difficult technique to master inasmuch as it simply takes a bit of practice so that the investigators understand how it is intended to work and become accustomed to working with each other so that their moves are smoothly coordinated. It is very important that the investigators get together to discuss and practice their strategies before attempting the actual surveillance if successful results are to be realized.

When employing the A-B-C method (see Figure 1), the lead man (A) follows the subject (S). The second investigator (B) follows "A" while the third investigator (C) walks abreast of either the subject or, less commonly, the lead man. When approaching a corner at an intersection, the investigator occupying position C should increase his pace so that he can reach the corner just ahead of the subject who is across the street from him. Upon reaching the corner, the investigator can either pause or cross the street, and then proceed straight ahead if the subject continues straight ahead, or if the subject turns, he can turn in the same direction, thus being able to keep the subject in view for the investigator occupying position A, who may have lost visual contact with the subject depending upon which way he has turned. Should the subject stop or enter a building after turning the corner, this information can be passed on to the others by using previously arranged signals.

When using the A-B-C method, the investigators can smoothly rotate their positions each time the subject turns a corner, regardless of whether he stops before turning. Figures 2 through 5 show examples of possibilities for rotating when the subject turns a corner. When it is felt that the investigator in position "A" has been in that position long enough, the investigator in position "B" can switch positions with him by increasing his pace while "A" drops back or steps into a building.

When there is little or no pedestrian traffic in the area, it may be desirable to have man "A" precede the subject as shown in Figure 6. If the amount of traffic is unusually heavy, it may be better to have all the investigators on the same side of the street with man "A" quite close to the subject so that he can be adequately observed at all times and also so that he is not lost. Rotations under these conditions should be very frequent.

When engaged in the A-B-C method of surveillance, the man occupying position "B" should be alert for a *convoy*, which is an associate of the subject who follows him for the purpose of detecting the presence of a surveillance. In the event that a convoy is detected, the focal point of the surveillance should be switched from the subject to the convoy as he will follow fairly close behind the subject wherever he goes.

When a subject walks very slowly, stopping frequently to talk with people, to look into store windows and so forth, it may again be desirable to alter the positioning of the investigators in relation to the subject so that position "A" is in front of the sub-

# Foot Surveillance

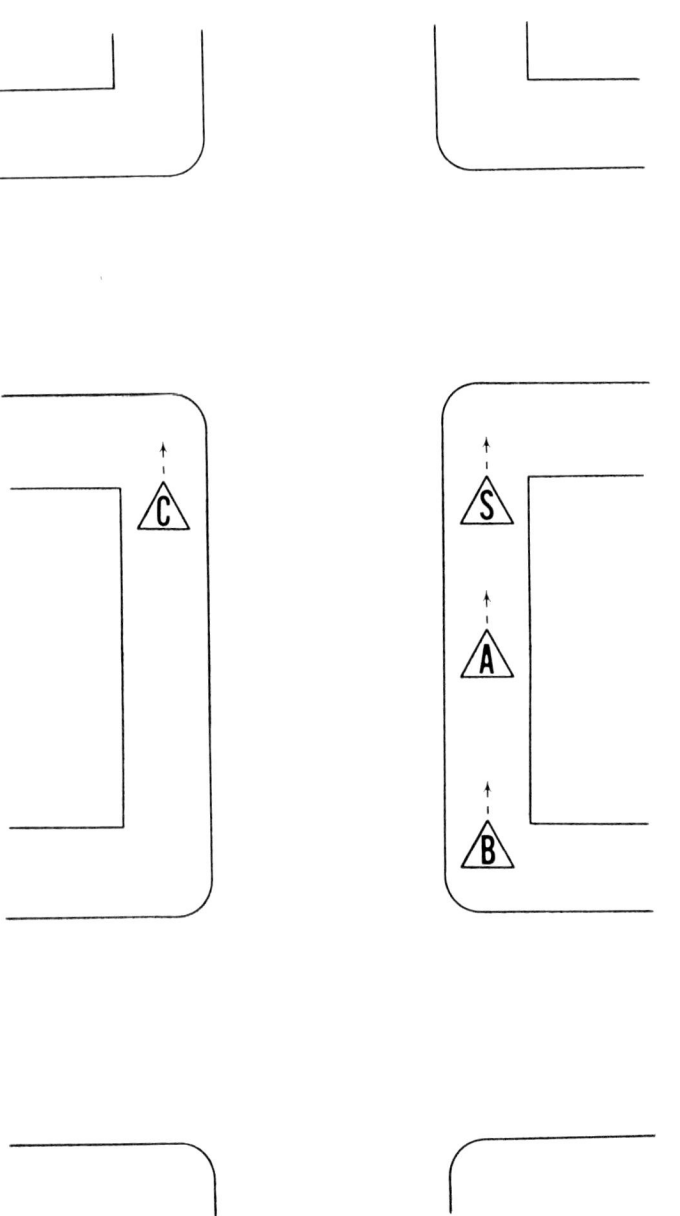

Figure 1. A typical multiple man foot surveillance technique involves having one investigator (A) follow the subject (S) while a second investigator (B) follows the first investigator (A). A third investigator (C) walks abreast of the subject.

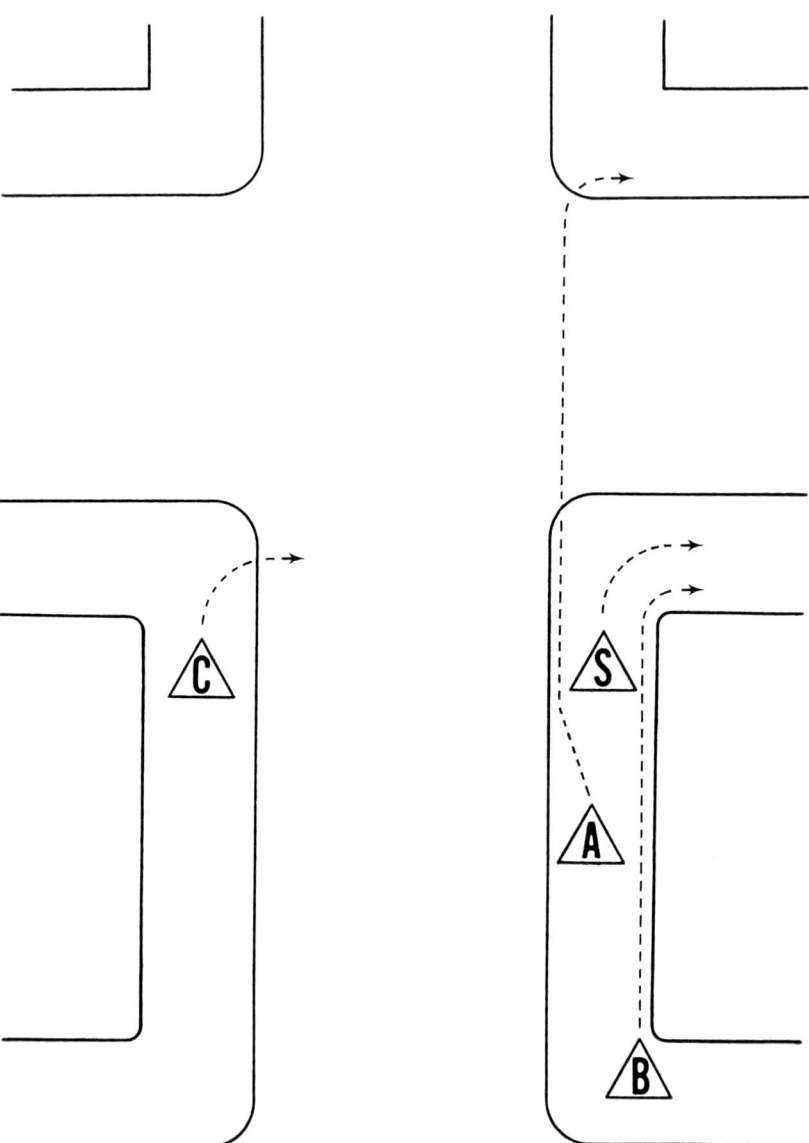

Figure 2. In the event that the subject turns right, man "A" can cross the intersection, thus assuming the "C" position. Man "B" turns the corner and assumes the "A" position. Man "C" assumes the "B" position.

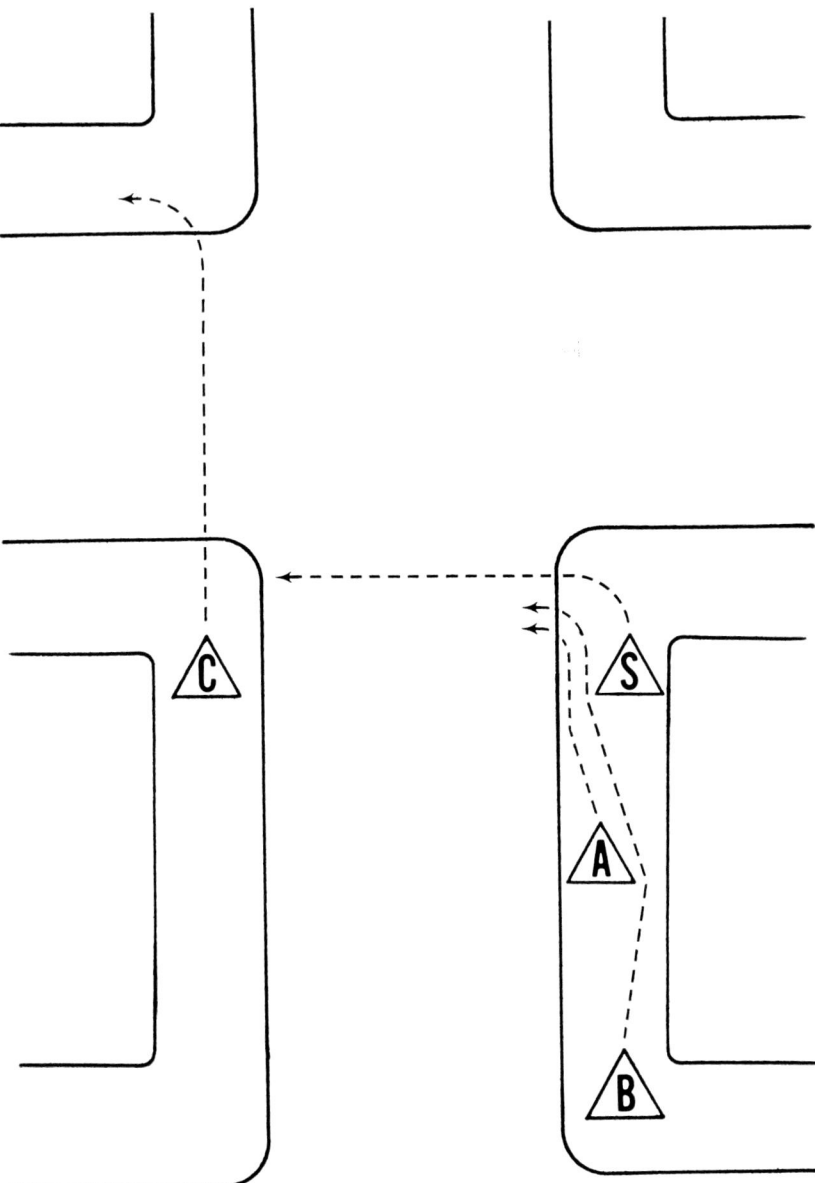

Figure 3. Subject turns left before crossing the intersection. Man "A" follows the subject while Man "B" follows "A." Man "C" crosses and turns left. All have maintained their original position except that Man "C" is now on the opposite side of the subject.

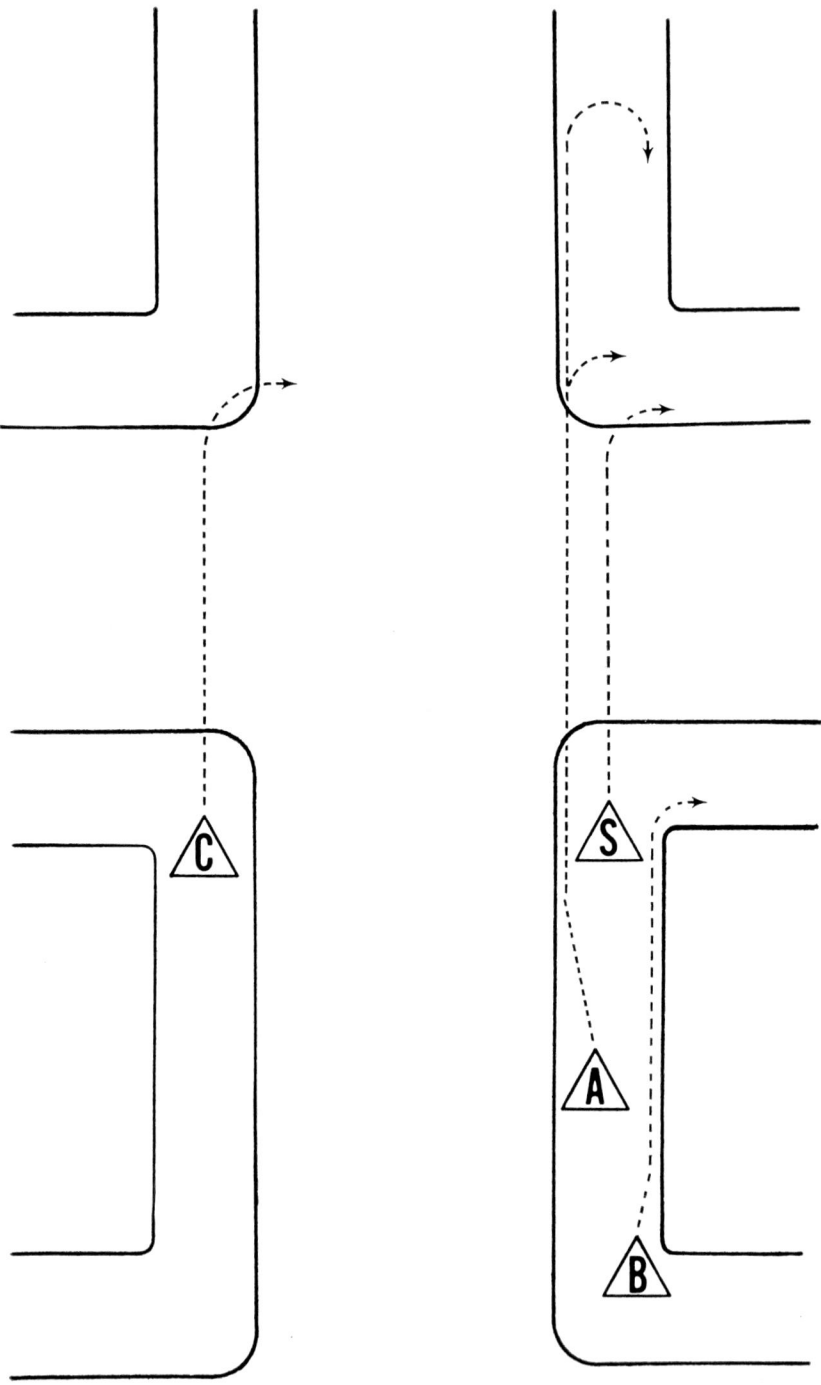

Figure 4. Subject crosses the intersection and then turns right. Man "A" crosses and either turns right thus maintaining the "A" position, or goes straight, only to double back and assume the "B" position after Man "C" has taken the lead position. Man "B" turns before crossing thus assuming the "C" position.

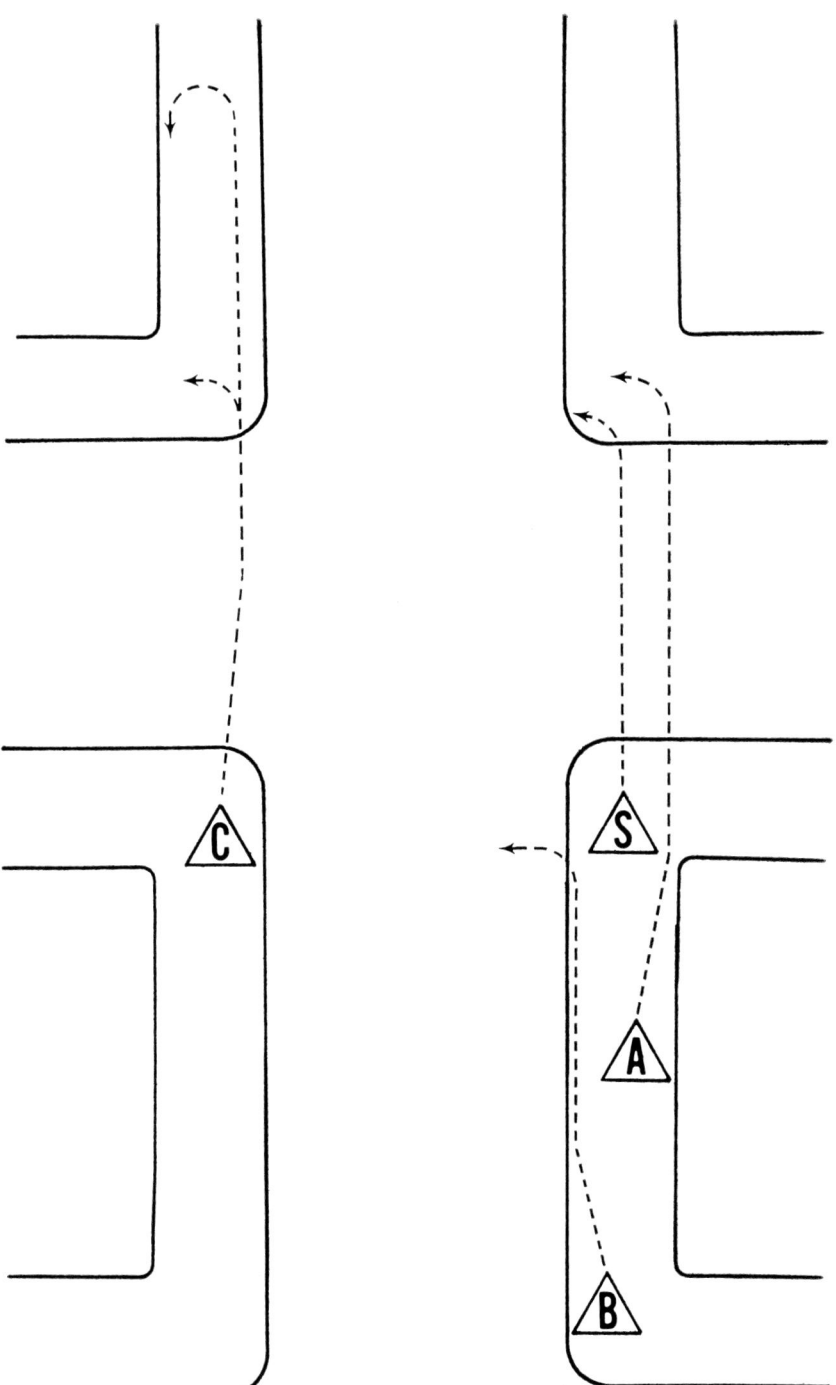

Figure 5. Subject crosses the intersection and turns left. Man "A" follows. Man "B" turns before crossing, thus assuming the "C" position. Man "C" crosses the intersection and either turns left, thus assuming the "A" position, or goes straight, only to double back to assume the "B" position.

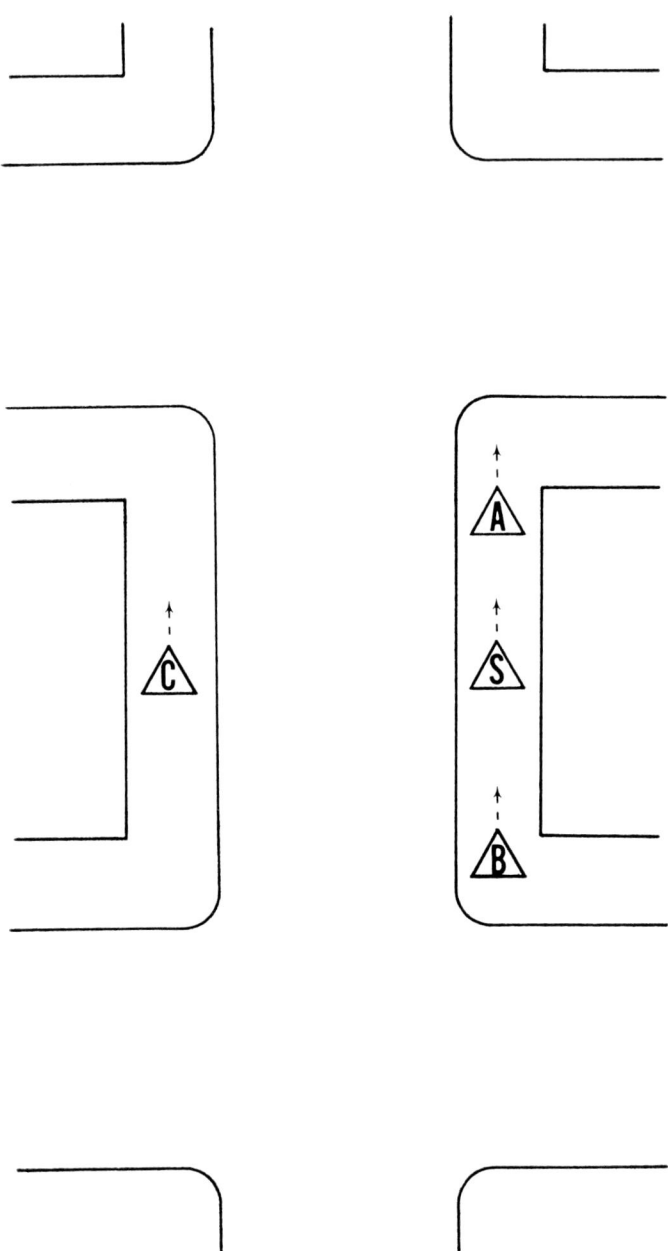

Figure 6. A simple variation of the standard multiple man technique involves having Man "A" precede the subject. This variation is sometimes useful if there is limited pedestrian traffic.

ject as illustrated in Figure 6. In the event that the subject enters a building, it may be desirable for one investigator to follow him inside with the others taking up positions at various exits. In some instances, it will be desirable for all investigators to take up positions on the exits with no one going inside.

## COMMON TACTICS FOR DETECTION AND EVASION

When a subject suspects or fears that he may be under surveillance, there are a number of ways in which he may respond in an effort to detect and/or lose anyone who may be following him. Some of the more common evasive tactics which investigators should be aware of are discussed with hopes that they will make the inexperienced investigator a bit better prepared to handle such situations as they arise. It must be stressed, however, that these are only ideas. One cannot expect that all subjects will react in such a fashion. In some instances, the subject's reaction may be a variation of the things that are discussed here and the investigator must be capable of reacting accordingly.

### Detecting a Surveillant

1. SUBJECT: Stop after turning a corner and study the reaction of the other people as they reach the corner. SURVEILLANT: Proceed on past the subject as though nothing were wrong.

2. SUBJECT: Board a public conveyance such as a bus, wait until it is about to start, then jump off to see if anyone else does likewise. SURVEILLANT: Ride the vehicle to the next stop, get off and wait to board the next bus. If the subject did wish to travel in that direction, he may be on the next bus.

3. SUBJECT: Casually look around. SURVEILLANT: Act in a normal manner, appearing to be just another person on the street going about his own business without any apparent interest in anyone else.

4. SUBJECT: Enter a building and immediately leave by another exit. SURVEILLANT: If not following the subject into the building, assume position at a corner of the building to watch the exits on two sides, thus decreasing the chance of the subject slipping out unnoticed. If following the subject into the building, continue in the manner best suited for the circumstances.

5. SUBJECT: Use a convoy. SURVEILLANT: Shift the focal point of the surveillance from the subject to the convoy, as the person acting as a convoy will follow the subject wherever he goes.

6. SUBJECT: Watch reflections in store windows. SURVEILLANT: Act in a normal manner. If using a multiple man technique, frequent rotations are desirable.

7. SUBJECT: Drop a scrap of paper to see if anyone in the area retrieves it. SURVEILLANT: If working alone, attempt to kick it off to the side for later retrieval. If using a multiple man technique, the investigator occupying position "B" should attempt to retrieve the paper.

8. SUBJECT: Walk at irregular paces, sometimes fast and sometimes slow. SURVEILLANT: Attempt to settle on a pace that is an average of the two extremes.

9. SUBJECT: Arrange with people in the area to be alert for the possibility of a surveillance. SURVEILLANT: Act in manner characteristic of persons in the neighborhood, so that subject will not be alerted and persons in area will not notice unnatural actions.

10. SUBJECT: Use binoculars from a room or a roof across the street to examine the occupants and contents of the rooms adjoining subject's for indications of a surveillance. SURVEILLANT: Keep all equipment in the room out of sight. It may also be desirable to keep the curtains drawn.

11. SUBJECT: Attempt to look into adjoining rooms when someone enters or leaves; an accomplice may be used for this purpose. A pretext inquiry of the occupants of adjoining rooms may be made to get a look inside. SURVEILLANT: Any equipment should be placed out of view.

12. SUBJECT: Open and close hotel room door to make it sound as if leaving room. If someone leaves an adjoining room, subject will then leave to observe the person and note his appearance. SURVEILLANT: If this occurs, another investigator should be assigned to the case.

13. SUBJECT: Watch people in the hotel lobby to see if anyone appears to be overly observant of individuals in the area. SURVEILLANT: Avoid sitting in the lobby and, as characteristic in fic-

tion, looking over the top of a newspaper or magazine. Sit in front of a window or lamp to be backlighted—this will make it difficult for anyone else to get a good look at the surveillant's features and thus remember him.

14. SUBJECT: Pretend to leave the hotel room and listen for sounds that may indicate a surveillance. Then make enough noise to be heard to see if sounds from an adjoining room quickly cease. SURVEILLANT: Never make sounds that indicate a surveillance, whether or not the subject is believed to be able to hear.

15. SUBJECT: Start to leave the hotel lobby and then turn back to see if anyone has gotten up to follow. SURVEILLANT: Do not stop abruptly but continue as if unconcerned. It is best to wait to react until sure the reaction is appropriate.

16. SUBJECT: Take a suicidal chance crossing a street during heavy traffic and then look back to see if someone else has done likewise. SURVEILLANT: Do not take unnecessary chances.

17. SUBJECT: Converse with an associate while facing each other—look in opposite directions for evidence of a surveillance. SURVEILLANT: Continue past the subject with investigators "B" and "C" waiting until the subject continues on his way. It may be desirable at this point to rotate the position of the investigators in relation to the subject.

18. SUBJECT: Pass through a large open area such as a parking lot or park; choose such an area for the purpose of meeting someone. SURVEILLANT: Observe from a distance using available cover. A small pocket binocular or monocular is a useful item.

19. SUBJECT: Suddenly reverse the direction of travel and carefully study the people now traveling in the opposite direction. SURVEILLANT: Continue past the subject. The position of the investigators in relation to the subject rotates.

20. SUBJECT: Approach and accuse the investigator of following. SURVEILLANT: The most appropriate response will depend upon the circumstances. Pretending anger and indignation or offering a suitable pretext supported with identification or business cards may be in order. Repositioning of the investigators in relation to the subject is definitely in order and it may be advisable to withdraw that investigator from the assignment.

## Eluding a Surveillant

Some of the better ways of eluding a surveillant follow.

1. Go into some favorable location, such as a public restroom, and change clothes to alter appearance.
2. Jump off a public conveyance just as it is about to leave.
3. Cross a street against very heavy traffic.
4. Take the last taxi at a stand.
5. Circle the block in a taxi.
6. Enter a building by one door and immediately leave by another.
7. Become lost in a crowd.

## CHAPTER 4

# Automobile Surveillance

### GENERAL CONSIDERATIONS

WHEN A SUBJECT who is to be followed uses some type of motor vehicle transportation, it is necessary also for the investigator to use a motor vehicle. In this endeavor, there are many motor vehicle surveillance techniques, variations of which may be employed depending upon the conditions under which the surveillance is being conducted. Some of the factors that will influence the choice of technique, or variation thereof, are the following:

1. Whether the surveillance is being conducted during daylight hours or at night.
2. The wariness of the subject.
3. The amount of vehicle traffic in the area.
4. The number of investigators and vehicles available for the operation.
5. The importance of the case.
6. The physical layout of the area.

In situations where the nature of the case is very serious or important, the use of two or more surveillance vehicles, equipped for effective radio communications is encouraged. Ideally each vehicle should be of a different color and also contain two investigators. The driver can then concentrate on his driving while the other investigator concentrates on the movements of the subject, directs the driver, communicates with any other investigators that may be involved, keeps notes, and alights to follow the subject on foot if necessary.

As an alternative to using two or more surveillance vehicles, it is possible to use an *electronic locating and tracking system*, often referred to as a *bumper beeper*. These systems consist of a small radio transmitter about the size of a pack of cigarettes that is inconspicuously affixed to the subject vehicle and a special radio receiver that picks up the signal, usually pulsating, that is emitted by the transmitter. Some such systems feature a direction finding capability while others do not. Nevertheless, even the less sophisticated systems (nondirectional) are a great asset for surveillance operations.

When a moving surveillance is to be conducted using a motor vehicle, it is important that the driver be proficient and capable of reacting quickly to the ever-changing traffic conditions. It is also important that he be willing to drive very aggressively at times to avoid losing the subject. This point is important because many otherwise capable investigators have failed as surveillants simply because they were unwilling to drive in the aggressive manner so often necessary. When driving in an aggressive manner, however, the driver must remain very alert to traffic conditions, look ahead, and anticipate possible hazards so that he can drive in such a manner in a reasonably safe fashion.

## PREPARING FOR AN AUTOMOBILE SURVEILLANCE

Any physical surveillance operation, whether it be stationary or moving, on foot or by vehicle, in a rural or urban setting, should be preceded by a preliminary survey of the surrounding area in which the surveillance activity will either take place or begin, and by accumulating sufficient information regarding the subject with an emphasis placed on the subject's identity and appearance. The preliminary survey is important because it helps to know what kind of vehicle and mode of dress will be consistent with the area, and a better selection can be made insofar as to when and from where the investigator will watch and wait for the subject to appear. It should be remembered that most moving surveillances are preceded by a period of time in which the investigator must simply sit and wait for the subject to appear.

When the subject does appear and begins moving from the area, it will be much to the investigator's advantage if he has *anticipated* the various routes by which the subject may leave the area and also considered the course of action he will take in each case. Many motor vehicle surveillances that are unsuccessful prove to be so within the first few blocks because of poor positioning and a failure on the part of the investigator to *anticipate* and to *think ahead*. When anticipating which way the subject may go and what one will do as a result, one should not overlook the feasibility of starting the surveillance in the lead (ahead of the subject) for a while when the subject first starts out and later falling in behind him. One should not make the mistake of thinking that a surveillant must *always* be behind his subject in order to monitor his movements effectively.

While preparing for a vehicle surveillance, it is a good idea to have various items in the car to enable one to alter his general appearance from time to time. This is especially important if an investigator must attempt to conduct the entire operation by himself, a task that is not normally recommended. Such items may consist of a hat or two, a wig, sunglasses and sometimes regular eyeglasses, a reversible jacket, and anything else that may seem appropriate under the particular circumstances (see Figure 7).

During the preparation stage, one must consider some means of note taking. A pad of paper on a clip board works well. If this method is chosen, it will be found that the clip board is easier to write on while driving, assuming that there is not a second investigator to record notes, if the clip board is elevated by placing it on a five-inch attaché case next to the driver. For night

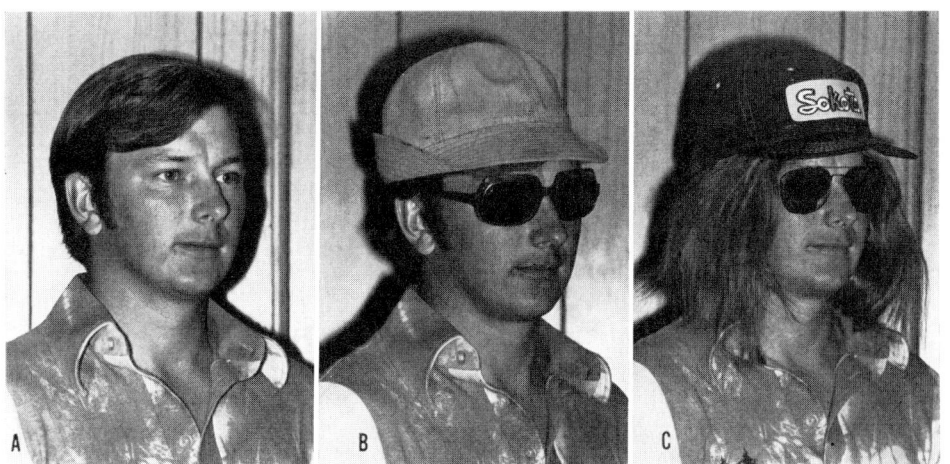

Figure 7. (A) Surveillant with nothing to alter his general appearance. (B) Investigator wearing a hat and sun glasses which causes a change in his general appearance. (C) Wearing a wig, ball cap, and sun glasses causes a considerable change and can be done quickly and easily while in the field.

work it is worth considering some means of softly illuminating the paper so that one can see what he is doing when writing. In cases where a lone investigator must conduct the surveillance, a cassette recorder with a dictamike is a very worthwhile consideration because it permits one to make a prompt and precise record of important items such as times, locations, directions of turns, addresses, and vehicle registration numbers. Using the dictamike enables one to start and stop the recorder by simply manipulating an "on-off" switch on the recorder's microphone, thus enabling the driver to concentrate on the important tasks of observing the subject and driving. When using a dictamike, it is important to wait a second between activitating the recorder and talking so as to permit the recorder's motor to attain its maximum speed. If this is not done, the error will become painfully evident when one attempts to listen to the tape and prepare a written report.

## VEHICLE SURVEILLANCE TECHNIQUES
### General Considerations

As was previously stated, there are a number of different surveillance techniques that may be used, depending upon the circumstances. These techniques will be discussed; however, before becoming involved with them, it would be desirable to discuss some of the more general aspects of vehicle surveillance operations.

Naturally, the amount of traffic on the road will have a large influence on how close the surveillant can be to the subject without his presence becoming obvious. Because the possibility of losing the subject increases with an increase in the distance between the two vehicles, and because the possibility of being detected increases the closer the surveillant is to the subject, it is desirable to remain as close to the subject as possible to avoid losing him, but not so close that the possibility of detection becomes a probability. If more than one vehicle is available, it is desirable to alternate positions frequently to avoid having any one vehicle behind the subject for prolonged periods of time.

In an effort to remain within constant view of the subject, but to avoid being detected, the investigator can employ a number of simple techniques that will make minor alterations in the general appearance of the surveillance vehicle and its occupants.

To disguise the vehicle, items can be hung and removed from the rear view mirror, items such as a facial tissue box can be placed onto and removed from the dash, license plates may be changed, the seating position of occupants may be rearranged, and special switches may be used to permit the dimming or eliminating of various lights at night. One should also consider using a rental agency and changing cars daily.

When installing cut-out switches for lights, one must decide how elaborate he wants to get. Some investigators install only a few switches: one so that the parking lights can be turned on or off without affecting the head lamps, a second switch that will eliminate one of the head lamps, and a third switch to eliminate the brake lights. Other investigators have chosen to install a large number of switches so that they can control virtually all the lights of the vehicle (see Figure 8). Installing this many switches

Figure 8. Panel of switches by which the surveillant can eliminate various lights on the vehicle to alter its general appearance at night.

is fine except for the fact that it is easy to become confused when driving at night and trying to keep an eye on the subject. However, it will be observed that the driver of this vehicle has also installed indicator lights which aid greatly in eliminating this problem.

In addition to employing various techniques to alter the appearance of the surveillant vehicle, it is possible also to alter the appearance of the occupants through the use of reversible jackets, adding or changing hats, eyeglasses, etc. (refer back to Figure 7). To be avoided are theatrical types of disguises such as imitation beards, mustaches, and noses, as they will generally not appear as natural as they should. Utilization of simple disguise methods is naturally more effective during daylight hours than after dark.

In addition to disguise techniques, the driver of the surveillant vehicle should also alter his driving technique occasionally. For example, if there are two or more driving lanes, each should be

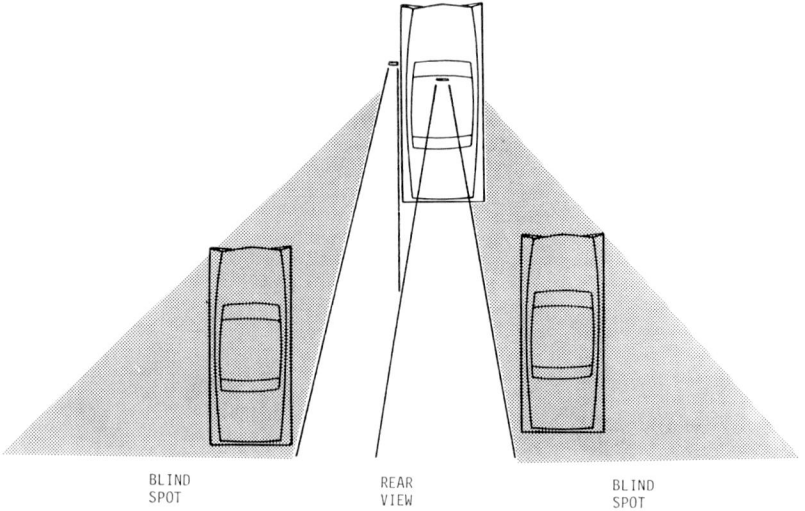

Figure 9. Although mirrors do provide rear vision, there exists a blind spot in the area outside that portion covered by the mirrors and to the rear of the driver's side vision. Blind spots should be taken advantage of when following a vehicle, or when surreptitiously approaching a stationary (occupied) vehicle on foot.

## Automobile Surveillance

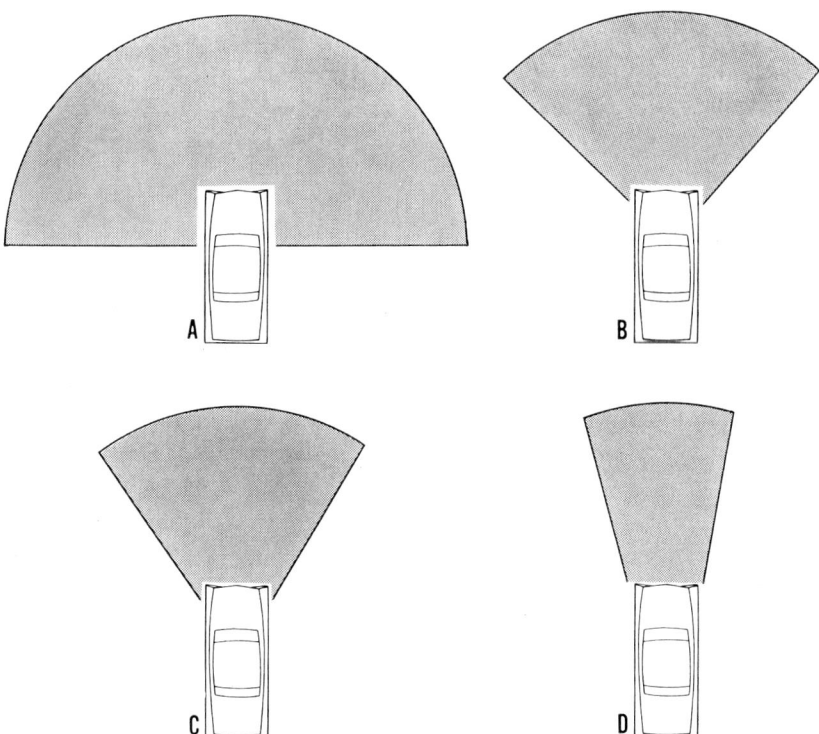

Figure 10. (A) When a vehicle is stationary, the driver's field of vision covers an area of 180 degrees or more. (B) When the vehicle is traveling 20 M.P.H., the driver's field of vision is reduced to approximately ⅔. (C) When the vehicle is traveling 40 M.P.H., the driver's field of vision is reduced to approximately ⅖. (D) When the vehicle is traveling 60 M.P.H., the driver's field of vision is reduced to approximately ⅕.

used intermittently. Another important consideration that should be recognized by the driver of a surveillance vehicle is that there exists for all drivers a rear vision blind spot; when conditions are such that one must drive reasonably close to the subject on a multilane freeway, every effort should be made to stay within one of the subject's blind spots. The blind spots exist just outside the area covered by the rear view mirrors and to the rear of that area covered by the driver's normal vision, which is normally seen from the rear side windows. If a vehicle on either the right or left side of the subject vehicle is positioned far enough back so that it is necessary for the driver to turn his head sharply to see it, and far enough to either side of the vehicle so that the mirrors do not disclose its presence, it will most likely go unnoticed by the driver unless he does turn his head sharply (see Figure 9).

Another factor that will have an effect on the likelihood of the driver observing a vehicle within the blind spots is the fact that the faster a vehicle travels, the narrower becomes the angle of the driver's perception (see Figure 10).

When driving within another driver's blind spot, it is important to remain alert so that appropriate evasive action can be taken in the event that the subject makes a lane change; he may do so unaware of the surveillance vehicle's presence.

### Parallel Surveillance (Automobile)

Parallel surveillance is a method employed when the amount of traffic is very light and the surveillance would therefore be easily detected by the subject if an attempt were made to follow him from the rear. This method of surveillance is also used to a considerable degree by patrol officers using marked squad cars when they desire to follow and observe the activity of a motorist who has in some manner aroused their suspicions or curiosity but probable cause for stopping the vehicle does not yet exist.

When conducting a parallel surveillance, the surveillant drives parallel with the subject vehicle on a street that is one block to either his right or left. This form of surveillance has its greatest advantage in that it greatly reduces the possibility of detection over that existing were the surveillant traveling behind the subject on the same street. Its primary disadvantage lies in the fact that the subject is not under constant observation inasmuch as the surveillant will see the subject vehicle at an intersection, then speed up and watch for it at the next intersection. It is not normally possible to observe the subject between such points. When the subject fails to appear at the next intersection, it can be presumed that he has stopped, turned off into an alley or driveway, or parked his vehicle, in which case the investigator will drive to that intersection in an effort to see where he is or where he may have turned off. It should be apparent now that this form of sur-

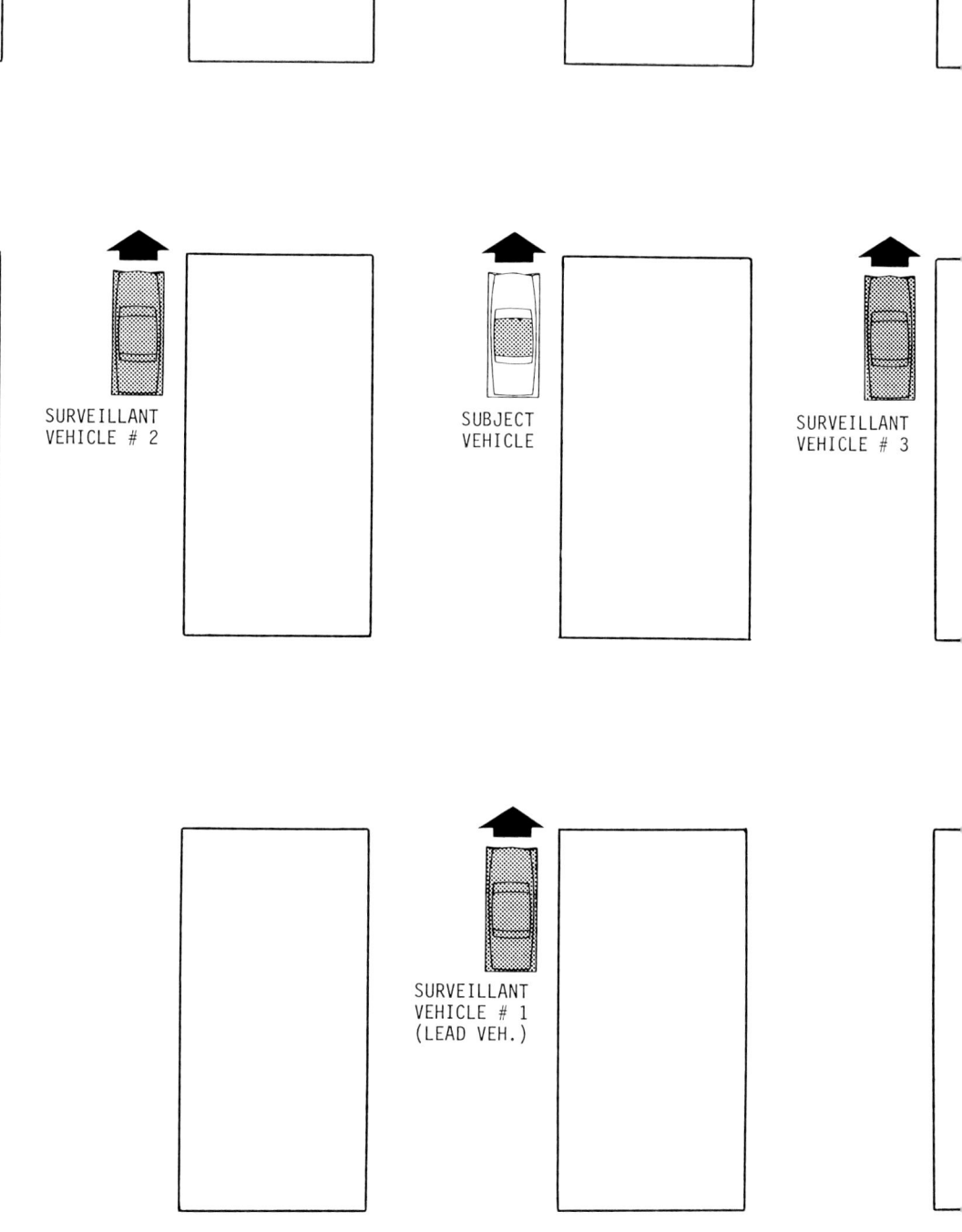

Figure 11. Parallel surveillance is an effective technique when the topographical conditions favor it. Generally most effective in residential areas.

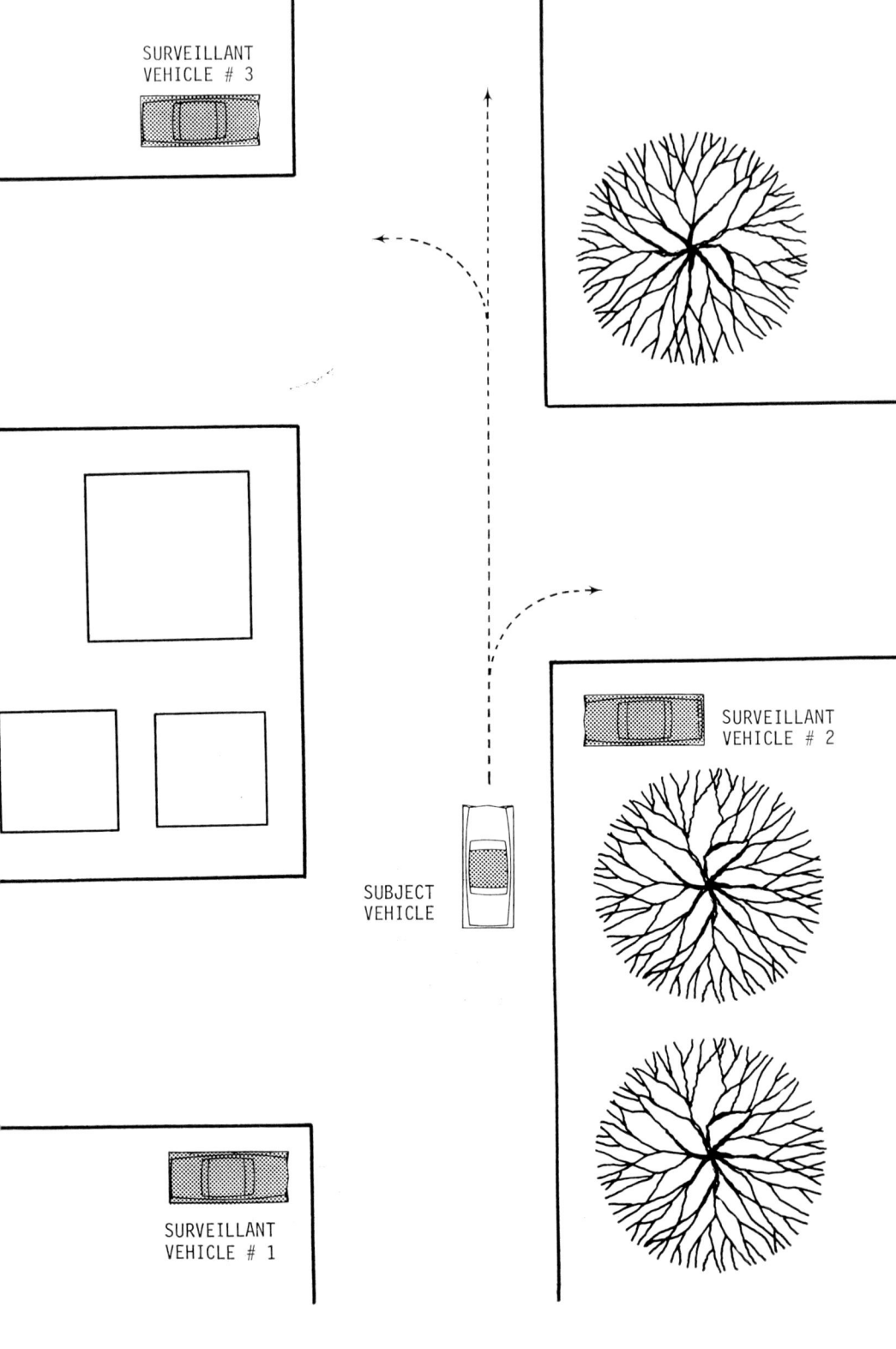

veillance has an inherent weakness in that the subject can easily be lost. However, on cases of a very sensitive nature where one cannot afford to be discovered by the subject, or when attempting to follow and observe a vehicle while patrolling with a marked squad car, this method has considerable merit.

It will be found that in a surveillance method such as this, residential areas will tend to be more favorable than industrial and commercial districts. However, the possibility of this technique producing successful results should never be discarded without consideration if some other method is not suitable under the circumstances.

When conditions warrant or justify the use of two vehicles for a surveillance, one may follow the subject while the other parallels him, or the two vehicles can position themselves so that the subject is flanked on two sides, thus having a surveillance vehicle on both his right and left. These positions would naturally be varied in accordance with the layout of the area. When three vehicles are used to conduct this type of a surveillance, the subject vehicle will often have a vehicle on both his right and left with the third vehicle either following or preceding him, depending upon the circumstances (see Figure 11). In the event that the third vehicle is preceding the subject, observations can be made using the rear view mirror.

When more than one vehicle is used to conduct a surveillance, it is important that provisions be made for effective radio communications between the vehicles involved and also that it has been established which investigator is to be in charge of the surveillance so as to ensure smooth coordination of the operation. It may be decided that one individual will give the instructions

---

Figure 12. Progressive surveillance. Can be accomplished using one or several surveillance vehicles. The first day the subject is observed leaving and watched until he passes from view. The following day a position is taken further along the route. The subject is again observed as he comes into and passes from view. This procedure is continued until the subject's destination is learned. This technique is useful only when the subject consistently travels the same route to the same destination.

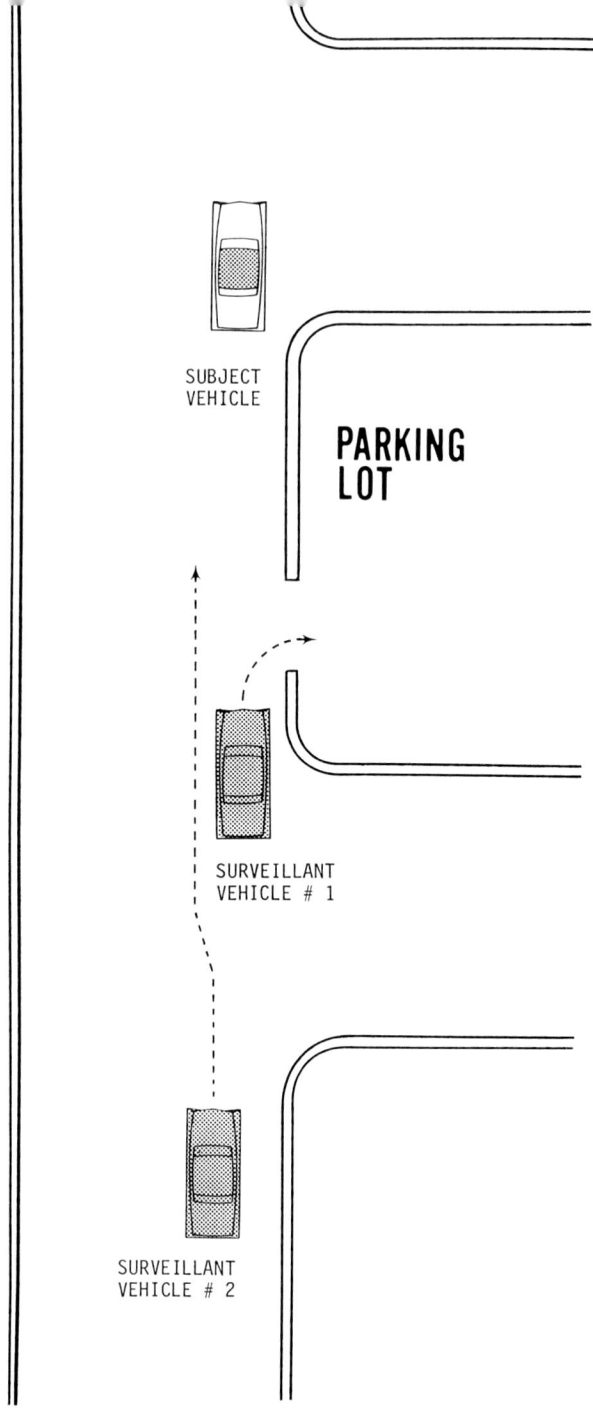

Figure 13. To rotate the position of the surveillance vehicles in relation to the subject, vehicle #2 increases his speed while vehicle #1 turns off, allowing #2 to assume the lead position.

throughout the entire operation; however, the investigator in the *lead* position will generally be in the best position to give instructions.

## Progressive Surveillance

There are instances, such as when a subject is extremely wary or when he travels through sparsely populated areas, that the possibility of following him for any reasonable period of time does not exist. If the individual in question is believed to have an unbroken routine, or if it is suspected that he has a specific destination to which he goes each day, perhaps making a delivery on certain days, a *progressive surveillance* may be the most appropriate technique to use.

When using this technique, the investigator will position himself where he can observe the subject when he leaves the area and thus learn the direction in which he goes. He may then follow for a very short distance or he may not, depending upon the circumstances. The following day the investigator will position himself farther along the subject's route, either where he lost sight of him the previous day or at some point beyond where he could make a turn. Again, the investigator will observe the subject as he comes into view, passes by, and proceeds on his way. This process will be repeated until the subject's destination is learned. As can be seen, this can involve a lot of time.

In many instances this technique can be effectively employed using several investigators who will be positioned at various points along possible routes by which the subject may leave the area (see Figure 12). By using several investigators, several days work can be accomplished in one day.

## Miscellaneous Surveillance Techniques

In Figures 13 through 25 are a number of situations an investigator is likely to encounter when conducting a vehicle surveillance. Studying the illustrations should enable one to develop a number of ideas in regard to possible ways of dealing with a variety of situations that are not really uncommon when engaged in work of this nature.

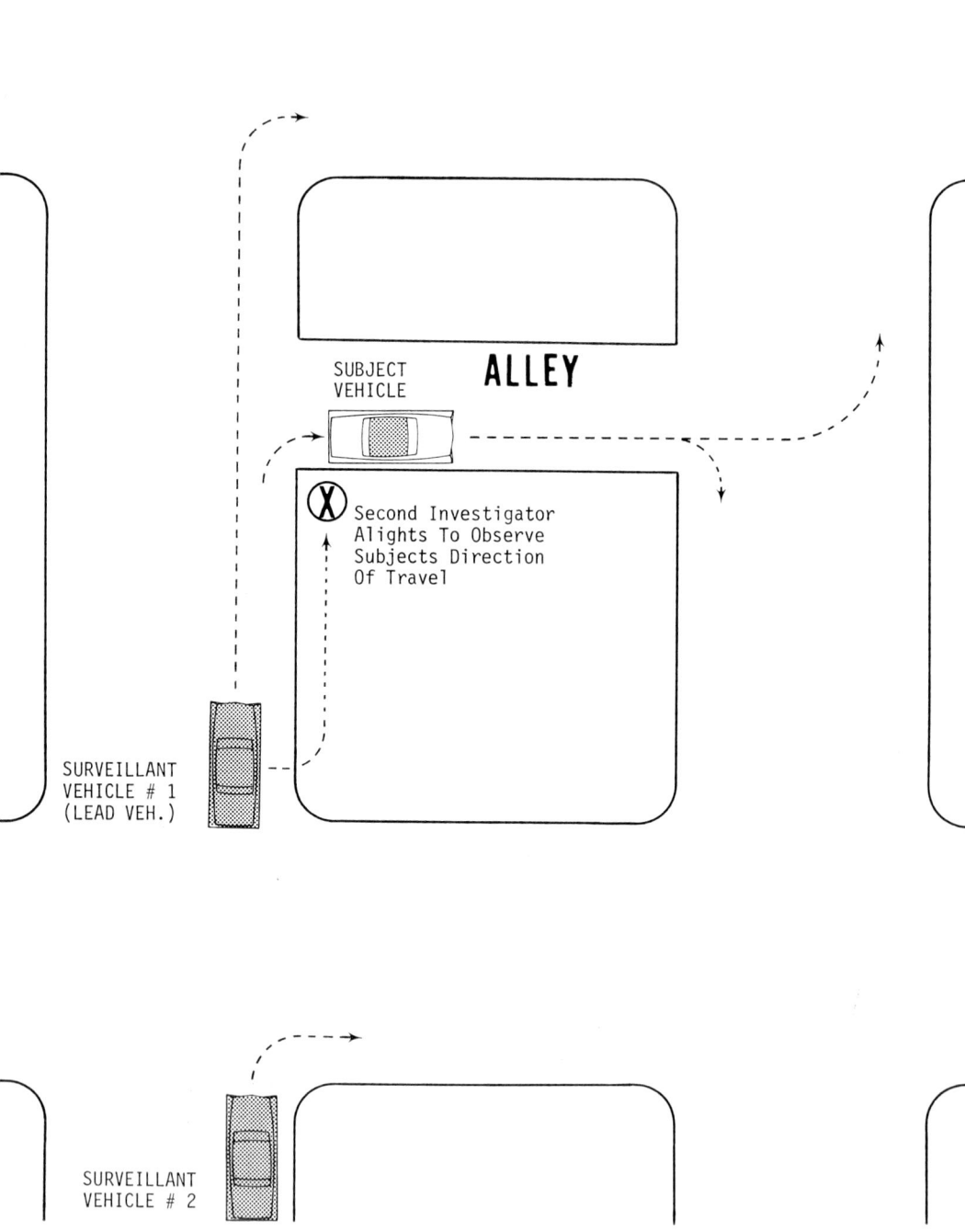

## Tailing at Night Without Lights

When attempting to follow a vehicle in an urban setting during early morning hours after most of the traffic has died down, it is often desirable and sometimes essential to drive without lights to avoid detection. If there is a reasonable degree of traffic on the streets, however, driving without lights is not normally necessary and doing so can present a safety hazard. This is not to suggest that it is not desirable under such circumstances to travel a short stretch occasionally in this manner.

The technique of driving without lights to follow a vehicle is especially useful if the surveillance is being done by a uniformed patrol officer using a marked squad car. Surveillance operations are not normally conducted using marked squad cars; however, there are many occasions in which a patrol officer while on duty will observe something that he feels warrants further observation and, as a result, will attempt to follow a vehicle for a distance. In so doing, he is conducting a physical surveillance in every sense of the word.

When driving without lights, the driver must be very alert for any traffic that could pull away from a curb or pull out from a side street or private drive, for it is very likely that the driver of such a vehicle will not see the surveillant vehicle for the same reason that the subject does not see it. Because such hazards exist, the surveillant should keep one hand on the light switch and be prepared to take evasive action.

## Detecting and Eluding a Tail

When following a vehicle, the investigator should be alert for indications that the subject has become aware of him. However, he must guard against the feeling that everyone is aware of who

---

Figure 14. Subject turns into an alley. Lead vehicle (#1) stops short of the alley, allowing the second investigator to go on foot to see if the subject stops or passes through the alley and turns. If he turns the direction of the turn is indicated. Vehicle #2 turns a block early. Both vehicles are in position to assume the lead position depending upon which way the subject may turn.

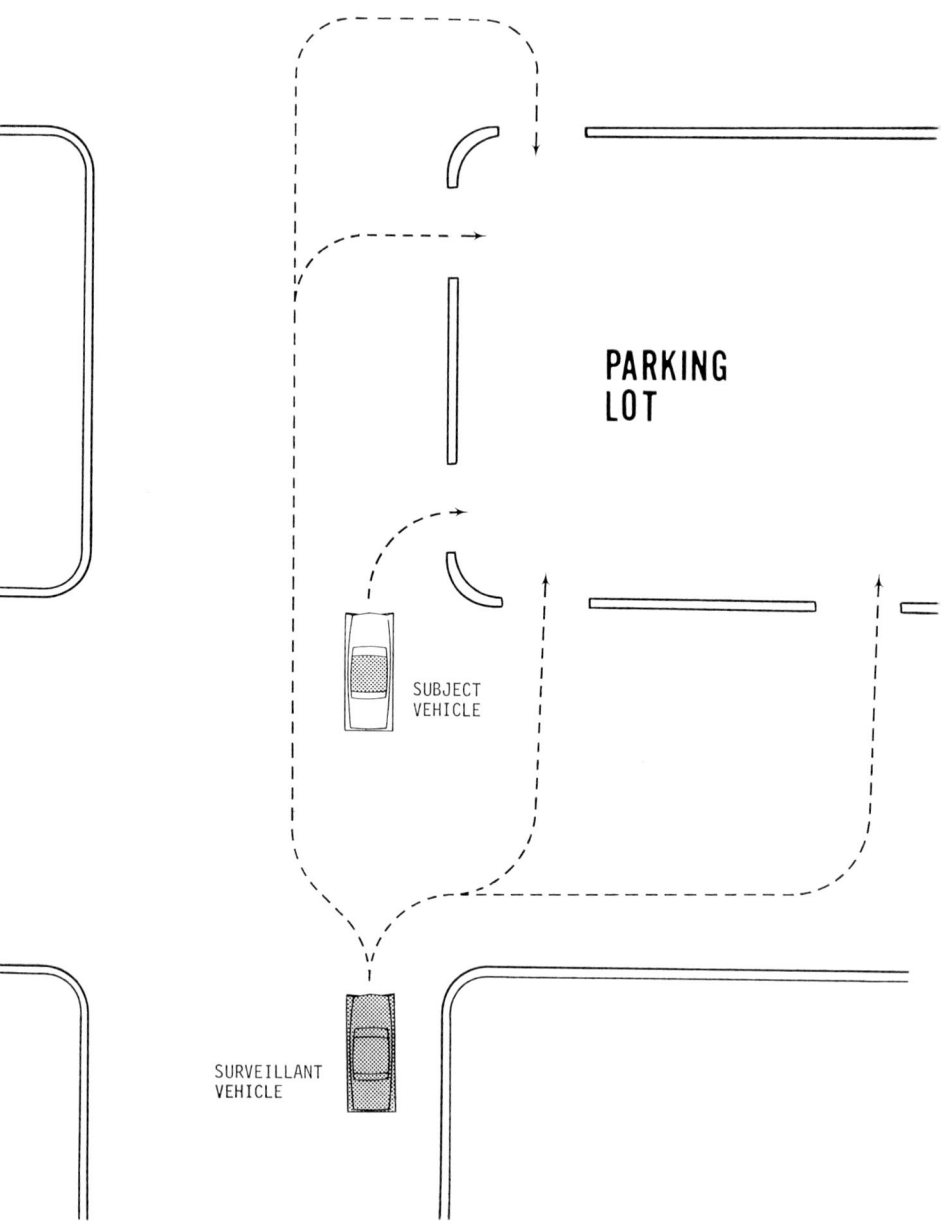

Figure 15. When the subject turns into a parking lot, it is desirable to avoid following him using the same entrance. Generally, if conditions permit, it is best to pass by and use a farther entrance.

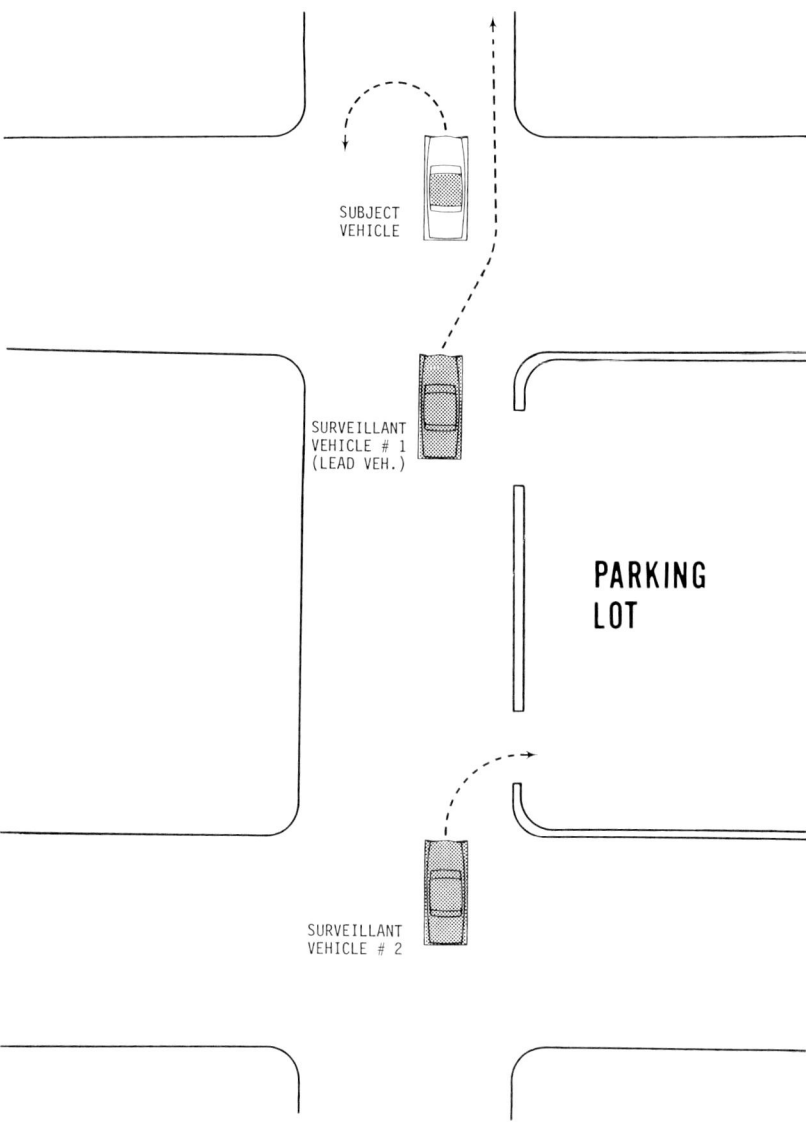

Figure 16. Subject makes a "U" turn. The lead vehicle (#1) should continue on and radio to #2 who will turn off, wait for the subject to appear and then assume the lead position. Vehicle #1, which was originally in the lead, will pass from the subject's view and make a "U" turn to assume the #2 position.

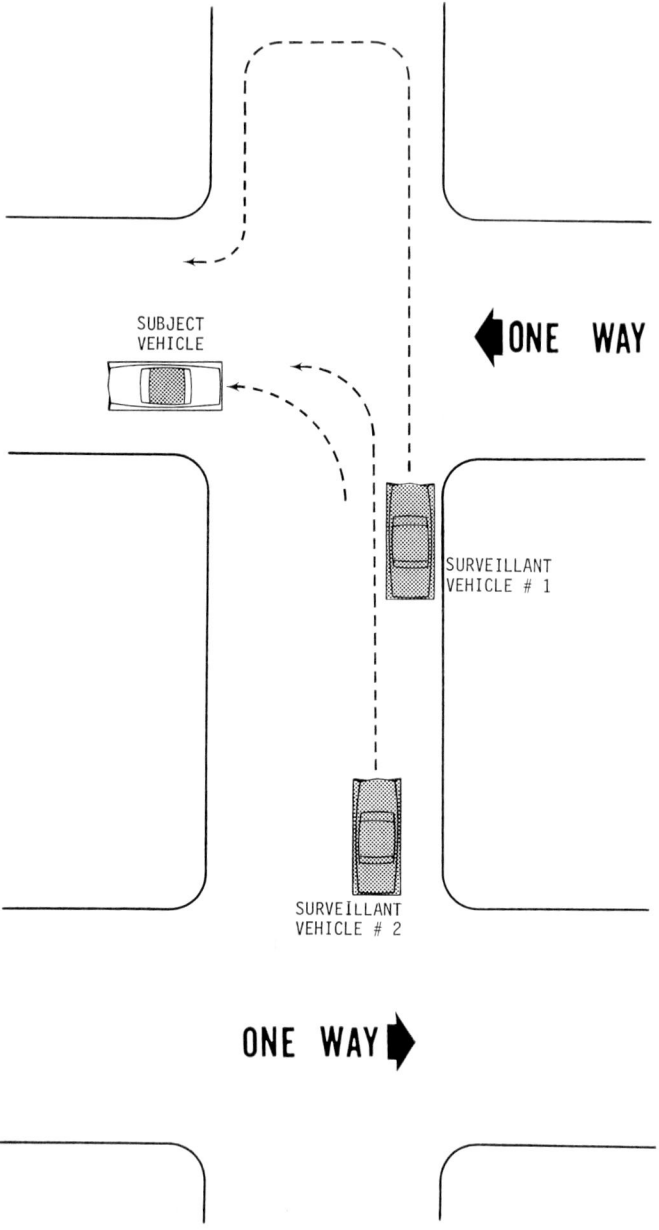

Figure 17. Subject turns onto a one-way street. The lead vehicle may continue following, or he may continue straight, allowing vehicle #2 to assume the lead position. The original lead vehicle will, after passing through the intersection, circle the block or make a "U" turn to assume the #2 position.

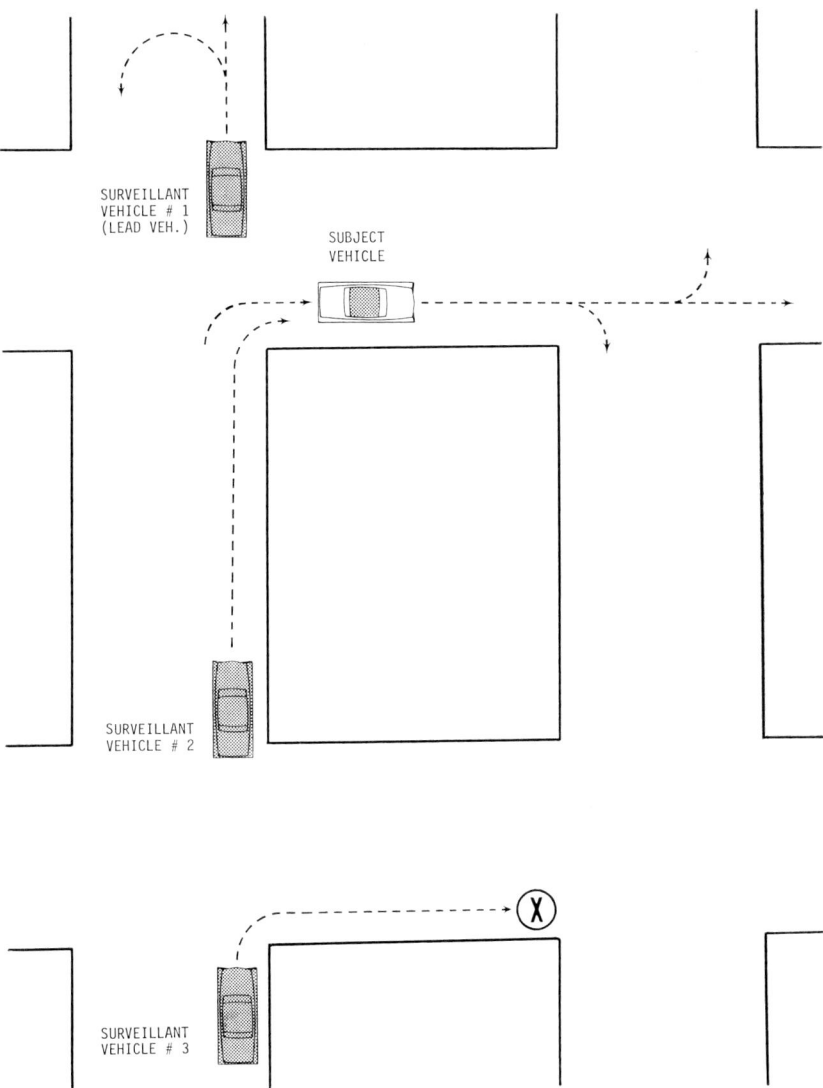

Figure 18. Subject turns a corner. The lead vehicle (#1) passes by and later makes a "U" turn or circles the block. Vehicle #2 turns the corner and follows the subject. Vehicle #3 turns a block early and waits for instructions from Vehicle #2 who has assumed the lead position.

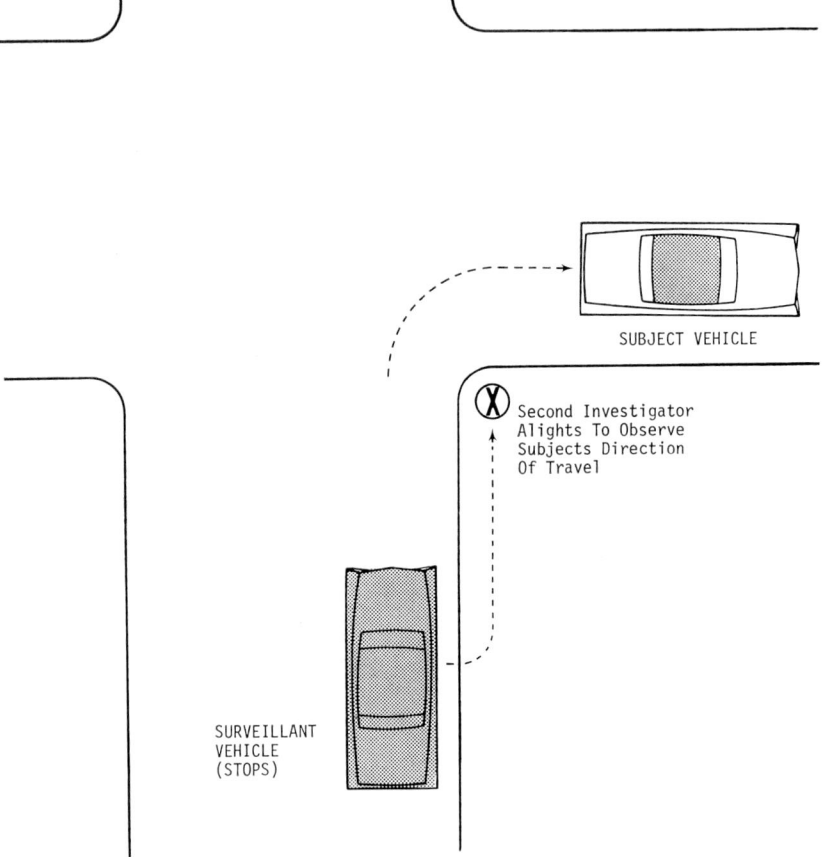

Figure 19. When the subject turns a corner, it is often desirable to stop before reaching the corner and have the second investigator go on foot to the corner to observe which way the subject goes. When traffic is heavy and the surveillant vehicle cannot get to the corner, this tactic is essential.

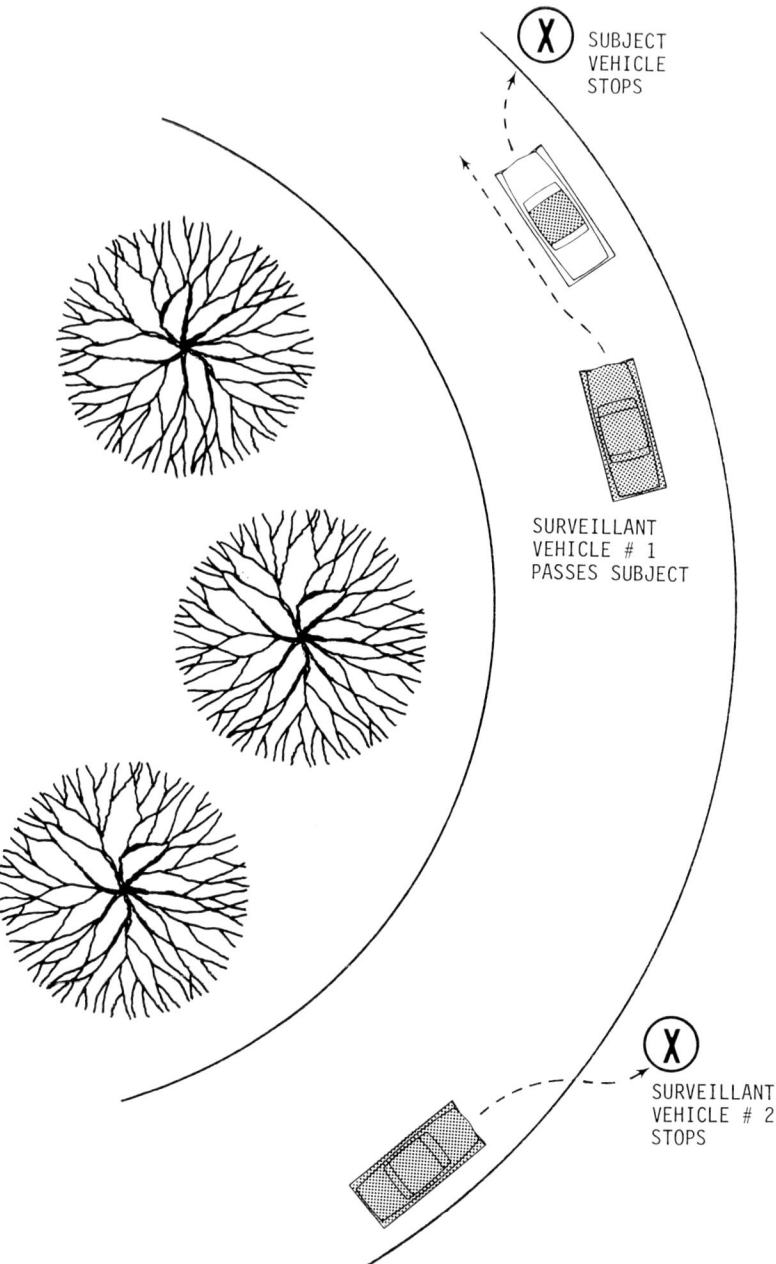

Figure 20. Subject stops after rounding a curve or passing over the crest of a hill. The lead vehicle should pass by and radio to Vehicle #2 which will pull off the road and wait. The lead vehicle will also pull off the road when conditions permit. When the subject resumes travel, one of the surveillance vehicles will assume the lead position depending upon which direction he goes.

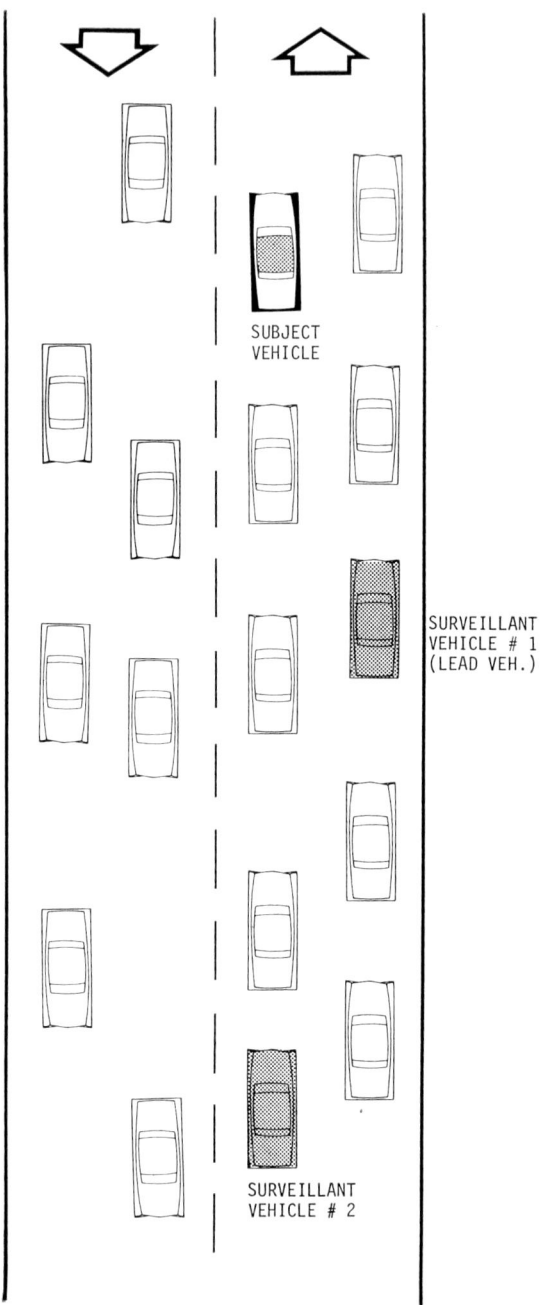

Figure 21. When conducting a surveillance in heavy traffic, it is desirable for the lead vehicle (#1) to remain fairly close to the subject vehicle taking full advantage of his *blind spot*. Frequent rotations of the surveillance vehicles in reference to the subject is desirable. See Figure 9 for example of the location of blind spots.

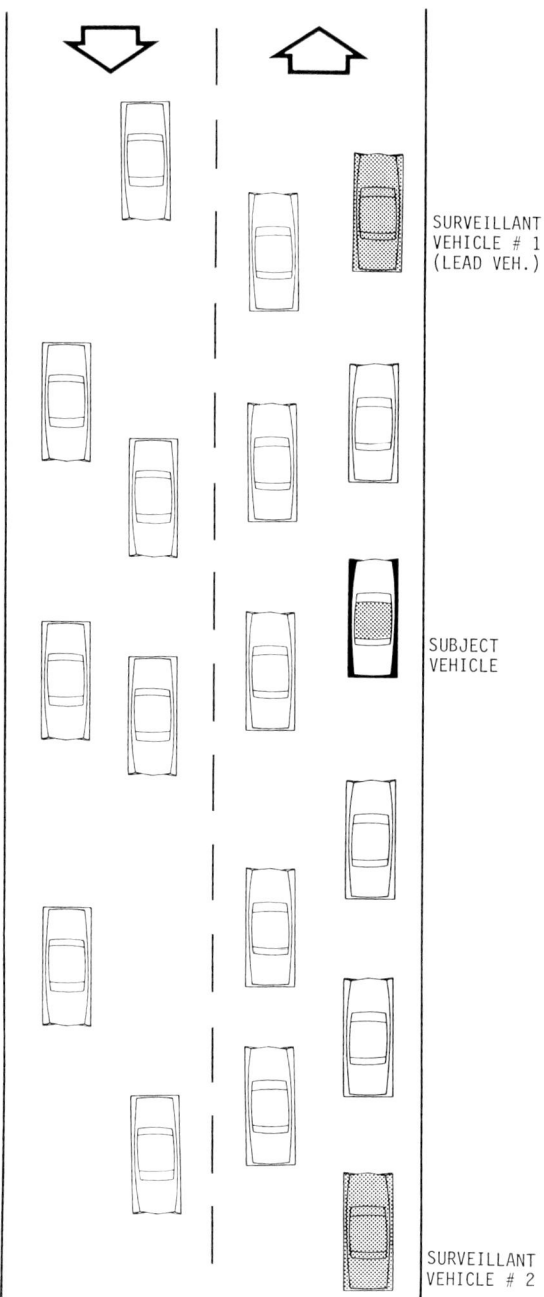

Figure 22. The surveillant vehicle (#1) may, under certain circumstances, lead the subject and observe him in the rear view mirror. When more than one vehicle is involved, the other vehicles should remain behind the subject.

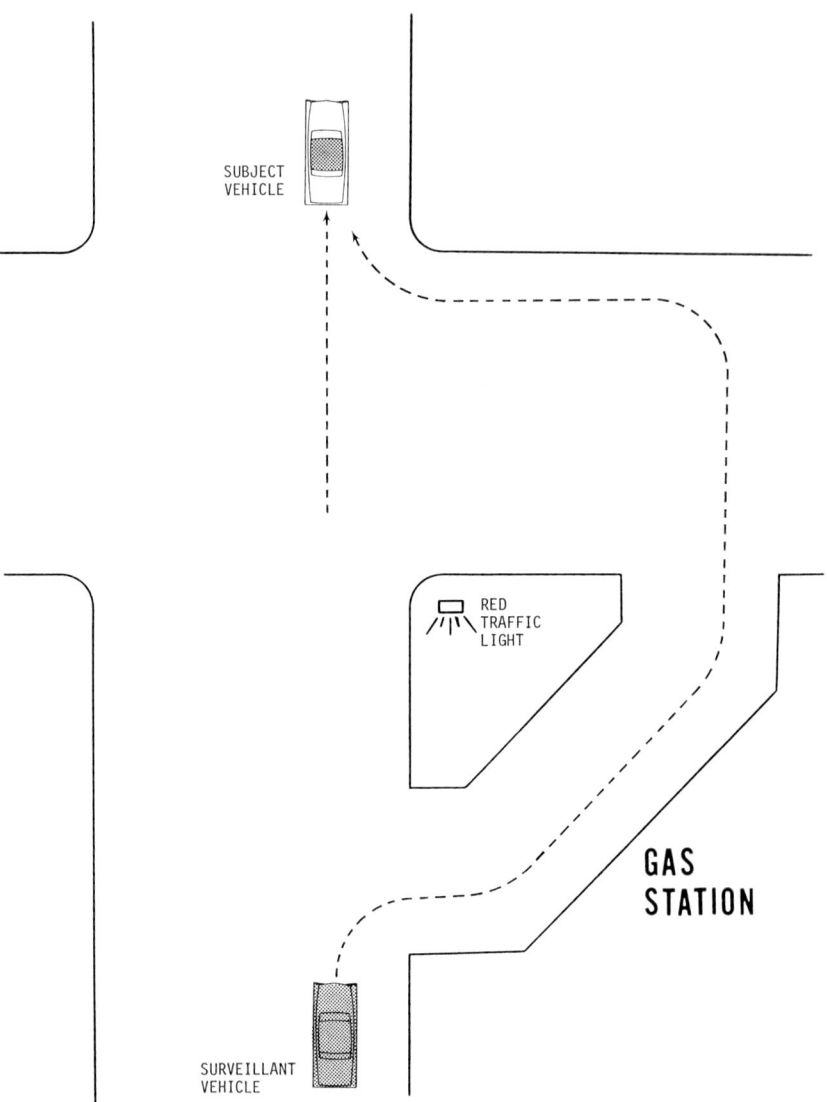

Figure 23. When a subject passes through an intersection just as a signal light turns red, the surveillant may find it necessary to go through the light to avoid losing contact with him. This can be accomplished by simply disobeying the light or, if conditions permit, by-passing the light as shown.

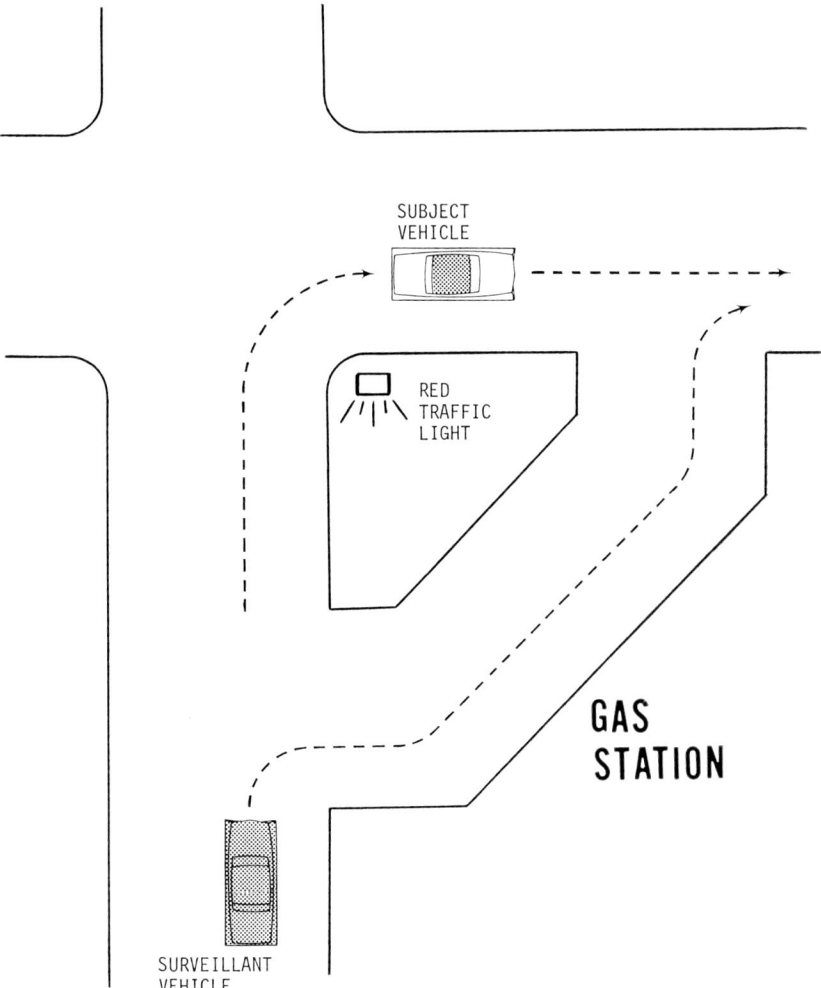

Figure 24. When a subject vehicle makes a right turn just as a signal light turns red, the surveillant may make the turn against the red light (legal in some states after first stopping) or, if other traffic blocks such a move or if making such a move would alert the subject, consider by-passing the light as shown.

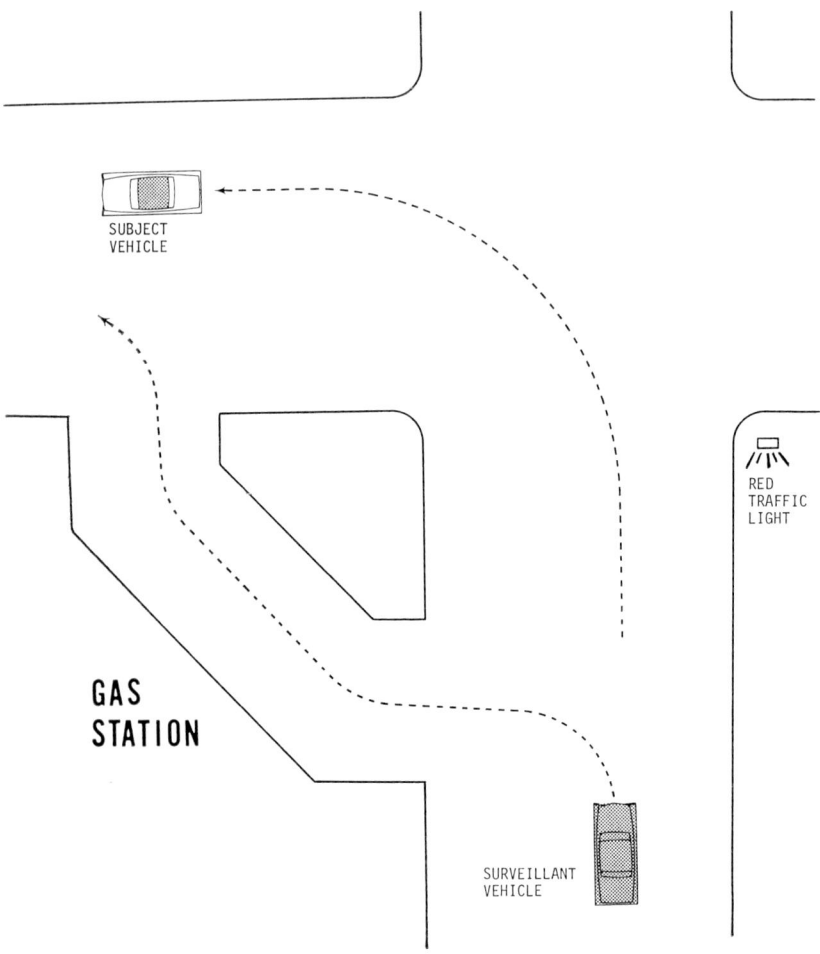

Figure 25. When a subject vehicle makes a left turn just as a signal light turns red, the surveillant may find it necessary to go through the light to avoid losing contact with him. Unfortunately such a move can alert a subject and if possible the light should be by-passed as shown.

and what he is. This feeling of self-consciousness is typical of almost all investigators the first few times they engage in surveillance activity.

When a subject engages in activity that is apparently intended to elude a tail, it may be something that he routinely does as a precautionary measure, or it may be an indication that he has detected the surveillant and is attempting to elude him.

The following are some methods that a subject will frequently employ to either detect or elude a tail. The reader should realize, however, that a subject may do something that is not indicated here, or he may use a variation of one of these techniques. This listing should, nevertheless, provide some ideas as to the type of thing to expect.

1. SUBJECT: Turn a corner and immediately park. SURVEILLANT: The lead vehicle should proceed on by and appropriately advise the second vehicle, if there is one, so that he can stop somewhere behind the subject and assume the lead position in the event that the subject continues on. If there is no second vehicle, it is still better for the surveillant to pass the subject and turn off a short distance ahead rather than stopping behind him.

2. SUBJECT: Drive up to the curb as if to park, and then pull away abruptly. SURVEILLANT: Lead vehicle may pass the subject allowing the second vehicle to assume the lead position. If one vehicle is involved, it may be better to pass the subject and then later turn off, allowing the subject to pass by, and then discreetly move in behind him.

3. SUBJECT: Use excessive and/or irregular speeds. SURVEILLANT: If possible, settle on an average speed.

4. SUBJECT: Use devious routes. SURVEILLANT: The lead vehicle should remain at as great a distance as possible to avoid detection. If more than one surveillance vehicle is involved, frequent trade-offs of the lead position should be made.

5. SUBJECT: If the subject is with an accomplice, leave the vehicle and then double back and hide in the vehicle while accomplice drives out of the area. SURVEILLANT: The vehicle should be followed long enough to ascertain whether the subject is in fact in the vehicle.

6. SUBJECT: Drive the wrong direction on a one-way street. SURVEILLANT: During daylight hours, attempt to parallel the subject on the next street, watching at intersections. After dark, consideration should be given to the possibility of following without lights. In the event that the street is only one block long, wait until the subject has made a turn at the far end and then follow either directly or by using a parallel street.

7. SUBJECT: Make a midblock "U" turn. SURVEILLANT: If two or more vehicles are being used, the lead vehicle should proceed straight and advise the second vehicle of the subject's move so that the driver can turn off and take up the lead position when the subject passes by. The original lead vehicle may then double back and assume the number two position. If only one surveillant is involved, an attempt should be made to circle the block or to turn around out of sight of the subject. At night consideration should be given to the feasibility of maneuvering without lights.

8. SUBJECT: Go through red traffic lights, or time one's arrival at lights so that the subject goes through on the yellow; watch the rear view mirror to see if anyone goes through against the red light. SURVEILLANT: If it is necessary to go through the red light to avoid losing the subject, every effort should be made to accomplish it without the subject observing the action because such an act will serve to alert him. If there is a gas station or parking lot on the corner, consider going through it to get onto the street that is running perpendicular so that a turn with the green light can be made (see Figures 23, 24, and 25).

9. SUBJECT: Make false starts to lure the investigator into making a premature move. SURVEILLANT: Be sure that the subject does in fact intend to leave before leaving one's position to follow.

10. SUBJECT: Ride a bicycle which is too slow for automobile surveillance and too fast for foot surveillance. SURVEILLANT: This is a most difficult situation to contend with successfully; however, there are a number of methods, all of which leave something to be desired, that may be considered depending upon the circumstances. Consider using another bicycle, or paralleling with an automobile and spotting the subject at intersections. Con-

sider also dropping off a foot man and picking him up frequently, or circling the blocks.

11. SUBJECT: Drive into dead-end streets to see who follows. SURVEILLANT: Normally, do not follow the subject onto such streets. In this instance, knowledge of the area is desirable. Fortunately, many such streets are appropriately marked.

12. SUBJECT: Drive through alleys. SURVEILLANT: The lead vehicle stops before arriving at the alley and allows the second investigator (riding in the lead vehicle) to alight and proceed to the alley on foot to see if the vehicle has stopped therein or passed through. In the event that the subject passed through, the direction of his turn is made known to the other members of the team. The lead vehicle may then proceed to the corner and make the appropriate turn so as to continue the surveillance, or the second vehicle, which has turned at the previous intersection, may pick up the subject and assume the lead position, depending, of course, upon the direction in which the subject turned after passing through the alley (see Figure 14).

13. SUBJECT: Abandon the vehicle. SURVEILLANT: If there is more than one investigator involved, the subject should be followed on foot while a second investigator watches the car as a precautionary measure against the subject's doubling back and attempting to leave the area unnoticed.

14. SUBJECT: Have a confederate follow to detect the presence of a surveillance. SURVEILLANT: When a convoy is detected, the focal point of the surveillance should be shifted from the subject to the convoy.

15. SUBJECT: Use radio monitors in an effort to detect the presence of a surveillance. SURVEILLANT: For this reason it is desirable to use radios that are on a frequency that would not be likely to be monitored. Transmissions should also be as brief as possible.

16. SUBJECT: Stop after descending a hill or rounding a curve. SURVEILLANT: The lead vehicle should proceed on by in a normal manner and advise the second vehicle, which should pull off the road and wait until the subject resumes travel. The lead vehicle, once out of sight of the subject, should also pull off the road and wait. When the subject resumes travel, whether the lead vehicle

or the number two vehicle will assume the lead position will depend on whether the subject proceeds straight ahead or doubles back (see Figure 20).

17. SUBJECT: Drive at a very low rate of speed forcing other traffic to pass. SURVEILLANT: Frequently pull into drives, parking lots, and other available places from which to keep watch on the subject while remaining essentially out of view himself. To be considered also is the feasibility of driving ahead of the subject.

## Reestablishing Contact in a Broken Surveillance

To benefit from this section, it will be necessary for the reader to follow both the subject and surveillance vehicle along on a map as they go about their ways. Of the two examples that are given, one is fairly complex while the other is simple. The first example is that of a live surveillance in which the subject was lost from view and quickly relocated through the use of a very definite and systematic procedure. The second example is quite simple and is intended to aid in understanding the logic that lies behind the technique that was employed by the surveillant in the first example. It should be pointed out that this method of reestablishing contact with a lost vehicle works equally well whether the surveillant is a plainclothes investigator or a uniformed officer on patrol who has lost sight of a vehicle.

For the first example, refer to Figure 26. The surveillance vehicle is on Third Street paralleling a subject who is traveling north on College Drive. At Lyon Street the subject makes a left (west) turn. The investigator also turns left onto Lyon Street and proceeds to the intersection of Lyon and College. The subject at that time has reached First Street and has turned right (north). The investigator turns right onto College Drive and quickly proceeds to Main Street. The subject, however, who is traveling on First Street, fails to appear at Main Street, so the investigator turns left and proceeds on Main Street to First Street. Upon arriving at the intersection, the subject is observed turning into a private drive. The investigator turns right (north) and proceeds to the parking area of a local trucking firm to wait for the subject to reappear. Just as the investigator is making a left

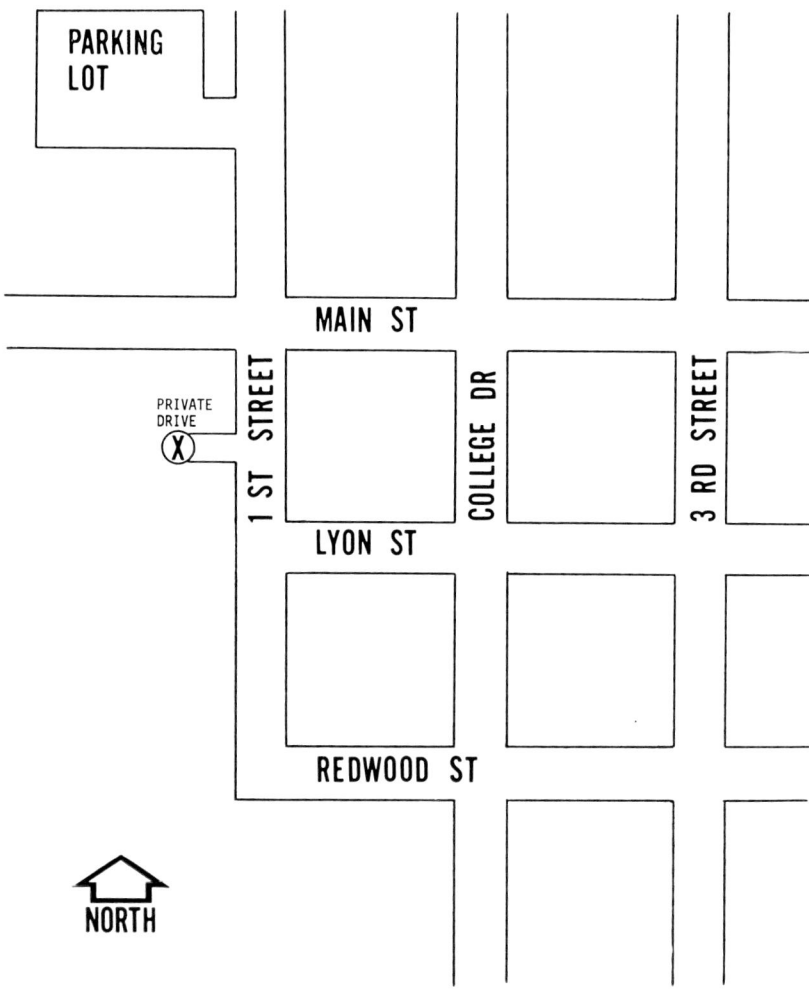

Figure 26.

turn into the lot, he observes in the rear view mirror that the subject vehicle is preparing to drive back onto First Street; however, the investigator is interrupted by another vehicle while turning around in the lot and the resultant loss of time enables the subject to leave the drive and proceed out of sight. As can be seen by studying the map, there are a number of directions in which the subject may have gone. The investigator must act quickly and decisively if contact with the subject is to be reestablished.

The investigator knows that the subject did not go north on First Street and cross Main, for if he had, they would have met. The subject would have had time, however, to have traveled north on First Street and then turned either right or left on Main Street. The investigator quickly proceeds south on First Street to Main and looks in both directions. Because Main Street to the west is a long, straight stretch, and because the subject vehicle is not observed traveling along that stretch of road, it is evident that it did not go in that direction. If the vehicle had made a right turn onto Main Street, it would then have turned either right or left onto College Drive, for it is not observed traveling on Main Street in that direction either. The investigator quickly proceeds on Main Street to College Drive and looks north, a fairly long stretch of road and observes that the subject did not go in that direction. It is possible, however, that the subject, when he left the private drive, traveled south and then turned onto either Lyon or Redwood Streets, or he may have taken either Lyon or Redwood Streets to College Drive, turned south, and is at that time just beyond a curve that is south of Redwood Street. The investigator turns south on College Drive and proceeds south at a rapid rate of speed, observing closely the roadways on both his right and left as he goes. After going around the curve, he observes a vehicle matching the description of the subject's a few blocks ahead. Upon catching up to the vehicle in question, he determines it to be that of the subject.

While it is true that the subject, once lost from view, can turn a corner and pull into another drive or alley and thereby elude the surveillant, it should be apparent that the investigator or officer who practices this concept will be at a decided advantage when conducting a physical surveillance.

Because a subject will occasionally be lost from view simply as a result of evasive tactics, a method such as this can often serve to reestablish contact. In the example that was just given, the time involved in reestablishing contact was only a minute or two.

While the foregoing example of a live surveillance may ap-

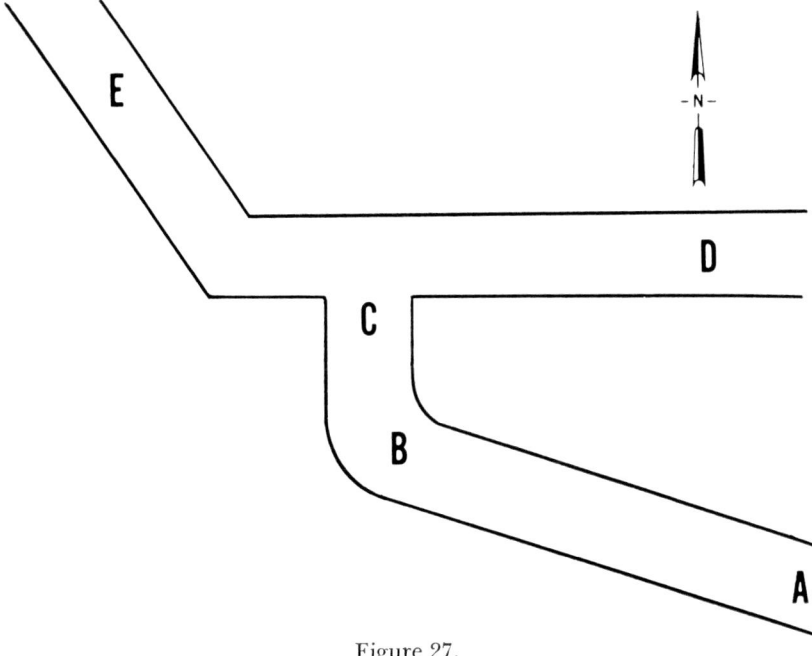

Figure 27.

pear to be a bit complex, it really is not. Consider it in the light of this simplified version. This example, Figure 27, although overly simplified, should serve to clarify the logic of this technique. Let us assume that an investigator at point A is following a subject who is at point B. Assume also that the curve in the road prevents the investigator from seeing which way the subject turned upon reaching point C. After traveling around the curve and arriving at point C, the investigator looks to the right and realize that if the subject had turned right, he should be able to see his vehicle in the vicinity of D. Because he is not observed traveling along that long straight stretch of road, it is safe to assume that the subject has turned left and is just around the bend at point E.

This is the logic that was employed by the investigator in the first example. It is simply a process of elimination. Needless to say, it is much to the investigator's advantage to know the area in which the surveillance is being conducted.

## Violating Traffic Laws

When conducting a moving surveillance involving motor vehicles, it often becomes necessary to violate traffic laws to prevent losing the subject. When so doing, however, the investigator has the responsibility to do so in a safe manner. Should the investigator be involved in an accident, the fact that he was conducting a surveillance will not release him from assuming responsibility for his actions. The fact that he was conducting a surveillance will not change the fact that he, and innocent people, could be injured seriously by his actions should he become involved in an accident, and the surveillance will most assuredly not be a successful one. Therefore, although it is often necessary to violate traffic laws, the investigator has the responsibility of doing so safely.

When it is necessary to go through a red light, never approach the intersection at a rate of speed that will make it impossible to stop to avoid any vehicles approaching the intersection from the right or left. When it is necessary to exceed the speed limit, remain alert for the possibility of vehicles entering the roadway from side streets or driveways, or for oncoming traffic that may turn across in front of the surveillant vehicle. When it is necessary to make illegal turns, be sure to yield to all other traffic in the area. Good judgment and alertness will enable one to accomplish these things in a reasonably safe manner.

When violating a traffic law to stay with a subject, do so without the subject's being able to see the act. Many subjects will, for example, time their arrival at a controlled intersection so that they go through on the yellow light and then watch their rear view mirror to see if anyone traveling behind him goes through the red light. If they do, he will become suspicious.

## Binoculars for Automobile Surveillance

When one conducts a moving automobile surveillance, it will prove advantageous to have a pair of uncased binoculars lying on the seat to be picked up for quick examinations from time to time. Having binoculars handy can aid in determining which way a subject may have gone in situations where the investigator may have been held up in traffic while the subject proceeded on his way, turned a corner, and gained too great a lead. When this happens it is easy for the subject to get far enough ahead so that the investigator, with the unaided eye, is unable to distinguish the subject vehicle from others in his immediate vicinity. This problem can prove to be very real after dark inasmuch as it is difficult to distinguish the tail lights of the subject from those of others in the area. If, for example, while the investigator was tied up in traffic, the subject reached an intersection but it is not known to the investigator whether he proceeded straight through or made a right or left turn, this determination can often be made by pausing at the intersection and quickly looking in each direction with binoculars. Once it has been determined which way the subject has gone, the investigator has only to attempt closing the gap without alerting or losing the subject.

Binoculars are also useful in many instances before the actual surveillance is begun as they enable the investigator to watch for the subject from a distance that precludes accidental discovery. Similarly, binoculars can prove to be a valuable aid once the subject has reached his destination as they enable the investigator to remain at a distance that precludes detection and yet observe such things as the subject's actions, pertinent vehicle registration numbers, identifying features of persons with whom the subject may interact, and building numbers.

When binoculars are used in conjunction with an automobile surveillance, the compactness of 6×30's, 7×35's, and 8×40's will prove to be an asset during daytime hours; however, after dark a pair of 7×50 binoculars is recommended because of their superb light gathering capability. Worth noting also is the fact that a binocular whose magnifying power exceeds seven or eight times will generally prove to be too strong for applications such as this, because one is frequently making observations from a vehicle while the engine is running and the vibrations can cause severe problems. Furthermore, when using binoculars for quick and brief examinations, the lower power instruments will generally make it easier to quickly locate the subject and keep him within the field of view. Again, a magnifying power of seven or eight times will prove in most instances to be the most practical.

## Bumper Beepers

The all too difficult task of following a vehicle can be greatly simplified through the use of an *electronic locating and tracking system,* often referred to as a *bumper beeper.* Such a system consists primarily of a miniature radio transmitter (see Figure 28) about the size of a pack of cigarettes or smaller, which is concealed on the subject vehicle. The radio signal that is emitted by the beeper is picked up by a special radio receiver in the investigator's vehicle (see Figure 29). Some such receivers feature a direction finding capability while others do not.

There are two distinct advantages offered by a beeper system. The first is being able to follow a vehicle while remaining out of sight of that vehicle. Some systems accomplish this better than others. The second benefit is being able to relocate a vehicle once it has been lost during a surveillance, or to locate a vehicle at any time its whereabouts must be known. These systems are especially useful for moving surveillance in situations where one lone in-

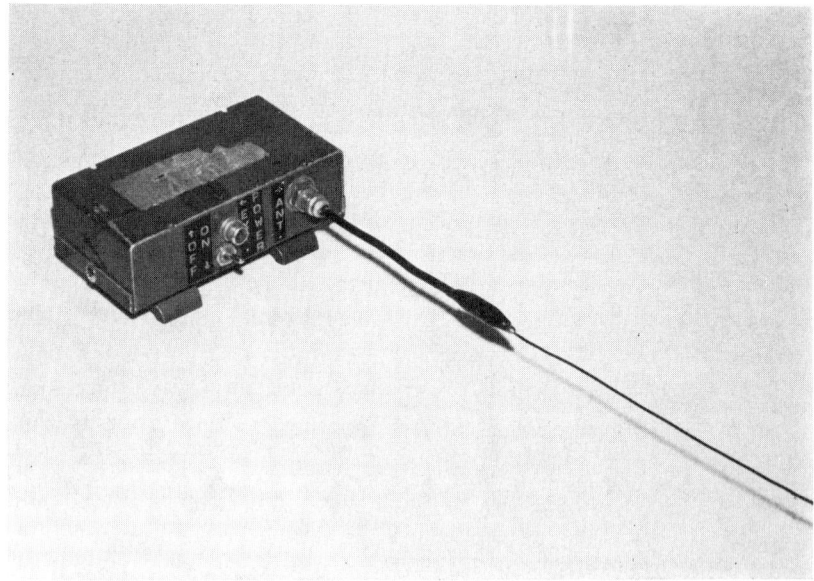

Figure 28. Miniature radio transmitter (bumper beeper) that is affixed to a subject vehicle for purposes of following it with a radio receiving unit.

# Automobile Surveillance

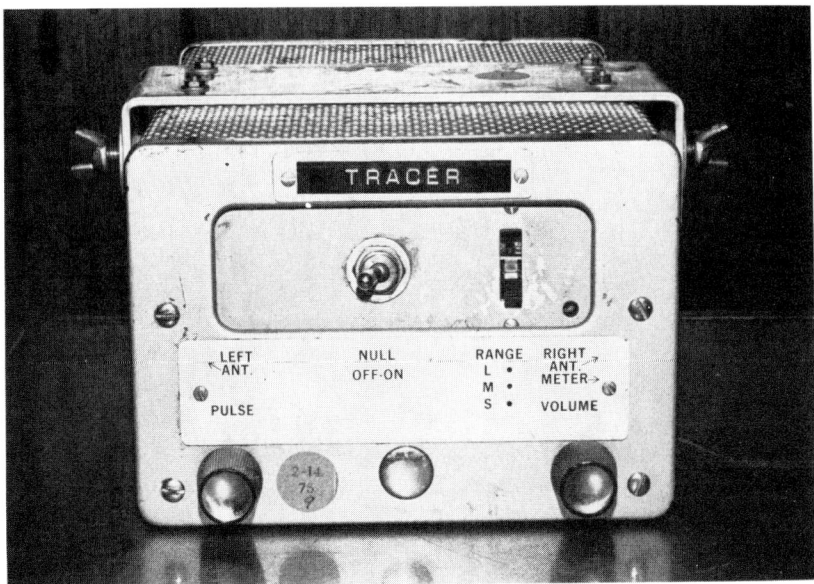

Figure 29. Special radio receiver for determining the approximate range and direction of the beeper shown in Figure 28.

vestigator must attempt to surveil a vehicle himself. This is very often the case with private investigators because of a client's unwillingness to pay the fee necessary for more than one investigator and vehicle.

Beepers may be affixed to almost any type of vehicle, such as a car, truck, boat, or airplane. Although most beepers contain strong magnets, some have a clamp with which they can be secured to a vehicle. In Figure 30 is illustrated a typical method of concealing a beeper upon an automobile. Note that the beeper has been positioned on the forward portion of the vehicle's gas tank with the antenna directed downward. When the vehicle is sitting on the ground, all that is visible is a short length of the antenna. The antenna is not highly noticeable, however, because it is dark in color and positioned several feet forward from the rear of the vehicle.

Some beepers emit a continuous signal while others emit a pulsating signal. The latter has an increased battery life because

Figure 30. Typical method of concealing a beeper (transmitter) on an automobile. Note that the beeper has been positioned just forward of the vehicle's gas tank with the antenna directed downward.

it is not transmitting continuously. Some beepers also contain their own power source (batteries) while others are intended to draw their power from the vehicle's electrical system. The latter are called *parasitic beepers*. Beepers that contain their own batteries typically will operate from four to ten days before it becomes necessary to replace the batteries. Parasitic beepers will operate indefinitely.

The Wackenhut Security Systems markets a parasitic beeper that is placed between a vehicle's radio and antenna by simply unplugging the antenna from the radio, plugging the beeper into the radio and then plugging the antenna lead into the beeper. A lead from the beeper must then be connected to a 12-volt wire from which it will receive its power. There are two distinct advantages to a beeper of this type over those that must be affixed to a vehicle's undercarriage. First, because this beeper is parasitic it will continue to operate as long as it is needed with no change of batteries being necessary. Secondly, because the signal is transmitted from the car's radio antenna, which is considerably higher than would be an antenna positioned under the car, the effective range is greater. The weakness of this type of a beeper lies in the fact that it takes several minutes to install and it is also necessary to gain entrance to the vehicle. The beeper shown in Figures 28 and 30 can be installed in a matter of just a few seconds. When a beeper is placed between the car's radio and its antenna, there is no interference with the radio's normal operation.

The typical range of most beepers is anywhere from two to five miles on the open road when the receiver is in another vehicle. In a downtown area the same beeper will have an effective range of only a few blocks. The range will be better if the vehicle is parked high on a parking ramp, but the signal may be lost entirely if the subject vehicle parks in an underground lot or garage. Should the receiver be placed in an aircraft, the effective range will be increased from two to five miles to well over twenty-five miles.

It will be found that the effective range of *any* beeper is significantly greater when either the transmitter (beeper) or receiver is elevated. Thus, when the distance between the two vehicles involved becomes too great and contact is lost, it is recommended that the surveillant drive quickly to high ground in an effort to reestablish contact. In some cities, the freeways are a good place to go when this situation occurs, for they are often elevated. In this respect, it helps to be familiar with the area. It is also for this reason that, when a semitrailer truck is to be followed, consideration should be given to the possibility of placing the beeper on top rather than under the trailer.

It was stated that most beeper receivers contain a direction finding capability. Some of the less sophisticated systems, however, will enable the investigator to determine the approximate distance between his vehicle and that of the subject based upon the strength of the signal, but possess no direction finding capability. Even these systems afford the investigator a considerable advantage over simply trying to maintain visual contact with the subject. Consider for a moment the benefit of knowing when one

70                Fundamentals of Physical Surveillance

is getting close to the subject after having lost sight of him during a surveillance. If the signal continues to get stronger, one is obviously getting closer. Should the signal begin to diminish, the distance between the vehicles is increasing. Many receivers have a three position switch that controls the sensitivity of the receiver, thus enabling one to better gauge the approximate distance from which the signal is being received.

Next in line insofar as sophistication is concerned are systems that enable one to determine when the subject vehicle is either directly in front of or to one side of the surveillant vehicle. This is illustrated in Figure 31. With this type of a system, the sound of the signal is distinctly different when it is received from the *null zone* directly ahead of the surveillant vehicle as opposed to the areas on either side. This being the case, when the subject

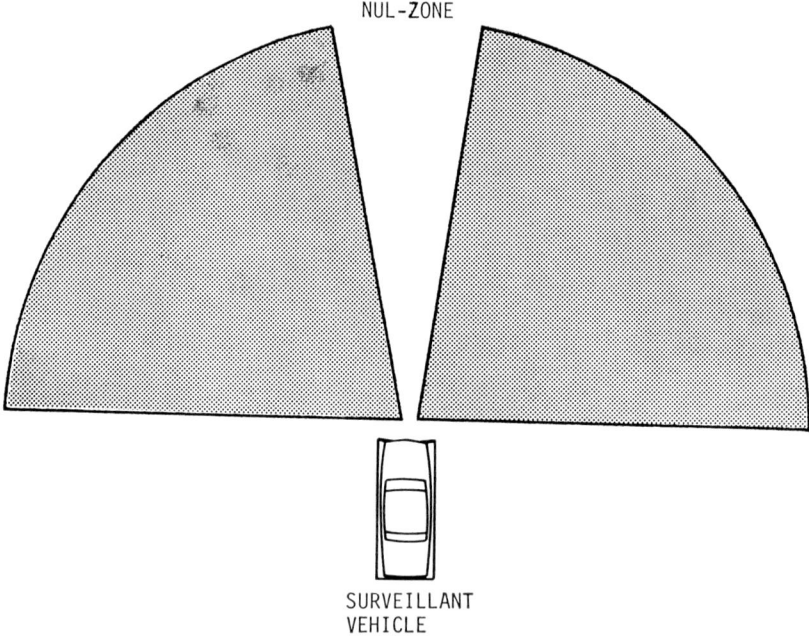

Figure 31. Illustrated is the *rough* area of coverage of the beeper's receiver with the center portion that has been left open indicative of the *null zone,* an area that will register a distinctly different sounding signal when the beeper transmits from within.

# Automobile Surveillance 71

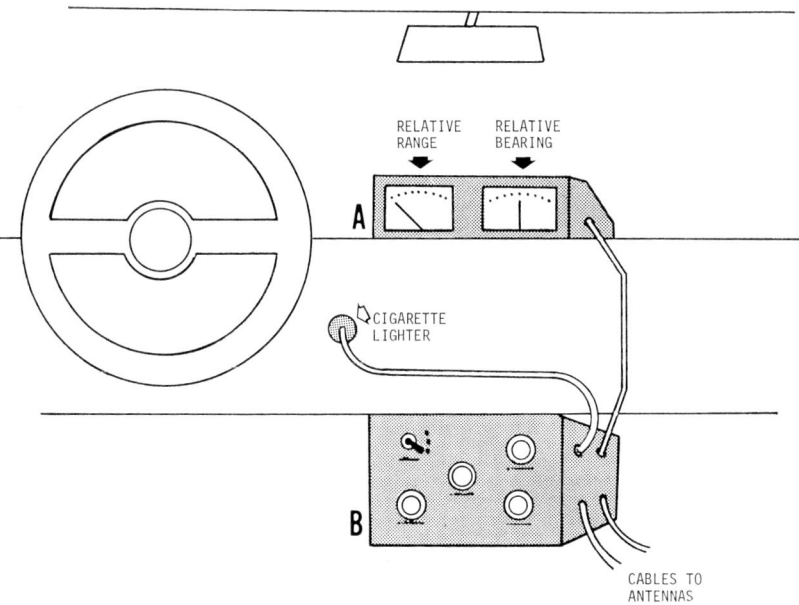

Figure 32. Sophisticated beeper system manufactured and marketed by The Wackenhut Corporation. With this system, a needle deflection indicates the direction from which the beeper's signal is received.

vehicle is directly in front of the surveillant vehicle, the investigator will be aware of its position based upon the tone of the signal. When the subject vehicle makes a turn, the move will be evident by a notable change in the tone of the signal. There is no indication, however, which way the subject vehicle has turned and it is necessary to make this determination by manipulating the surveillant vehicle in either direction until the subject is once again within the null zone. With this type of a system, as with all such systems, the relative range of the subject vehicle is determined by the pitch and/or strength of the signal.

A very sophisticated beeper system is the Bloodhound® manufactured by The Wackenhut Security Systems (see Figure 32). With this system, the direction from which the signal is being received is indicated by a vertical needle which will deflect in the direction from which the signal is received each time the beeper transmits a brief signal. When the subject vehicle is directly in front of the surveillant vehicle, the needle will remain vertical. In the event that the subject vehicle should go around a curve or turn a corner, the needle will deflect in the direction of the turn, thus enabling the surveillant to know immediately the subject's direction of travel.

Beeper systems, although they are not difficult to use, do require a certain amount of training and practice so as to correctly interpret the information that is provided. Even the Wackenhut system (Bloodhound), in spite of its high degree of sophistication, requires some experience. For example, it is possible, because of reflecting signals, to get a needle deflection to the right while the subject has in fact made a left turn. (The reason for this is illustrated in Figure 33.) The faster the vehicles involved are traveling, however, the less deceiving such signals will tend to be.

As was previously stated, beeper systems are useful not only as an aid for following another vehicle, but also for locating vehicles. If, for example, a beeper has been placed upon a suspect's vehicle and for some reason the vehicle must later be located, all one need do is drive back and forth (a grid pattern) through the area, making a sweep every couple of miles, depending, of course, upon the effective range of the beeper in the particular area. For example, if the beeper emits a signal that can be picked up from a distance of 1.5 miles, then one can drive back and forth through the area making three mile sweeps.

When attempting to locate a vehicle once its signal has been detected and the direction from which it is coming is determined, one can begin driving towards it, or he can attempt to pinpoint the vehicle's location, provided, of course, that the vehicle is stationary, by a process referred to as triangulation (see Figure 34). This can be accomplished with one vehicle, but a second vehicle equipped with a receiver will make it possible to pinpoint the vehicle's location much more quickly since they can take a reading from two different points simultaneously.

To determine the location of the subject vehicle, one should have a map of the area covered with clear plastic, a straight edge, and a grease pencil. The map must be positioned to coincide with the direction of the streets. The position of the surveil-

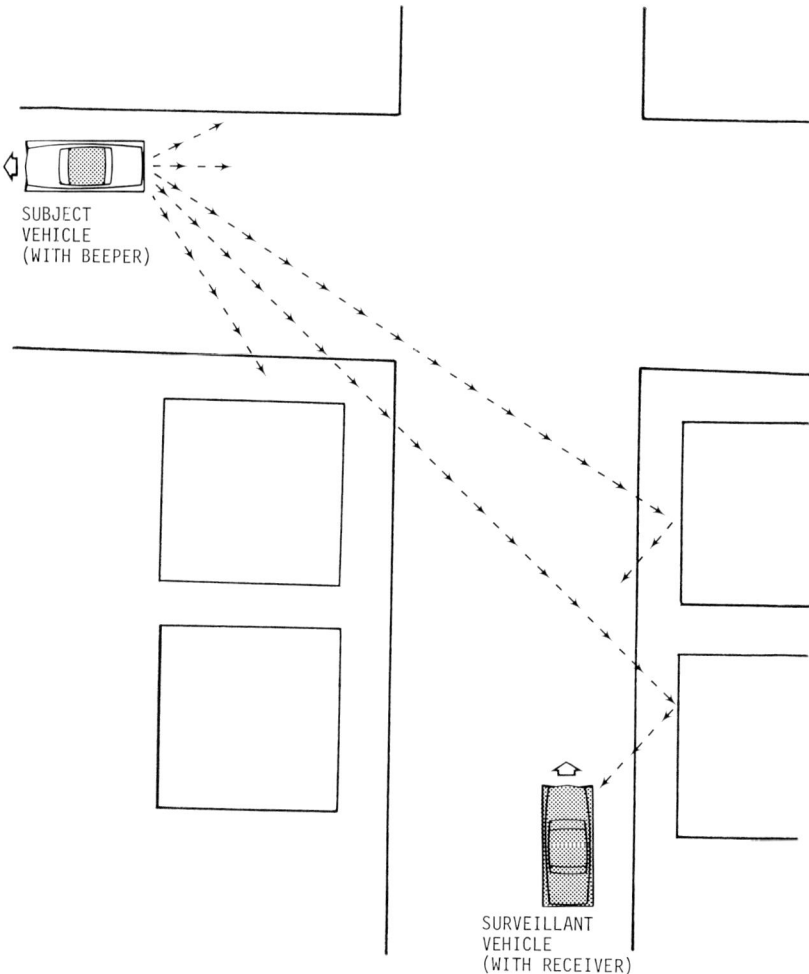

Figure 33. With a beeper system that features a direction finding capability, it is possible to get a false direction reading because of reflected signals. The faster the vehicles are traveling, however, the less deceiving such signals will tend to be.

lance vehicles is marked and a line drawn from each position to coincide with the direction (compass bearing in degrees) from which the signal is being received. As stated, this is done from two different locations. The point at which the two lines cross is the subject vehicle's approximate location. One may then move into the area to conduct a visual search for the vehicle in question. Should the subject be moving, it is possible to keep a running triangulation in this manner.

Because of the great range from which a beeper's signal may be detected when working from an aircraft and because of the speed of aircraft, a vehicle may be located much more quickly by this method if a very large area must be searched. Once the vehicle's approximate location has been determined, automobiles may move into the area to continue the search.

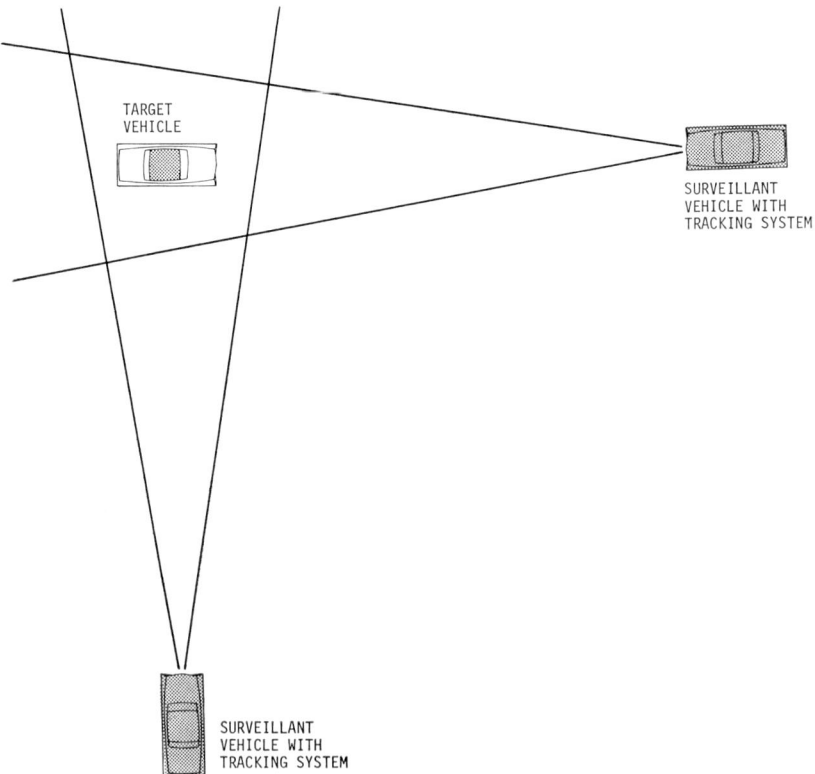

Figure 34. Two surveillance vehicles equipped with beeper receivers using a *triangulation technique* to determine the approximate location of a subject vehicle carrying a beeper.

One should also be aware, when using beeper systems in a metropolitan area, that if the subject gets onto a freeway, he can be lost within just a minute or two if the investigator does not follow suit. Consider that if the beeper has a range of two miles, and the subject enters a freeway and travels away at a speed of 60 M.P.H., it will take only two minutes to exceed the range of the beeper. If the subject was on the outer fringes of the beeper's range when entering the freeway, he may be lost in a matter of seconds. Again, it helps to know the area.

The reader should be aware that at the time of this writing there have been a couple of Federal Court decisions regarding the use of bumper beepers; see Chapter 13, Legal Aspects of Surveillance.

## CHAPTER 5

# Stationary Surveillance (Urban)

### GENERAL CONSIDERATIONS

STATIONARY SURVEILLANCE, often referred to as a *fixed surveillance* or *stake-out,* is a surveillance technique in which one will endeavor to observe a subject or area that is stationary, i.e. a given address and everyone who frequents it. When preparing for a stationary surveillance, the most important consideration to be made is that of selecting an observation post that provides both maximum cover and an unobstructed view of the area in question. In order to select the most appropriate observation post available, one should conduct a preliminary survey of the area. A preliminary survey will also enable investigators to select a mode of dress and a vehicle that is consistent with the area in which they will be working.

There are many reasons why a stationary surveillance operation will be initiated. This method of surveillance is almost always used as a preliminary to a moving surveillance to make contact with the subject. Law enforcement officers will also stake a place out for various other reasons as well. There are times, for example, when an informant has advised the police that a crime such as a burglary or robbery is planned for a given establishment within a certain time period. The police will naturally surveil the area in an effort to apprehend any offenders. It is not uncommon also for officers to surveil a given establishment to determine whether there is criminal activity taking place and also to identify those persons who frequent the premises. Investigations of offenses such as contraband sales and fencing operations will typically involve an operation of this nature along with other investigative techniques. Additionally, it is not uncommon for a uniformed patrol officer to stake out an individual's home or vehicle to effect an apprehension, or perhaps simply to issue a citation when an individual whose driver's license is under suspension gets into his vehicle and attempts to drive.

Civil and private investigators also engage in stationary surveillance for a number of reasons. A very common reason is a situation in which it is suspected that an individual has filed a *false disability claim*. When such is the case, civil investigators will surveil a subject's home or place of employment in an effort to observe him engaged in some type of activity that is inconsistent with his alleged disability. In most cases of this nature, a motion picture camera is used to document any activity that may be of significance.

Civil investigators are also employed for such things as surveilling a place of business when it is suspected that dishonest employees are passing merchandise out of the building to a confederate who removes it from the area. Again, photographic equipment may or may not be used to document the activity.

Whether a civil or a criminal case, the reasons for conducting a stationary surveillance operation are many. However, the techniques and methods employed remain basically the same.

During planning for a stationary surveillance, the needs of the case will generally suggest such things as the number of investigators that should be assigned to the case, the time duration of the operation, and the equipment to be employed.

When conducting a stake-out in an urban setting for an extended period of time, having two investigators assigned to the case is better than one. By assigning two investigators, one can make observations while the other writes notes and utilizes the radio. When the distance between the observation post and the subject necessitates the use of optical aids, having two investigators will enable them to alternate and thus help to eliminate fatigue.

## OBSERVATION POSTS

During a stationary surveillance, some form of cover is essential. In many instances it is desirable to select a point that is a considerable distance from the subject and make all observations using some type of optical aid such as binoculars or a telescope. Often, when working with optics from a long distance, the distance itself provides a considerable degree of cover. This being the case, the effectiveness of the actual cover is not so important as it is when working from a short distance. Normally, it is possible to work from a much greater distance during daylight hours than after dark. When darkness does necessitate selecting a position that is fairly close to the subject, the added cover provided by the darkness helps to offset the added danger of detection that is created by being closer to the subject.

There are a number of possibilities that suggest themselves when selecting an observation post in an urban setting. As one would expect, the effectiveness of any post is relative to the needs of the case and the specific circumstances under which the surveillance is being conducted.

*Automobiles* are often used as an observation post for surveillance operations of very short duration and in situations requiring a vehicle for the purpose of making an apprehension in the event that a violation is observed. Unfortunately, automobiles are not ideally suited for use as observation posts because cars are basically intended as a means of transportation, not as a place to sit for extended periods of time. This being the case, when an automobile is being used for such purposes, it is sometimes desirable to make use of several different vantage points and frequently move the vehicle from one to the next to avoid being in any one place for prolonged periods of time. When moving the vehicle, however, it should be done in an inconspicuous manner. Moving will help to avoid arousing undue worry and/or suspicion on the part of residents in the area.

When moving from one vantage point to another cannot be accomplished because there is only one suitable point from which to observe the subject, or when moving cannot be accomplished without leaving the subject area uncovered, one should consider the use of a suitable pretext for the purpose of adding an air of legitimacy to being in the area. The investigator may, for example, use a counter or a printed *traffic volume survey form* to give the appearance of making a traffic volume survey or he may raise the hood to simulate mechanical trouble. The appropriateness of a pretext will depend upon such factors as the nature of the neighborhood, the expected duration of the surveillance, and the specific needs of the case, to name only a few.

When it is known that one will be working in a given area, it is often advisable to contact the local law enforcement authorities, identify one's self, and explain that one will be working in a given area. When this is done, the police will not become suspicious when they see the same individual in the area for long periods. However, one should not become careless in his manner, feeling that because the police are aware of the operation it will be of no consequence if someone in the area becomes suspicious and makes a report to the police. One should remember that many people who have contacted the police regarding suspicious activity will watch to see what kind of action is taken. For this reason, if the police do not explain to the complainant what is taking place, nor approach the surveillant, questions are likely to be raised by an irate citizen.

When working from an automobile, one should drive to the desired position in a normal manner so as to not attract attention. Furthermore, a position on the next block is much better than being on the same block as the subject. Upon parking the car, one will tend to be less conspicuous if he sits in the passenger's seat and appears to be waiting for the driver rather than sitting behind the wheel. As an alternative, one may not be noticed at all if he sits in the back seat; when this is done, lowering the visors and raising the head rests will help a little to conceal one's presence. Another point worth noting is that a couple sitting in a car will draw less attention than will a lone male or two men.

Vans and campers have proven to be ideal for use as observation posts in situations where more suitable vantage points are for some reason not available. This is especially true when photographic equipment is employed. There are different schools of thought regarding how surveillance trucks should be equipped. Some investigators feel that one-way glass is the answer. Others feel that the mirror effect of the one-way glass has a tendency to betray the purpose of the vehicle.

One investigator attempted to conceal the purpose of the one-way glass on the sides of his van by having a fictitious *TV Repair* name painted on the sides with a picture of a television set also painted on the truck. The screen of the television set was then fitted with one-way glass. Investigators who do not use one-way glass often have curtains that can be drawn to darken the interior, thus allowing them to secretly observe or photograph out one of the windows that is only partially covered. Another technique that has proven to work well is the painting of a ficticious business name on the windows with the center portion of letters and numbers left unpainted, leaving a space through which observations and photographs can be made. Finally, some such vehicles have a blind that can be placed against the windows that gives the appearance of boxes and similar items stacked up. Camouflaged peep holes are provided in the blind.

When one is working from a truck, *all* unnecessary conversation and activity should be held to an absolute minimum to prevent anyone outside the vehicle from becoming aware of the fact that there are people inside. It is also for this reason that the volume of the radio should be checked to prevent its sounding loudly at an inappropriate time.

When a truck is being moved into position, the procedure will appear more natural if the driver alights and walks away after parking rather than remaining in the vehicle. When the surveillance is to be conducted for any reasonable length of time, provisions should be made for food, water, and a portable sanitary facility.

*Rooms in neighboring buildings* that provide an unobstructed view of the subject area make excellent observation posts and should be considered. Law enforcement officers will often find local merchants more than willing to give them a key to their establishment so that it may be used for such purposes during hours that it is not open for business. When considering contacting a building or business owner regarding the use of his premises as an observation post, it is important to consider the degree of his trustworthiness; if he is contacted, he must be made to understand the importance of maintaining absolute secrecy by telling no one about the operation.

When working from a room, one should make every effort to avoid being visible from the outside. *After the room has been darkened a bit, one will generally not be seen if a position is taken several feet from the glass.* In situations where it is necessary for some reason to be close to the glass, some means of camouflage should be employed so that people on the outside will not see the form of a person in the room. A lot can be accomplished by simply drawing the drapes part way, looking over the top of a shade, or placing a mirror within the room at the proper angle so that it provides a view of the area in question while the investigator himself remains out of view of anyone outside. *Never* should one peek out by pulling the shade or curtain to the side because both the movement and the unnatural position of the shade or curtain will attract attention.

When selecting a room in a building for a surveillance operation, one must make provisions for a discreet means of entering and leaving the area. Furthermore, if the owner of the building is not aware of the operation, nothing should ever be left unattended that would disclose the nature of the operation. Similarly, when the operation has been concluded, nothing should be left behind, even paper scraps, to indicate what has taken place.

*Roof tops* also make good observation posts in many instances. When working from a roof top, however, one should avoid a position directly across the street from the subject because a suspicious or wary subject will often make a visual check of the roof tops in his vicinity. One will be much less likely to be spotted if a roof top on the next block is selected, both because the subject will be less likely to be suspicious of the possibility of his being surveilled from that far away and because the added distance itself provides cover.

When considering roof tops, recognize that weather can be a problem at times. Recognize also that a person on a roof top who is silhouetted against the sky is easily noticed, and for this reason an effort should be made to have something behind one's self so as not to extend above the skyline.

*Outdoor observation posts* should be considered when there is no room, roof top, or ideal vehicle location from which to discreetly surveil an area. In many instances it is possible to obtain the permission of a homeowner to sit on his property for such purposes.

When an outdoor post is used, weather conditions are an important consideration. If it is cold out, it will take much more clothing to remain warm while sitting motionless than when moving about. If it is raining, appropriate rain gear is essential. Insect repellant should be taken if there is a chance that mosquitoes and other pests may be about.

In regard to cover, such things as fences, bushes, or lawn chairs can be effectively used to break up one's form, especially at night.

*Undercover techniques* may be in order in situations where there is no appropriate cover available. This is often referred to as using a *pretext*. A pretext may involve posing as a painter, a motorist with mechanical trouble, or whatever else would seem appropriate and natural under the circumstances.

CHAPTER 6

# Physical Surveillance by Uniformed Officers Using Marked Squad Cars

## GENERAL CONSIDERATIONS

THE BACKBONE of any police organization is its uniformed patrol force, consequently it is to this division that the greatest number of any department's personnel are assigned. In any community of reasonable size, there are uniformed patrol officers on duty twenty-four hours a day, 365 days a year. These officers, while on duty, are naturally available to respond to calls, but between calls they are concerned primarily with patroling and making visual observations, being alert for anything that may appear to be out of the ordinary.

Because of the amount of time that is spent by patrol officers making visual observations, it stands to reason that they will frequently see something that they feel warrants further observation. If the activity is taking place at a given location, binoculars can often be used to make observations from a distance that precludes detection; however, if the subject to be surveilled happens to be a moving vehicle, the officer is faced with the task of following it. With a marked squad car, this is at best a most challenging task because of the vehicle's distinctive appearance and silhouette.

## STATIONARY SURVEILLANCE

As was stated, the uniformed patrol officer has frequent occasion, for a number of reasons, to engage in surveillance while on duty with much of the activity calling for a stationary surveillance. Some reasons for this activity include observing a subject whose actions have in some way aroused the officer's suspicions or curiosity, waiting to see if someone whose driver's license has been revoked may attempt to drive, waiting to apprehend some-

one who is wanted, or perhaps discreetly returning to observe the scene of a disturbance to see if it will flare up again after the officer has left, to name only a few.

When positioning the squad car, the officer should endeavor to place it so that it is partially hidden from view as shown in Figure 35, or so that its distinctive silhouette is broken up by the background against which someone might see it. It is also helpful when conditions permit to position the vehicle so that it is within a shadowed area rather than on the sunlit side of some large object such as a building. Along these same lines is the positioning of the vehicle among or behind other parked vehicles on a street rather than along a stretch of road where there are no other parked vehicles. By so doing, a person will have a tendency to perceive only a string of parked vehicles and may not notice the squad car, at least not as readily as if the squad car were sitting in the open by itself (see Figure 36).

In some situations it is desirable to park the vehicle so that it is facing away from the area of the subject, and observations then made using the rear view mirror. Positioning the vehicle in this manner is desirable if the subject may attempt to leave the area by traveling in the direction in which the squad car is located and the possibility of a pursuit exists. This technique is also useful if the vehicle cannot for some reason be positioned out of the subject's view because it tends to give the impression that the driver is interested in something other than the subject. The primary disadvantage lies in the fact that one cannot discern detail as well using the rear view mirror as when viewing something directly. Whether this will prove to be a problem will depend upon the specific circumstances involved.

Another technique that may assist the patrol officer when conducting a stationary surveillance using a marked squad car is to

---

Figure 35. (A) The officer has positioned his vehicle so that he can view the subject's car, which is in a parking lot about 400 feet away, through a gap in the fence (see arrow). (B) View of the squad car taken from the position of the subject's vehicle (note arrow). (C) Closer view showing the squad car from the subject's line of view (note arrow).

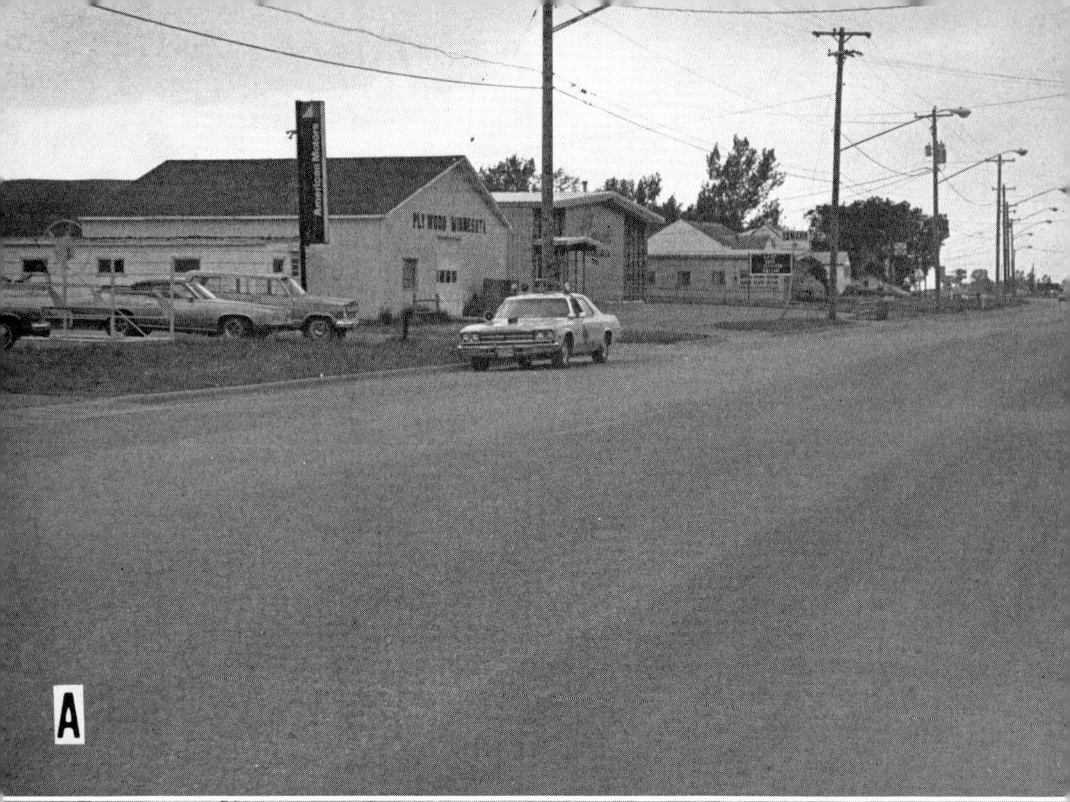
PLYWOOD MINNESOTA

A

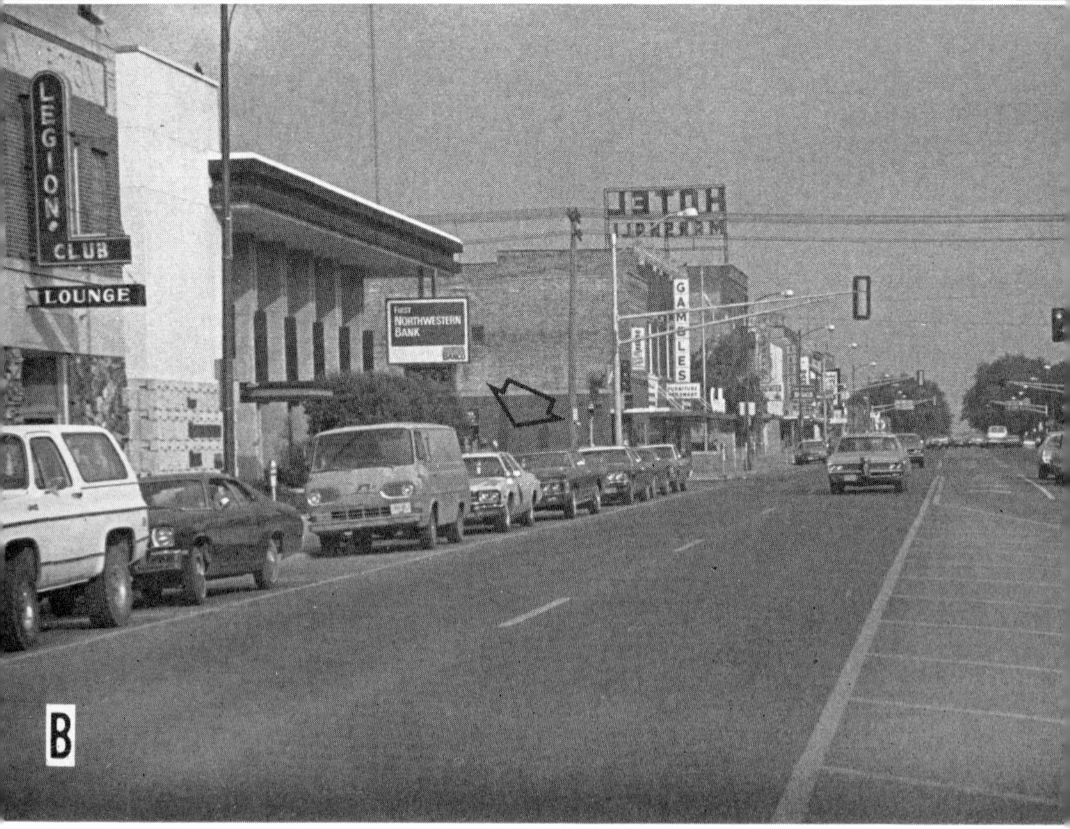
LEGION
CLUB
LOUNGE
FIRST NORTHWESTERN BANK
HOTEL
GAMBLES

B

appear to be making a traffic speed survey if the vehicle is equipped with a radar unit or one can appear to be making a traffic volume count. This pretext may or may not be supported with printed survey forms.

When a stationary surveillance is conducted using a marked vehicle at night, the cover provided by the darkness can be a real asset. To use the darkness effectively as a cover, it will in many instances be necessary to move into the area with the headlights off so that those being observed are not aware that a vehicle has moved into the area. In many cases in which the patrol officer, while patrolling at night, sees something that warrants further observation, if he can quickly extinguish his headlights, the subject may not become aware of his presence; he can then watch from his present position or possibly move to a better one without his lights. If, however, the lights cannot be extinguished before the subject has become aware of the squad car, it is sometimes better to proceed on by as if one had no particular interest in the subject and then return without lights. When moving into the area without lights, it is best to drive slowly to reduce the likelihood of the vehicle's being heard. One should also keep one hand on the headlight switch for safety purposes.

During movement without headlamps, the brake lights while stopping and the backup lights after stopping can serve as a giveaway, with the brake lights being the more serious of the two. Unfortunately, many administrators will not agree to having cut-out switches installed so that these lights can be deactivated. A common argument against such switches, and it is a valid concern, is the safety hazard that will exist if the brake light switch is forgotten in the *off* position. An alternative to an on-off switch is a pressure switch that would require the driver to hold pressure on the switch while using the brakes. Such a setup would naturally be a bit inconvenient, but it is a reasonable compromise between efficiency and safety.

---

Figure 36. (A) The presence of a squad car parked along a street that is free of other parked vehicles is very obvious. (B) A squad car parked among other parked vehicles is much less noticeable (note arrow).

When using a vehicle that does not have a cut-out switch for the brake lights, one may use the emergency brakes by either disconnecting the spring that holds the release lever in place or by holding pressure on the release lever. When using the emergency brake, one will observe that if more than moderate pressure is applied, a tire will tend to drag, causing a considerable amount of noise. For this reason the braking should be fairly gradual. The fact that the vehicle will be moving slowly will help considerably. It also helps a bit to put the vehicle in *neutral* when stopping. With most vehicles having automatic transmissions, if a forward gear is selected the vehicle will begin moving forward. By putting the vehicle into *neutral* when stopping, it will not be necessary for the emergency brake to overcome this force, even though limited.

After stopping, when the shift lever is moved from the drive or neutral position to the park position, it should be done very quickly so that the backup lights will not be on for any longer than a fraction of a second. This will lessen the chance of detection. The fact that the backup lights will in most cases be facing away from the subject will help considerably.

Any vehicle that will be used for any type of night surveillance activity should have the courtesy light switch disconnected so that the dome light will not come on when the door is opened. Failure to do so can very easily disclose one's presence if he must get out of the vehicle. Disconnecting the door switch is easily accomplished by removing the switch, disconnecting one of the wires and then remounting the switch in its original position. When the dome light is needed, it can be turned on using the switch in the dash.

Another problem that frequently occurs when one is attempting to surveil a subject at night using a marked squad car is the reflections from the chrome of the emergency equipment above the vehicle. Generally the bar on which these items are mounted is also chrome plated. Except for these undesirable reflections, a marked squad car can appear, at night, much the same as any other vehicle on the road. To eliminate this problem some officers cover the chrome with tape. Unless covered with tape, the problems of reflections from the overhead chrome can manifest themselves whether the vehicle is used for moving or stationary surveillance.

It will be found that the many rules of thumb that apply to the conducting of a stationary surveillance from an automobile do not always apply when using a marked squad car. Normally, when seated in a vehicle for the purpose of making observations, it is recommended that the surveillant sit either in the passenger's seat or in the back seat so as to appear more natural or to be less conspicuous. This does not apply to the uniformed officer using a marked squad car because his presence will naturally be obvious to those in the immediate area. Furthermore, the residents are not inclined to become as suspicious and worried about the officer sitting for a period of time in one spot as they would were he an individual who was not known in the neighborhood. The people may very well become curious as to why the officer is lingering in the area, but they will not become suspicious and call the local police department with a complaint.

It is also recommended that, when an unmarked vehicle is being used as an observation post, it not normally remain in any one spot too long, but that it be moved to a new position from time to time to avoid suspicion on the part of local residents. This naturally does not apply to the marked squad car. This is not to infer that it is not desirable in some situations to move a marked vehicle to a new position from time to time, but it is not done to minimize suspicion that the driver is a negative element of society and is perhaps up to no good.

The patrol officer will find that, when sitting in a marked squad car for any reasonable period of time during hours that children will be outside playing, they will often wander over and begin asking questions. This can in some instances present a problem, and whether it will be best to find a new position, ask them to leave, or simply tolerate them will depend upon the circumstances. If one is using the pretext of making a traffic volume count or a speed survey, he can so indicate when the children inquire as to what he is doing. In this way, inquisitive children can be used to advantage in some instances. The officer will also find that local residents who have had something on their mind will sometimes take the liberty of approaching him and making an informal complaint. How these people should be handled will, of course, depend upon the circumstances. But regardless of how the officer handles these people, they must be treated courteously. In many instances, they too can be used to advantage if they are permitted to leave believing that the officer is engaged in something other than his actual task.

### MOVING SURVEILLANCE

When it becomes necessary to discreetly follow a vehicle using a marked squad car, the officer is at a distinct disadvantage for obvious reasons; however, there are a few techniques that are somewhat effective and if practiced, they will increase the chances of success.

During daylight hours, a marked squad car is highly visible and a technique that would normally work well with an unmarked vehicle will not necessarily work when using a marked vehicle. For example, a common technique employed when using an unmarked vehicle is to keep a couple of unrelated vehicles between the subject vehicle and the surveillance vehicle. With a marked vehicle, however, this technique is not effective for obvious reasons. A more suitable alternative might be a *parallel* method if the layout of the area favors it. The parallel method will often work well in residential areas (refer to the section on *Parallel Surveillance* in Chapter 4).

In many instances distance is the patrol officer's best cover; however, the greater the distance that is maintained between the two vehicles involved, the greater will be the possibility of losing the subject. Traffic conditions will have a significant influence on the best distance to maintain.

At night, if there is no other traffic on the road, following a subject with lights off can prove to be very effective. When one is using this procedure, it is recommended that one hand be kept on the light switch for safety purposes. One must also not only watch the subject and for obstacles in or along the roadway such as parked vehicles, but he must be extremely alert for the possi-

# Uniformed Officers Using Marked Squad Cars 91

Figure 37. (A) Officer in full uniform. (B) By replacing the uniform cap with a wig and ball cap, adding a pair of sunglasses, and covering the uniform with a jacket, one no longer appears to be a uniformed officer.

bility of another vehicle pulling away from the curb or entering the roadway from a side street or driveway.

When the uniformed officer desires to follow a vehicle discreetly at night but the subject is aware of the squad car, it will sometimes work to either turn off the road and then double back without lights or wait until the subject turns off, at which point the officer would continue going straight ahead until out of sight and then double back without lights.

In surveillance activity using a marked squad car, just as was the case when using an unmarked vehicle, it is desirable to have lying on the seat next to the driver a pair of binoculars that can be picked up and used without delay. (Refer to the section *Binoculars for Automobile Surveillance* in Chapter 4.)

**UNDERCOVER TECHNIQUE FOR UNIFORMED OFFICERS**

There are times when a uniformed officer working with a marked squad car will observe activity that is of interest to him, but the circumstances are such that, if he leaves his position in an attempt to make an apprehension or to confiscate contraband or seize evidence, the subject(s) will see him before he can get to them and the evidence or contraband will either be destroyed or disposed of. There is also the danger that the people will flee and get away.

In some instances, the officer can direct a second officer in from another direction using the radio, and once he has reached the subject's position, the first officer can safely leave his position to assist. In some instances, however, this is not possible. In this case, it is often possible for the officer to put on a shirt or jacket that is long enough to cover his duty belt and the equipment hanging from it, and also a fairly long wig and/or cap. Depending upon the time of day, it may be desirable to include even sunglasses. When these things are worn over the uniform, it is not difficult to walk up to almost anyone without his realizing that it is a uniformed police officer approaching (see Figure 37). By the time the officer is close enough to the subjects for them to discern that something is wrong, he will be close enough to effect an apprehension.

CHAPTER 7

# Surveillance in Rural Areas

## GENERAL CONSIDERATIONS

WHILE MUNICIPAL LAW enforcement officers are generally not concerned with surveillance techniques that are applicable to rural areas, there are many enforcement officers and investigators, both governmental and private, whose work frequently takes them into such areas. Consider, for example, the investigators employed by the Federal Bureau of Investigation, the Bureau of Alcohol, Tobacco and Firearms, and the Conservation Department. The jurisdiction of these agencies includes such areas. This holds true also for sheriff's departments whose area of jurisdiction typically includes far more rural than urban area. Among the many private investigative companies are a few very large firms having offices not only throughout the United States, but the entire free world, with Pinkerton's, Incorporated, being the oldest, largest, and most widely known of such companies. Although the majority of the investigative work engaged in by such companies is for business and industry, and therefore concentrated largely in urban areas, investigations conducted by these companies do frequently take their investigators into rural areas.

In this chapter, an attempt is made to provide the reader with the necessary information to give him understanding of physical surveillance techniques applicable to the rural setting.

## THE PRELIMINARY SURVEY

When preparing for surveillance activity in a rural area, it is important, as always, to conduct a thorough preliminary survey of the area in question. This preliminary survey is important if one is to benefit from a vantage point that offers both good concealment and an unobstructed view of the area to be surveilled. A preliminary survey will also alert the surveillant to such things as the type of dress and vehicle that will be consistent with the surroundings and the most appropriate routes by which to enter and leave the area.

When conducting the initial survey, one should pay close attention to all roads in the area, including field roads, roads created by logging crews, and the like. This is especially important if the surveillance is likely to result in a pursuit. To attempt a pursuit in such areas without being reasonably familiar with the area is hazardous and the likelihood of apprehending a suspect who is familiar with the area will be greatly reduced. When one conducts the initial survey of an area, it is not uncommon to survey an area as great as several miles in all directions from the subject's location. In many instances this can be effectively accomplished using aircraft along with maps of the area (see Figure 38).

## RURAL VANTAGE POINTS

After the preliminary survey has been conducted, the information obtained should be used to select a good vantage point and the most appropriate route by which to travel to and from that location. When selecting a vantage point, the primary concern is a position that both conceals the observer from the view of those being observed and possibly others in the area, and a location that affords the surveillant with an unobstructed view of the area to be observed. In some cases it is also necessary that the vantage point be situated so that the investigators can move quickly to make an apprehension. If there is no such vantage point, it may be necessary to have one investigator positioned where he can observe effectively, and have additional investigators positioned at a point from which they can effectively make an apprehension when so advised by the observer. Radio communication in such instances is essential. When using radios, it is important that the volume be kept low enough so that it does not alert the subject.

Figure 38. Aerial photographs are often useful for studying an area prior to conducting a surveillance operation in a rural area. (A) Taken at an altitude of about 700 feet above the ground (not sea level). (B) Taken from an altitude of about 5,000 feet above the ground.

While it was stated that the vantage point should conceal the observer from the subject's view, it is not always necessary to be completely concealed from view so much as it is necessary to blend with the surroundings. The subject should not be able to detect a notable color difference between the surveillant and the surroundings, nor should he be able to detect an outline that is characteristic of man. In this respect, one would be well advised to utilize camouflaging techniques when conditions warrant it (see section on Camouflaging).

The possibilities for vantage points in a rural area are many, and one is encouraged to use his imagination. Trees are useful, since people seldom look up into them. The surveillant may dig out a shallow foxhole and lie on a tarp in it. If the foxhole is in an open area, it may be desirable to cover one's self up with a camouflage tarp. Tall weeds, crops, bushes, rocks, and tree stumps are also effective (see Figure 39). Large bushes, brush piles, and windfalls can be hollowed out to some degree without altering their original appearance and then used to sit in; they make excellent blinds. Natural contours in the land such as ravines and gullies are often located in desirable places and should be used (see Figure 40). Actually, any place a person can effectively secrete himself will prove to be effective in most instances. Care should be taken, however, so that the location selected is not one that is likely to be discovered accidentally by the subject, children at play, domestic animals, hunters, and so forth. Should people by chance pass near the investigator's position, it is desirable that the investigator not look directly at them as they pass, for if he does, they are likely to sense his presence. Additionally, the less movement there is on the part of the surveillant, the less chance there will be of anyone becoming aware of him. It must be remembered that the human eye is quick to detect movement, but if the surveillant is dressed in a color that blends well with

---

Figure 39. (A) Standing in the open in a rural area will make one's presence obvious. (B) By standing behind some natural object, one's presence will be much less noticeable.

his surroundings and he remains motionless, it is quite likely that someone could look directly at him and not notice him.

When moving into position in a rural area, it will at times be necessary to move into the area under cover of darkness. It may also be necessary in some situations to remain on post for several days. For this reason, provisions for food and water should be taken into consideration. Care should also be taken to ensure a reasonable degree of comfort, for an uncomfortable surveillant will not remain as alert as he otherwise would. In cold weather it must be remembered that it takes considerably more clothing to keep warm when sitting motionless than when moving.

Depending upon the circumstances involved, observations in a rural area can sometimes be made from a motor vehicle with the use of binoculars or a telescope. When this is done, it is important to position the vehicle so that it is not in direct view of the subject (see Figure 41). It is also recommended that the vehicle be of a subtle color that will blend with the background (brown, green, dark gray, etc.) rather than a color that is outstanding. In addition to the color of the vehicle, it is equally important that the chrome parts of the vehicle be toned down, perhaps with a layer of dirt or with vehicle wax. This will prevent light reflections. It is also desirable in many instances to cover the windshield and the rear window with a tarp or blanket because glass can also reflect light, thus betraying the presence of the vehicle.

## MOVING INTO THE SURVEILLANCE AREA

After the initial survey has been completed and a vantage point selected, it must be determined when the surveillance activity will provide the most desired results. After these things have been decided upon, it will be necessary for the surveillant to move unobtrusively into the area. Whether this will best be accomplished during daylight hours or under cover of darkness,

---

Figure 40. (A) Natural contour in the land being used by a surveillant for cover while surveilling a rural area. (B) Subject's view of the surveillant as he is positioned in A (note arrow).

by foot or by vehicle, will depend upon the circumstances. In either case, however, the main objective is to move into the area and take up one's position in a manner that does not serve to alert others to the fact, or to arouse someone's curiosity or suspicions.

When moving into an area by car during daylight hours, it is desirable in most cases to drive to one's destination in a manner that would be expected of one who belonged in the area and knew where he was going. In other instances, it is possible to move unnoticed into the area by using an alternate route. If, however, it is necessary to move into the area under cover of darkness, the procedure may be quite different.

When it is necessary to move by vehicle into an area under cover of darkness, it is often desirable to extinguish the headlights a considerable distance, sometimes several miles, from the area in question and proceed the remaining distance using a *blackout light* (see Section titled Blackout Lights). When nearing the vicinity of the subject, the speed of the vehicle should be reduced to about five to ten miles per hour to eliminate the tire hum that can be heard at night for a considerable distance. On a gravel road it is necessary to reduce the vehicle's speed more than on a hard surface road. In low gear, the proper rate of speed can often be maintained with the engine idling. A word of caution is in order. When night driving without headlamps, it is highly recommended that the surveillant begin by pulling over to the side of the road for ten to twenty minutes, thus allowing his eyes to readjust themselves to the change in illumination. This period of readjustment is necessary even if one will be using parking lights or a blackout light.

---

Figure 41. When working from an automobile in a rural area, it is important that the vehicle be covered in some way so that it is not in direct view of the subject. (A) Surveillant vehicle positioned so that the surveillant can view the subject through a break in the tree line (note arrow). (B) Note how subtle the presence of the vehicle is when positioned behind foliage, even though not completely hidden from view. It is important that the color of the vehicle be subtle.

If two or more surveillance vehicles will be traveling at night without lights, it is recommended that they move one at a time. If it is necessary that they move at the same time, it is extremely important that each driver know exactly where the other is at all times to prevent an accident between them. It has happened. The drivers should also be alert for other traffic which might present a potential hazard.

When one moves into an area on foot, it will sometimes be better to travel at night, sometimes by day. The following points of consideration will apply in some cases to daytime operations and in other cases to nighttime operations—in some instances, to both. Good judgment on the part of the investigator will generally dictate when each is more appropriate.

When moving into or through a rural area on foot, it is important that it be done in a manner that will not alert the subject to the surveillant's presence. The need to move very quietly logically increases the closer one gets to the subject. In situations where one will be moving in extremely close to the subject, extreme caution must be exercised.

There are a number of ways in which one can move very quietly and unnoticed in a rural setting. The fundamentals of this art will be discussed in this section. Naturally, the techniques that will work best will depend upon the part of the country in which one is working and upon the time of the year. However, the logic behind the techniques that are discussed here will apply to most situations so long as the reader makes whatever variations may be necessary to conform to his particular area and situation.

When one works in a rural area, it is desirable in many instances to utilize camouflaging techniques so as to blend with the surroundings and thus reduce the possibility of detection, not only while at the vantage point, but also in traveling to and from that point.

When moving on foot, it is desirable to avoid large open areas. however, when such areas must be crossed, one should take advantage of any natural cover that may be present such as natural contours of the land, weeds, shrubbery, and perhaps crops. In some instances it will be necessary for one to crawl on his belly

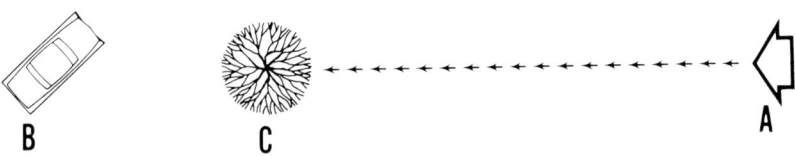

Figure 42. When attempting to approach a subject in a rural setting, there usually exists some kind of a blind spot that can be used for cover while approaching the subject. In this case, if the surveillant (A) keeps the tree (C) between himself and the subject (B) while moving, it is highly unlikely that he will be observed by the subject.

to avoid detection, while in other cases one will be forced to take the long way around.

When moving into a position that is very close to a subject, one can usually find a blind spot of some sort that will provide some degree of cover while moving. The blind spot may consist of nothing more than a bush. Figure 42 illustrates a subject's position, a tree, and a surveillant's course of travel as he approaches the subject. As will be observed, as long as the investigator keeps the tree between himself and the subject, the possibility of being detected will remain minimal. In some cases, it is necessary to crawl slowly through the grass and weeds to achieve the desired position. Never should one walk on the crest of a hill, thus becoming silhouetted against the sky, but rather, below the crest (see Figures 43 and 44).

When moving through a rural area, it is recommended that one not use any foot paths that may be in the area, even though they will make travel easier. It is better to travel a short distance to either side of the path, moving slowly, quietly, and remaining alert for anyone who may be using the path.

Dogs and domestic livestock can present both a nuisance and a hazard. One possible means of avoiding them, aside from the obvious need for slow, quiet movement, is to approach the area from down or across wind. In the event that one is discovered by such animals, it is generally better to pacify them in some manner rather than trying to chase them away.

When a surveillance is to be conducted for an extended period of time, there will necessarily be many trips made to and from

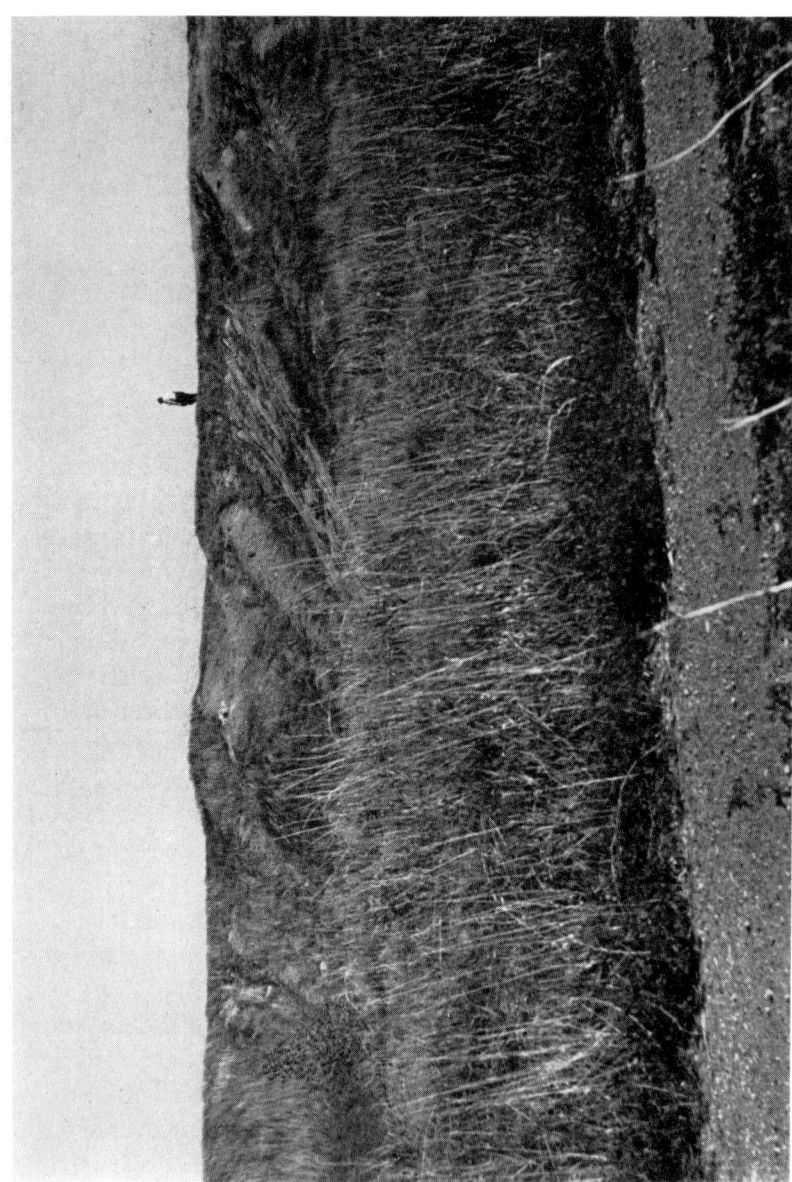

Figure 43. When moving through a rural area, one's presence will be obvious if he allows himself to become silhouetted against the sky.

# Surveillance in Rural Areas

Figure 44. A person walking below the skyline is much less noticeable.

the chosen vantage point. If the same route is used consistently, it will take only a short period of time before a telltale path has been formed, thus betraying the surveillant's activity in the area. For this reason, a slightly different route should be used each time if at all possible. If using different routes to avoid creating a path is not possible, an effort should be made to select a route that coincides with natural lines of the terrain such as along fences, along the edge of fields, etc. This consideration is especially important if there is a possibility that the subject will view the area from the air.

When moving through an area on foot, every effort should be made to walk on surfaces that are not only quiet, but those that will not leave tracks. When leaving tracks cannot be avoided, try walking on the balls of the feet because the resulting tracks will appear much less like those of a human. When following a creek, one often finds it difficult to walk on the banks without leaving a distinct trail. For this reason the banks should be avoided. In some instances it may be desirable to walk *in* a creek rather than beside it, provided, of course, that the mud stirred up from the bottom will not serve to alert someone.

It is comparatively easy to walk quietly after a rain has soaked the ground because fallen leaves, grass, and twigs do not have a tendency to crack or crunch as they do when dry. Similarly, ground that is covered with freshly fallen snow makes for very quiet movement. Unfortunately, fresh snow leaves testimony of one's having been in the area. Gravel is difficult to walk on quietly while grass is very good. Although walking through grass does tend to leave a trail, it will normally stand back up after a relatively short period of time and again look normal. When walking through grass, try taking high steps so that the grass is disturbed *only where the foot has been set down*. This is much better than walking through the area in a normal manner and simply plowing down the grass as one goes along his way.

Although rainy or stormy weather is not the most pleasant weather to travel in on foot, such weather provides ideal cover for movement. Windy days are also good because the noise of the wind blowing has a tendency to conceal any noise the surveillant may make. When difficulty is being experienced with quiet movement on a calm, dry day, consider placing a very large thick pair of wool socks over one's shoes because they have a great muffling effect. Moccasins are also a worthwhile consideration.

Snow that has formed a hard crust is often quite noisy to walk on because the surface collapses as one applies weight to the foot. A worthwhile technique to try involves poking a hole through the crust of the snow with the toe and then inserting the foot through the hole. When walking on crusty snow that simply makes a crunching sound but does not give way, try slowly setting the foot down with all the weight evenly distributed on the foot rather than bringing the heel into contact first and then rolling the weight as is characteristic of normal walking.

A variation of the walking technique that was just described is one that was used so successfully by the American Indians while hunting and in warfare. This technique involves the simple process of moving very slowly and setting the foot down by bringing the ball of the foot into contact with the ground first, then the heel. It is important to set the foot down where there is nothing that will tend to make a sound when weight is applied, such as a twig that could crack. One will do well to experiment a bit to determine what walking technique will work best for him. Consider also the possibility of one technique working better on some surfaces than on others.

In attempting to move quietly, it is absolutely essential that nothing be worn or carried that will make sounds, such as keys or loose change. Furthermore, the clothing should not be of a material that will create a scraping sound when walking.

When moving into the area, one should allow enough time so that it does not become necessary to hurry. One should move slowly, stopping frequently to look around and listen. One should be ever alert for alarm devices such as trip strings. Some devices will be designed to sound an alarm of some type while others will simply upset an object so that a later inspection by the subject will reveal the fact that someone has been in the area. Similarly, one should avoid leaving anything that could disclose his presence such as paper scraps or damaged vegetation. While walking, it is important to look from side to side and frequently to the rear.

As already stated, when moving to or from the vantage point, and while at the vantage point, one should take advantage of any natural cover that is available and keep all sound and movement to a minimum. If working with a partner, one should keep talking to a minimum, and when it is necessary to talk, it should be done in low tones.

When two investigators have been assigned, it is desirable for one to concentrate on the subject area while the other records notes and watches for anyone that may happen upon them. The second investigator can also move in for a closer examination if necessary. Furthermore, if it becomes necessary to change the vantage point, one of the investigators can meet the relief team and escort them to the new location.

Not to be overlooked when working in rural areas is the use of a suitable pretext. Desirable results can often be achieved by posing as a hunter, fisherman, camper, surveyor, or whatever else would appear natural under the particular circumstances.

The following is a listing of twelve points summarizing what has been discussed. If these considerations are adhered to and practiced, there is little reason why one should not be effective when moving through a rural area on foot.

   1. A recent rainfall or snowfall aids significantly in quiet movement through an area on foot.

   2. Walking quietly involves picking one's footsteps carefully while maintaining good balance as well as not trying to move too rapidly.

   3. Rainy, blustery weather, although a bit unpleasant, is ideal for discreet movement.

   4. When it is dry, and silent movement is difficult, try placing a very large thick pair of wool socks over the shoes. They have a great muffling effect. Moccasins are also a worthwhile consideration.

   5. Windy days are good because sounds made by the surveillant are covered by the rustling of leaves, bushes, and branches.

   6. When moving through an area, be alert and look from side

to side and frequently to the rear. Learn to see what is being looked at.

7. Use all available cover because it helps to break up the telltale form of man.

8. Avoid walking on dry leaves, dry limbs, twigs, or gravel.

9. Do not move continuously, but rather, move short distances, stopping frequently to look and listen.

10. When possible, move into or across the wind to avoid having one's scent detected by any dogs the subject may have.

11. Avoid unnecessary movement. Movement of a person can be quickly detected in a rural area because it is emphasized by the immobile background.

12. Do not be in a hurry. Plan ahead so that plenty of time is allotted for moving to the desired position.

## CAMOUFLAGING

When working from an outdoor observation post in a rural area, it is important that one take appropriate measures to blend effectively into the surroundings without altering its natural and original appearance. To achieve this end, it is often desirable to take advantage of various camouflage techniques that are appropriate to the specific locale.

When camouflaging one's self, the color of the clothing that is worn should blend with the *predominant* color of the background against which one may be observed. Furthermore, the skin and all light colored or shiny equipment should also be toned down for the same purpose. A sharp glint of sunlight reflecting from an item such as a belt buckle or watch, even though only for an instant, can alert a subject.

When using camouflage clothing and skin toning, one must remember that these measures will only assist one in remaining undetected while utilizing natural cover in the area. If one dons camouflage clothing and paints his face only to sit in the open, chances are he will be detected because camouflage techniques are intended not to make one completely unnoticeable, but only to enable one to blend effectively with the natural surroundings. To do this one should attempt to use the surroundings and the cam-

110   *Fundamentals of Physical Surveillance*

ouflaging together to prevent a contrast between his silhouette and the background. This can best be accomplished by positioning one's self not in the open, but among such things as shrubbery, in shadowed areas, among rocks, and by *remaining perfectly still*. If this is done, there is little reason why one should not experience a good deal of success at these endeavors.

When toning the skin, one can use a paint stick made specifically for this purpose, or he may use burnt cork, mud, carbon paper, and anything else that will cause the skin to blend better with the surroundings. When toning the skin, one may use an even color or he may use what is referred to as a disruptive painting technique. When using a disruptive technique, the patterns should cut across the nose lines, cheek bones, eye sockets, and chin lines. The color frontispiece depicts a subject among some shrubbery wearing camouflage clothing and skin toning. Skin toning should also be considered at night to prevent the moonlight from reflecting from the oil of the skin. Figure 45 shows an individual wearing *whites* to blend with the snow.

Figure 45. Investigator wearing white coveralls to blend better with snow.

It was stated that any equipment being used should be toned down so as to avoid detection. One way of doing this is to wrap the object with a cloth, possibly in strips, that is of a color that blends well with the background.

## COVERS

When working from an outdoor observation post, one will sometimes find that there is not sufficient natural cover in the area and it will be necessary to construct some type of a supplementary cover. Such cover should not, under normal circumstances, be isolated because such things as a lone clump of bushes will draw attention. This is especially true if the cover is in a location where there was previously nothing.

When constructing a cover, natural materials such as bushes and tree branches with leaves will naturally appear the most normal; however, it must be remembered that branches with leaves, once cut, will turn brown after a short period of time and, if not replaced, will serve to pinpoint the observer's position. For this reason, when such materials are used, it is extremely important that they be periodically replaced, with care being given as to how the dead foliage is disposed of.

As can be seen, there are certain problems that manifest themselves when natural materials are used for the construction of a cover. As an alternative to natural materials are various artificial materials which may effectively be used to simulate tall grass, bushes, stumps, rocks or whatever else the situation may call for.

In some situations a foxhole will prove effective. Whether one will dig a hole deep enough to simply lie in or deep enough to sit in will depend largely upon the individual situation. When a foxhole is dug, it will most often be done under cover of darkness with all evidence of the night's activity being removed before morning. The hole, after being dug, should be concealed with an appropriate cover. When the hole is dug, the dirt should be placed into sand bags or on a tarp and deposited in some suitable location such as on a dirt road, in a body of water or creek, out of sight under a bush, and so forth. If for some reason the dirt cannot be removed, it should be covered with natural materials such as leaves, branches, and sticks.

## BLACKOUT LIGHTS

Blackout lights, referred to by some investigators as *sneak lights,* were designed so that military convoys could move at night and yet remain undetected by opposing forces. These lights, for obvious reasons, have proven to be very useful for investigators who have a need to drive undetected at night through rural areas. Figure 46 illustrates how a blackout light works. As will be observed, the point from which the light is emitted is shielded from the view of anyone who may be in front of or to the side of the light, and as one would expect, the level of the illumination provided is quite low. Another factor favoring the efficiency of these lights is that the sides of pebbles, rocks, etc., that face the light source are illuminated while the opposite sides remain mostly shadowed and therefore less visible to anyone who may be in front of the investigator's vehicle. While the intensity of these lights is necessarily low, it provides for reasonably safe travel at low speeds (ten to twenty-five miles per hour).

The method of mounting these lights on a vehicle is very much an individual consideration. As shown in Figure 47, some investigators prefer to have a bracket mounted on their vehicle to which the light can be attached when needed, and when not in use, the light is removed and placed into the vehicle's trunk. The advantage of this type of a setup is that the light extends a few inches in front of the bumper and grill, thus avoiding reflection

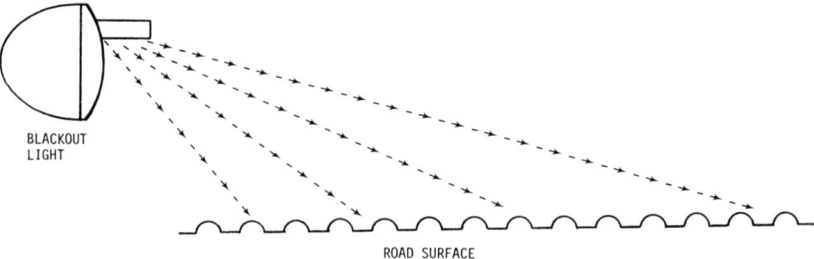

Figure 46. Blackout lights designed by the military for night movement of convoys have proven to be useful for investigators having a need to move through an area unnoticed at night. Note that the hooded light source prevents it from being seen by a subject. Note also that only the sides of objects facing the source of the light will be illuminated.

Figure 47. Blackout light mounted to a vehicle by a bracket which allows it to extend a few inches beyond the grill and bumper thus preventing unwanted reflections from the chromed surfaces.

from those surfaces. Furthermore, the higher the light is from the ground, the better and further it tends to illuminate the roadway. In Figure 48 is illustrated a surveillance vehicle with the blackout light mounted behind the grill. The advantage of this setup is primarily that of convenience because when the light is needed one has only to turn off the main headlamps and switch on the blackout light. The major drawback is a certain degree of reflection from the bumper and grill below the light. During periods that heavy use of the light is anticipated, the driver of this vehicle places black tape on the portion of the bumper and grill directly below the light, thus eliminating undesirable reflections. It is best to use a tape with a dull finish such as friction tape as opposed to electrician's tape that has a fairly shiny surface. Some investigators have fashioned a hinged bracket for the light that allows it to be positioned under the hood when not in use and swung out when needed.

Figure 48. Blackout light mounted behind the grill (note arrow).

Because blackout lights were not made for twelve-volt systems, they must be modified. This, however, presents no problem for it must simply be made to accept a twelve-volt bulb and can be accomplished by anyone with a very elementary knowledge of electricity.

While there are many instances in which one can drive without some means of artificial illumination, there are many cases in which illumination, even though weak, is essential. To travel a good road on a clear night is not normally a problem; however, if the road is in an area that is fairly heavily wooded, or if one is attempting to travel over a road that is little more than a couple of tire ruts through a field or woods, some means of artificial illumination is often essential. The degree of illumination that is provided by a blackout light will make it easier to see the sides of the road and will greatly aid in avoiding objects that may be in the vehicle's path. It will be found that the degree of illumination provided by a blackout light approximates (very roughly) that of parking lights, but the light source itself is much more difficult for someone else to detect.

## MOVING SURVEILLANCE

When one follows a subject in a rural area using automobiles, the most appropriate method to use will be governed very much by whether the road is a main road or a back road, and whether the surveillance is being conducted during daylight hours or at night.

During daylight hours, distance is perhaps the best cover if traffic is very light. If traffic is reasonably heavy, keeping one or two unrelated vehicles between one's self and the subject will provide reasonably good cover. In addition, using various techniques to alter the appearance of the vehicle and the driver will prove to be advantageous. On long stretches of road it may sometimes be desirable to pass the subject car a time or two, exiting at the next crossroad and waiting for the subject to reappear, thus resuming the surveillance.

When one follows a subject on a main road at night, reasonable distance and use of various cut-out switches for altering the appearance of the vehicle will in most cases prove to be the most appropriate approach. Utilization of cut-out switches make it appear as if a vehicle with two normal headlamps is following the subject for a distance. When the subject at some point passes from the view of the surveillant vehicle, a head lamp can be cut out, thus appearing as if a different vehicle is then behind the subject. On some vehicles, the position of the parking lights relative to the head lamps is such that the glare of the head lamps does not hide the parking lights from view. When this is the case, a cut-out switch for the parking lights is also effective.

When it is necessary to follow a subject through the country at night using back roads, a better method may be to travel without any lights at all. In this way, the subject will simply not be aware of the fact that there is a vehicle behind him. The most appropriate distance to be maintained will depend upon the conditions; however, enough distance must be maintained so that the subject cannot hear the surveillant vehicle or see it when the headlights of an oncoming vehicle illuminate it briefly. Furthermore, it is important that there be enough distance between the two vehicles so that if and when the subject makes a "U" turn, the surveillant vehicle can be turned around and gotten off the road so as not to be seen by the subject.

Because of the importance of getting the surveillant vehicle off the road and out of view should the subject make a "U" turn, one should make a mental note anytime a driveway or turn-off into a field is passed. In farming country, there are very frequent drives into fields that are used by farm equipment. Some investigators, for the purpose of quickly locating such drives, have fashioned a device that can be mounted to the spot light, thus restricting the large beam into a small beam that will not be as readily noticed by the subject. Ideally, when getting the vehicle off the roadway, one should drive it behind something. However, because it will often be possible to get the vehicle off the road only a very short distance with nothing to conceal it from view, it is important that the reflective surfaces (chrome and license plate) be toned down so that the subject will not detect a glint of light from such surfaces. Dirt and vehicle wax work reasonably well for this purpose. It is also essential that the surveillant vehicle have a cut-out switch for the brake lights.

*The hazards of driving without lights cannot be overemphasized.* It is desirable, therefore, to keep one hand on the light switch in certain cases, and when an oncoming vehicle is met, the surveillant vehicle should pull over and stop until it has passed. The hazards of driving without lights can be reduced by paying close attention to what the subject's lights reveal. In this way, the surveillant has a pretty good idea of what he is getting into.

## NIGHT DRIVING PERISCOPE

An interesting product manufactured by Lenzar Optics Corporation* is the night driving periscope with a zoom telephoto capability (see Figure 49). This instrument contains a second generation image intensifying unit that allows a vehicle to travel at daytime speeds at night without lights.

While this instrument was initially manufactured and intend-

---

* Lenzar Optics Corporation, 210 Brant Road, Lake Park, Florida 33403.

Figure 49. Night driving periscope with a zoom telephoto capability (*Courtesy of* Lenzar Optics Corporation).

ed primarily for installation in tanks, armored cars, and similar vehicles, its compact size (12 x 6 x 4 inches) makes it easily adaptable to Jeeps®, Land Rovers®, and most other vehicle types when a need arises to drive at night without lights. Such an instrument would without a doubt be a great aid for following a vehicle in rural areas at night without lights. The power for this instrument is provided by a 3.5-volt dry cell battery.

The field of view of this instrument zooms from fifty degrees to ten degrees. With this feature, the instrument can be set at a viewing angle of fifty degrees for normal driving, and in the event that something is observed and a closer examination is desired, one can easily zoom in on it (see Figure 50).

### AIRCRAFT FOR SURVEILLANCE OPERATIONS

Aircraft, both rotary and fixed wing, have proven to be very useful for vehicle surveillance applications, especially when the subject will be traveling cross country. To use an aircraft effectively for such an operation requires that there also be a surveil-

## Surveillance in Rural Areas 119

Figure 50. (A) Photographed observation of the zoom periscope at its widest viewing angle of 50 degrees. (B) Photographed again at its narrowest viewing angle of 10 degrees (*Courtesy of* Lenzar Optics Corporation).

lant vehicle involved and that the operation be a well coordinated effort between them. Naturally, the cost of such an operation will be very high because of the high operational cost of aircraft. Furthermore, it will be found that while the operational cost of any aircraft is high, it is significantly greater for rotary wing than for fixed wing aircraft.

It is necessary for an automobile to be involved in the surveillance so that when the subject stops for a reasonable period of time, the ground team can take over the surveillance, thus affording the aircraft an opportunity to land and refuel if necessary. When the subject resumes travel, he is tailed by the ground team until the pilot, who has been so notified, can again become airborne and into position to observe the subject. At that time the ground team will once again drop back far enough so that the subject cannot see them. Another reason a ground team is necessary is the fact that when the subject stops and extinguishes his head lamps at night, the air crew will lose sight of him.

Fixed wing aircraft have some advantages over a helicopter in that they are much less costly to operate, they have a greater range, they have greater speed for following fast vehicles cross country, and they are more comfortable to ride in for extended periods of time. It will also prove to be advantageous for the observer, when working with a fixed wing aircraft, to sit behind the pilot rather than beside him so that he can easily look out either side of the plane. This will make it easier to keep the subject in view while the airplane circles the area.

During aircraft surveillance, whether it be rotary or fixed wing, the usefulness of binoculars should not be slighted. The merits of these simple but remarkable instruments should be given serious consideration inasmuch as it is generally necessary to maintain a minimum altitude of about three thousand feet above the ground (actual ground level, not sea level) to ensure that the subject will not become aware of the surveillance. At such distances, binoculars will prove to be a great asset.

When considering the feasibility of using aircraft for such an operation, it must be remembered that weather conditions are an important factor. Inclement weather can render such an operation impossible.

## CHAPTER 8

# Undercover Surveillance

### GENERAL CONSIDERATIONS

UNDERCOVER SURVEILLANCE, sometimes referred to as *roping*, is an investigative technique or method employed by investigators when conventional investigative methods fail to produce the desired information. There are a wide variety of situations and types of cases which call for this method of surveillance depending upon whether the nature of the case is civil or criminal and upon the specific nature of the information needed.

Undercover operations may be of such a nature that an investigator will spend as much as several months to a year or more on one assignment (common in industrial cases), or as little as five or ten minutes as could be the case when interviewing someone using a *pretext* or when making a drug buy from a suspect. This wide variation in the time span of such operations results from the fact that undercover operations are conducted for a number of reasons by investigators in both the civil and criminal sectors. Similarly, the word *undercover* will have different meanings depending upon who is using the term and the type of operation they have in mind.

When law enforcement officers assigned to the narcotics division speak of undercover operations, they are generally speaking of officers making controlled drug buys from suspected dealers to whom they have been introduced by an informant. This is done to obtain evidence against the suspect. Law enforcement officers will use similar methods for the purchase of other types of contraband and to investigate other offenses of an organized nature.

In contrast to the operations conducted by law enforcement personnel are operations initiated by business and industry. When a company's security director refers to an undercover operation, he generally means an operation whereby a private investigator establishes a rapport with the company employees by securing a job within the firm and posing as an employee himself. Such operations typically run for a duration of several months to a year or more and can be very complex in nature because of the various hiring practices of companies, the presence of labor unions, lay-offs, etc.

When an insurance adjuster refers to an undercover operation, he is generally speaking in terms of an investigator using a suitable pretext to cloak his true identity and purpose to interview a claimant and his neighbors or relatives in regard to the claimant's alleged injuries that are for some reason suspected to be false. This type of an operation is often referred to by adjusters as *sub-rosa* and, as one would expect, such an operation lasts only as long as it takes to conduct the interviews.

Undercover work, although a form of surveillance, requires of the investigator a set of skills that are totally foreign to those necessary for other types of surveillance or investigative activity. Most notable is the investigator's *role playing ability* and his skill at what is referred to as *roping*.

Roping is a means of obtaining information from a person without asking direct questions about the matter or topic of interest, but rather, by inducing the subject to volunteer the information by very subtly leading the conversation in the desired direction. Naturally, to engage a subject effectively in conversation and rope him means to analyze him properly so as to gain an understanding of his wants and needs, and then subtly appeal to those things during the course of the conversation. To do so will aid in gaining his trust and confidence, and thus establishing a rapport with him.

## INITIAL CONTACT

The most critical phase of most undercover operations is the initial contact with the subject, or in the case of business and industrial undercover work, the initial penetration into the company whereby one completes an employment application (which naturally contains fictitious information) that will be scrutinized. The investigator is interviewed, and subjects (fellow employees) will decide from first impressions whether they do or do not like or trust the *new employee*. An important point to consider is that once a person has formed an opinion about something or someone, he has a tendency to acknowledge those things that support his opinion and discount things of a contradictory nature. This is human nature and can work to the investigator's advantage if a subject is favorably impressed initially. If the subject is not favorably impressed, it can present a severe stumbling block, so severe in some instances that it may be desirable to assign another investigator to the case and reassign the first man.

## ACT THE PART

When engaged in undercover work, the investigator should not only consider the feasibility of changing his name and offering a cover story concerning his personal history, *he must also act the part and the person he is portraying*. This is important because as the old saying goes, *actions speak louder than words*. If there is an inconsistency between what the investigator says and what he does, he will fail in his attempt to gain the confidence of his subject. If he fails in this respect, the operation will fail because *the success of any undercover operation is a direct result of the investigator's establishing a rapport with the subjects involved*. The extent to which a rapport is established will depend upon the nature of the case. When buying contraband, very little rapport may be established; however, some degree of trust must be developed or the subject would naturally not make the sale.

## UNDERSTAND WHAT THE SUBJECT MEANS

Finally, when engaged in conversation with a subject, the investigator must realize that people do not always say what they mean nor do they always mean what they say. This can result from the context in which certain things are said. Problems can also result in cases where the investigator is from another part of the country or from a different subculture than the subject, because a word or phrase may have a different meaning for each, thus resulting in an incorrect interpretation by the investigator. If there is any reason to question whether the subject means that which the investigator thinks he means, every effort should be made to clarify the point without arousing the subject's suspicion.

## INDUSTRIAL AND COMMERCIAL UNDERCOVER OPERATIONS

## Cover Jobs

When a private investigator seeks employment within a company for purposes of undercover surveillance, the particular position sought will naturally be determined by the needs of the case. If it is suspected that a loss is occurring on the loading dock, for example, it will be desirable for the investigator to secure a position that enables him to observe that area and establish a rapport with people working there. This may mean obtaining a job on the dock or, if such a position is not available, a custodial position may serve as an acceptable alternative. Similarly, if the position into which the investigator must work is such that specialized skills are needed, it will be necessary to recruit an investigator with those qualifications.

Generally, most commercial and industrial undercover jobs require no specialized skill on the part of the investigator. Reference here is being made not to skill as an investigator, but to skills needed to adequately perform the *cover job*. In many instances it is desirable to use a menial position as a cover. Such jobs as stock, custodial, or dock workers are common and do not require a high degree of specialized knowledge or skill on the part of the investigator. Such jobs are frequently desirable because they can be filled by almost any investigator regardless of his background and they are often fairly low paying, a fact which makes for a reasonably high rate of personnel turnover. Naturally, such jobs are easier to obtain for purposes of a cover. Because of the high turnover rate, company employees are more accustomed to seeing new faces frequently and therefore are less likely to regard each new face suspiciously. Similarly, the high turnover rate makes it more difficult for cost reasons to verify background information provided on application forms adequately and a cover is not as closely scrutinized by the personnel department. Another advantage of such jobs, and this is especially true of custodial positions, is the fact that they will often offer considerable freedom of movement within the company.

Finally, although it is expected that the investigator will work in a manner that is expected of any employee, low paying positions sometimes enable one to spend a bit more time conversing with other employees before supervisors are likely to object. This, however, is a generality, not an absolute rule.

### Establishing a Cover

When an investigator goes undercover, he abandons his official identity as an investigator and begins to play the role of another person. He may or may not utilize a fictitious name for this purpose, but in either case, he will prepare a cover story that will justify his being in certain places at certain times and conversing with certain people—a story that is intended to assist him in getting *next to* the subject(s).

When establishing a cover story for purposes of undercover investigations, whether the investigation is to be conducted by law enforcement officers or private investigators, highly elaborate preparations are generally not made as is the case with political espionage operations. However, the cover story must be prepared well enough to ensure a successful operation. The investigator must display an appearance and offer an explanation about himself that will satisfy the subject of the surveillance that he, the investigator, is all right.

Generally, when establishing a cover story, it is desirable to remain as close to the investigator's real life situation as possible. This will enable the investigator to remember the story easier, and will also make it more difficult for someone to discredit the story. Periods of time that must be covered can in some cases be done by extending military service, school time, claiming periods of self-employment, etc.

When preparing for an assignment in another city, it is sometimes desirable to go to that city and find an unrelated job to work while preparing a suitable cover. If the assignment takes one out of state, the period of time in which one prepares his cover should also be utilized to obtain a local driver's license and vehicle registration plates unless the fact that the investigator is from out of state will be incorporated into the cover story.

## Fictitious Names and Social Security

When an investigator is to secure employment within a company for purposes of undercover surveillance, it is sometimes desirable to do so using an assumed name. This is true, for example, in situations where it is not likely that someone may actually recognize the investigator by sight, or know him by name, but where a background investigation conducted by a suspicious subject would jeopardize the operation and perhaps also the personal safety of the investigator should his true identity and purpose be known.

To secure employment within a company using an assumed name will naturally necessitate obtaining a social security card bearing the assumed name. Obtaining such a card can be easily accomplished by completing the appropriate change of information form which is available at any social security office. When completing the form for name change purposes, it is necessary to indicate one's true name as it appears on his present social security card, and also the assumed name as it is to appear on the new card. *All other information such as date of birth, parents' names, etc., must remain unchanged.* At the top of the card write something to the effect, *name change for pen purposes*. This will prevent later confusion on the part of the Social Security Administration when the one number is used with a variety of names.

The new card thus obtained will reflect the desired new name but the original social security number. Several cards may be obtained in this manner as needed, each reflecting a different name, and used interchangeably without problems so long as the *number remains unchanged*.

Some investigative firms, when assigning an investigator to work within a client's plant, will request that the investigator keep the pay check he receives from the client company payroll office for the specific job he is engaged in as a cover, and will themselves also pay him an additional sum for his daily reports. When an operation is conducted in this fashion, the investigator is in fact receiving two separate paychecks. If a ficticious name is being used as a cover, then a check under two different names will be received. If the check received from the client's firm is made out to the assumed name, and the check received from the investigative firm is made out using the investigator's true name, there will be no problem in regard to social security so long as the number has remained unchanged in both cases. Both checks should not be negotiated at the same bank, however.

If the appropriate name change form is completed and then mailed to the social security office, there will naturally be a reasonable time delay before the new card is received in the mail. However, if one goes in person to the social security office with his present card or the stub thereof, a new card may be obtained the same day.

### Using Fictitious Names

When an investigator's cover requires the use of a fictitious name, he must not only make the name change, he must become that person. Anything the investigator has that may prove to be inconsistent with the new name or the role that will accompany the name must also be changed. For example, if eyeglasses are worn by the investigator and he has his name engraved on the inner surface of one of the bows, a new bow must be obtained. If the key chain has initials on it, a new chain must be obtained. If the investigator takes up a new residence while engaged in the particular assignment, he should arrange to have mail sent to his new name at that address. Be certain, however, that return addresses do not serve to betray the cover. If in a hotel, he may wish to consider having himself paged while in the cocktail lounge, etc. Anything that will tend to lend an air of credibility to the new name should be considered.

While working under a fictitious name, the investigator should carry nothing on his person or store anything in his room or vehicle that would either reveal his true identity or make someone question the authenticity of his cover name or story. This point cannot be stressed too strongly, for it is not a remote possibility that someone, desiring to satisfy himself that the investigator can be trusted, will rifle his room, his vehicle, or both, while he is absent.

## Entrapment

Regardless of the nature of the undercover operation the investigator is involved in, he must be aware of what constitutes *entrapment* so as to avoid the possibility of the subject using entrapment as a defense in court.

To avoid entrapment, the investigator must exercise care never to suggest that a crime or irregularity be committed, or in other words, induce the subject to commit an act he would not otherwise commit. The investigator may, however, go along with an idea once it has been suggested by someone else. In fact, he may even let it be known that he is receptive to suggestions or that he is seeking a means by which to make a little extra money, but he cannot actually suggest that an irregularity or crime be committed. This occurs, for example, when an undercover investigator makes a drug buy. He is, when purchasing drugs from the suspect, participating in an illegal transaction. However, he has not induced the seller to do something he would not otherwise do.

It must be remembered when considering entrapment that the purpose of any undercover operation is not to create new problems, but to solve existing ones. Entrapment, although a *major* concern of undercover investigators, is not something that pertains only to them, but it will be found to apply in varying degrees to practically all phases of investigative work, and each investigator would do well to be fully familiar with exactly what constitutes entrapment.

## CHAPTER 9

# Facts About Vision

### GENERAL CONSIDERATIONS

Because physical surveillance involves extensive use of one's vision, it would be fitting to examine some basic factors regarding vision, an understanding of which will help to ensure that the surveillant will utilize this essential sense to its maximum capability. This discussion, although it is brief and nontechnical in nature, will go into sufficient detail to provide an understanding that is necessary for effective use of one's vision, especially when working at night.

### DAY AND NIGHT VISION

As can be observed in Figure 51, the human eye and the camera have much in common inasmuch as the lens of the eye projects an image upon the retina while the lens of the camera projects an image upon the film plane. The eye and the camera are also similar inasmuch as the ultimate resolution of an image is determined by the grain of the film in the camera and the size and concentration of the light-sensitive cells in the retina of the eye. As light strikes the retina, the cells generate impulses to the optic nerve which are from there transported to the brain. The amount of light that can pass through the lens in both the eye and the camera is controlled by the size of the lens opening.

The retina of the eye contains two types of cells known as *cones* and *rods*. The cones are concentrated largely in the area of the *fovea* which lies within the optical axis of the eye and are responsible for normal daytime vision. The rods lie in the area around the fovea and are responsible primarily for night vision. Because the light sensitivity of these two types of cells differs greatly, the eye actually contains two distinct types of visual systems (see Figure 52).

The cones, which lie primarily within the optical axis of the eye, are not highly sensitive to light and it is these cells that are

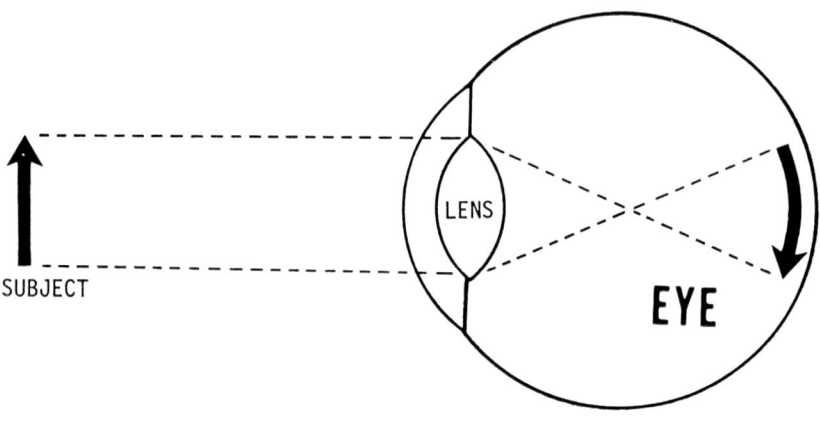

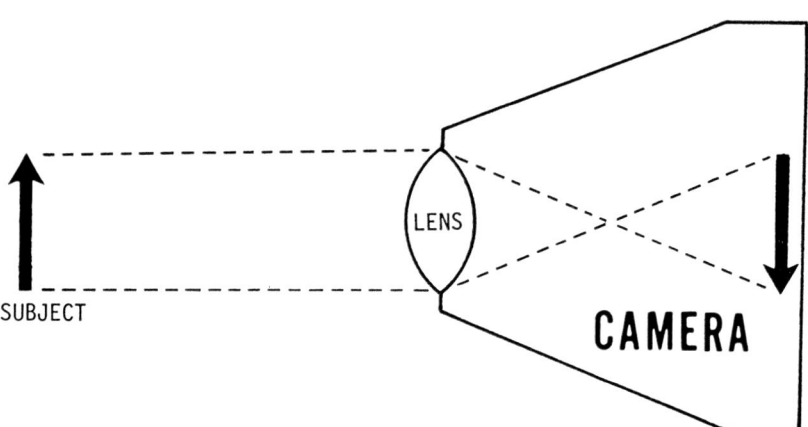

Figure 51. The eye and the camera are optically very similar inasmuch as they both possess a lens that projects an inverted image upon a light sensitive surface. Also, the amount of light that passes through the lens is regulated in both cases by the size of the opening. A camera is focused by changing the distance between the lens and the film while the eye focuses by changing the shape of the lens.

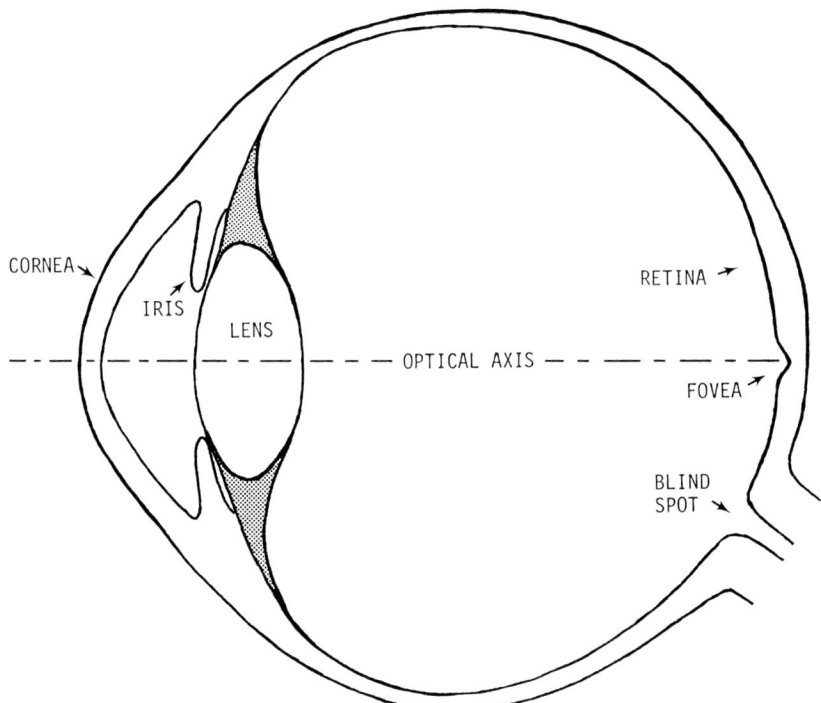

Figure 52. Horizontal section of the right eye. The small area of the fovea contains cones while the area around the fovea is comprised largely of rods. There are no cones or rods in the area of the optic disk thus resulting in a blind spot.

utilized for normal vision during the day or under reasonably strong artificial illumination. Because the cone section of the eye is much more densely supplied with cells than the rod area surrounding the fovea, the cone vision produces images that are clear and sharp. It is also the cones that are responsible for color vision. Thus, under conditions of good illumination, one is able to distinguish good sharp images in color.

The rods, which lie outside the area of the fovea, are *extremely* sensitive to dim light, but because they are much less densely supplied than are the cones, they produce an image that is rather blurred and lacking in detail. Furthermore, the rods do not provide color vision. When subjected to bright light, the rods lose their sensitivity. The reason for this phenomenon lies in the fact that the rods contain a rose-red pigment called *visual purple* which, when exposed to bright light, undergoes a chemical change that causes it to lose its color. This loss of color causes the rods to lose their sensitivity to light. The eye is, therefore, able to endure strong glaring light. When the eye moves from a brightly illuminated environment to one that is dimly lit, such as from a bright day outdoors to a movie theatre or barroom, there is a period of time in which the eye cannot see well if at all, depending, of course, upon the degree of difference between the two levels of illumination. After a period of a few minutes, visual purple will begin to be reformed in the retina and one will begin to see. As more visual purple is produced, the eye's sensitivity to light increases. After about twenty to thirty minutes or more, the eye can become several thousand times more sensitive to light.

It is worth noting at this point that visual purple can be produced only if the body has a sufficient quantity of vitamin A. Because vitamin A is not produced by the body, it is essential that one's diet contain a proper amount of this vitamin or night blindness (nyctalopia) can result.

Since the cones, which are the cells responsible for color vision, are relatively insensitive to low light levels, and the rods, while being highly sensitive to light, are unable to distinguish color, night vision is for the most part colorless. Also, since the rods produce images that are somewhat blurred and lacking in detail, while one will be able to see in near total darkness, only outlines or silhouettes of objects can be seen. Because the cones are concentrated in the area of the fovea, which lies in the optical axis of the eye's lens, and the rods are located in the area outside the fovea, when working under very low light levels one will not see as well if he looks directly at an object. To overcome this problem, one should look a little above or below objects to be viewed. The reason for this stems from the fact that the eyes must project the image upon the very sensitive rods rather than on the not so sensitive cones. This is why, for example, when one is night driving without lights, one will generally see better by looking a little above the road than directly at it.

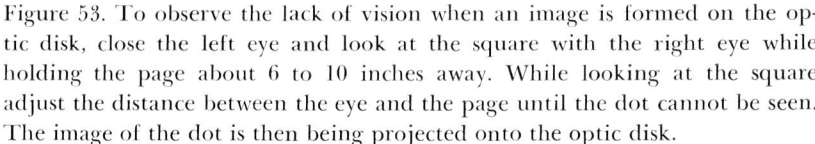

Figure 53. To observe the lack of vision when an image is formed on the optic disk, close the left eye and look at the square with the right eye while holding the page about 6 to 10 inches away. While looking at the square adjust the distance between the eye and the page until the dot cannot be seen. The image of the dot is then being projected onto the optic disk.

At this point it should be evident that two things must occur for one's eyes to become *dark adapted*. First, the pupil of the eye must dilate. This occurs quite quickly. Second, and more importantly, the retina of the eye must undergo a chemical change causing it to become more sensitive to light. However, this takes much longer than it did for the eye to dilate.

### BLIND SPOT

Because there are no light sensitive cells in the area in which the optic nerves connect to the retina, there is a resultant blind spot. However, we are not normally aware of this blind spot because the brain has a tendency to fill it in.

In Figure 53 are a dot and a square. Close the left eye and look at the square with the right eye while holding the page about six to ten inches from the eye. While looking at the square, adjust the distance between the eye and the page of the book until the dot can no longer be seen. When the dot disappears, it does so because the image of the dot is projected onto the area of the optic nerve where there are no rods or cones. Now, without moving the book, open the left eye and the dot should reappear. This explains in part how the brain is able to fill in the blind spot of each eye so that we are not aware of it.

### SUNGLASSES FOR EYE PROTECTION

It has been established that if sunglasses are not worn on bright days, the rods of the retina can become overstimulated and render them less sensitive to light, thus reducing one's optimum night vision. For this reason, it is recommended that anyone who relies in any manner on night vision obtain a pair of quality sunglasses to be worn on bright days.

## MOVEMENT

While the eye is quite quick to detect movement, the eye is unable to distinguish detail when an image is not stationary upon the retina. It is for this reason that the eye must follow a moving object in order to discern details. It is also for this reason that when one is surveilling a large area, it is recommended that the eyes not sweep the area, but rather, take it in sections and allow the eyes to come to rest and examine each section before moving on.

## FIELD OF VISION

When looking at a stationary object that is directly ahead of the viewer, a person will have a field of vision measuring about 180° horizontally and about 140° vertically (see Figures 54 and 55).

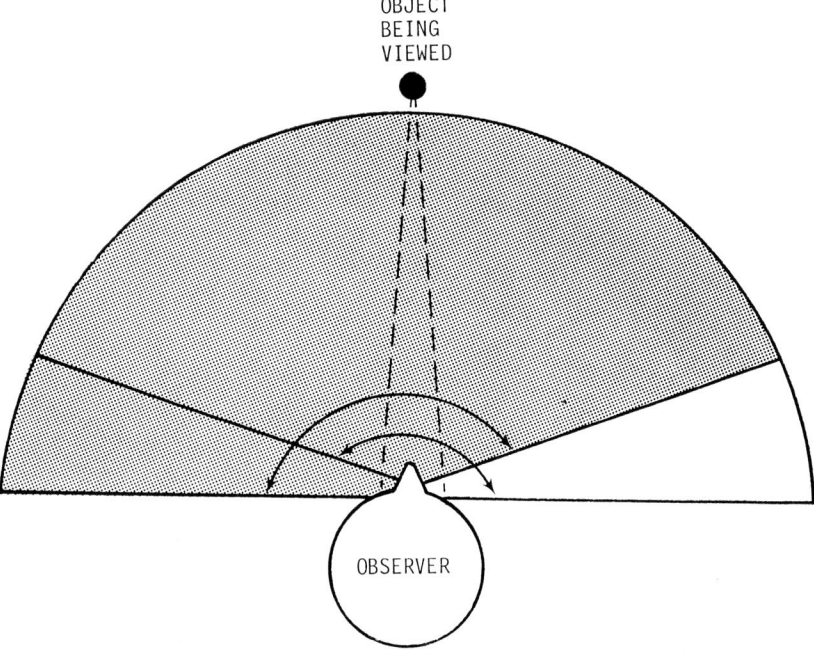

Figure 54. Each eye has a *horizontal field of view* of about 150° with both eyes together offering a total field of about 180°. Note how the field of each eye overlaps considerably with the other.

## Facts About Vision

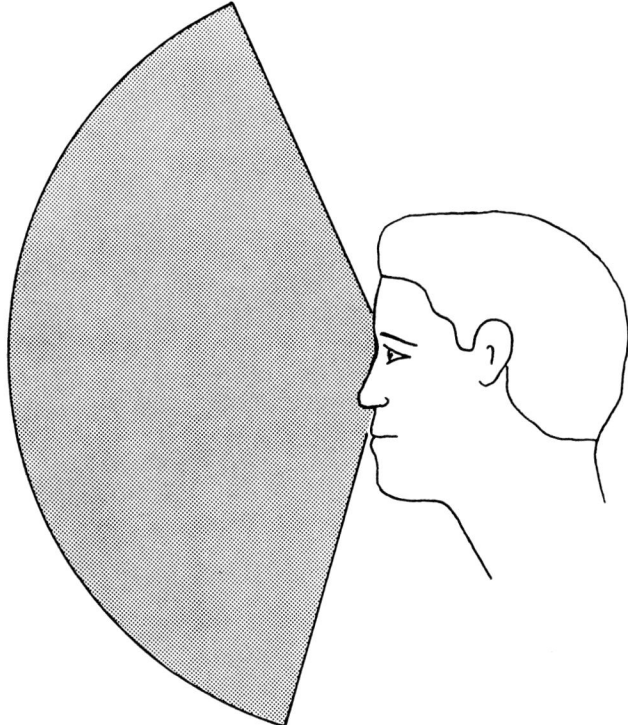

Figure 55. The *vertical range* of the eyes is about 140° and is bounded above by the brows and below the cheek bones.

As will be observed in Figure 54, each eye has a horizontal field of vision of about 150° with the field of each eye overlapping considerably with the other.

The vertical field of view, as stated, measures about 140° and is bounded above by the brows and below by the cheeks and does not change appreciably regardless of whether the eyes are directed upward or down unless the position of the head is also altered.

While man's field of vision is in reality quite wide, detail in the areas surrounding the object focused upon is quite limited. However, the eye is quick to detect motion in these outer areas, specially if the motion is accentuated against an immobile background.

CHAPTER 10

# Optical and Related Aids for Vision Extension

**INTRODUCTION**

PHYSICAL SURVEILLANCE involves making visual observations of people, of vehicles, and of activity that may be taking place at various locations. Because the practitioners of this art must rely so heavily on their sight when engaging in this form of activity, it is essential that they take advantage of the various tools that serve to extend their vision.

Although a lot of physical surveillance activity takes place during daytime hours, much of it takes place at night. It is for this reason that aids to extend one's vision under both day and nighttime conditions will be discussed. In this chapter, an examination will be made regarding the use of binoculars, telescopes, infrared viewers, and electronic light intensifiers. However, because of the frequency with which binoculars are used, the largest portion of this discussion will be devoted to them.

The investigator who does not utilize some means to extend his vision must either move in dangerously close to a subject to discern important details or, if he works from a safe distance, settle for results that are less precise; one cannot, for example, discern details such as vehicle license plate numbers from distances much in excess of 100 to 150 feet.

Optical equipment, especially binoculars, have proven to be extremely useful for uniformed patrol officers working with marked squad cars because they permit making observations from distances that preclude detection. While low powered telescopes are useful in many instances to the uniformed patrol officers, binoculars are handy because they can be placed on the seat next to the officer, picked up and hand held for immediate observations.

When it becomes necessary to observe a subject under low light conditions, the light gathering capability of large aperture binoculars will often produce the desired results. In other instances, it will be necessary to employ some other means such as infrared viewers or electronic light intensifiers.

In this chapter, an attempt is made to provide the reader with enough information concerning optical-related equipment so that he will have an understanding of the type of equipment available which will best suit his needs under various conditions. This information is provided in a nontechnical manner so that all readers, regardless of their present background, will benefit from it.

## BINOCULARS

### General Considerations

Because binoculars are a very important and frequently used optical accessory for extending the vision of those engaged in physical surveillance activity, police officers and investigators should be familiar with them and their proper use. This holds true for all optical-related equipment one may have occasion to use such as telescopes, infrared viewers, electronic light intensifiers, and photographic equipment.

A binocular is simply an optical device comprised of two telescope type systems which are mounted parallel to each other, enabling the user to view an enlarged image of some distant object using both eyes. While the term *binocular* may be applied to any device employing the parallel telescope principle, it is generally used in reference to *prism binoculars*.

Binoculars, in addition to providing an enlarged image of a distant object, provide an enhanced stereoscopic perception beyond that of normal vision. This effect is a result of both the separation of the axes of the objective lenses and the instrument's magnifying power.

When considering the purchase of binoculars, there are five essential factors to be addressed. These include
1. Magnifying power,
2. Illumination (light gathering capability),

3. Field of view,
4. Weight,
5. Durability.

While considering these five points, one should recognize that, aside from quality, binoculars differ primarily in

1. Magnifying power,
2. Field of view,
3. Illumination (light gathering capability).

Generally, if a particular binocular is advertised in a manner that places a strong emphasis on any single feature, it will be found that the feature has been made possible only at the expense of other features. For example, binoculars that are advertised as having extraordinary light gathering capabilities (large objective lenses) will prove to be fairly large and heavy, with size and weight increasing as the diameter of the objective lenses is increased. Similarly, binoculars with a strong magnifying power also prove to be fairly large and heavy, and the field of view generally decreases as the magnifying power increases. If a particular pair of binoculars is advertised as being very light in weight, it may be a result of lightweight but high quality materials or it could mean that the objective lenses are very small in diameter, a factor that will not only cause a reduction in size and weight, but will also have an adverse effect on the light gathering capability of the instrument.

The specific binocular features that will best serve one's needs will, of course, depend upon the intended use of the instrument. To be considered are such things as the subject matter, the distance, and the conditions under which viewing will be accomplished. This is important because some investigators work in urban settings while others work in rural settings. Some work in both areas. One must also consider whether the instrument will be used primarily during daylight hours or during dusk and at night. This consideration will influence whether one should select large or small aperture binoculars (large or small objective lenses). There will also be various other considerations that will manifest themselves in accordance with the intended use of the instrument.

When contemplating the purchase of a binocular, one must consider whether to purchase a low to moderately priced instrument or one in the high price category. Generally, it will be found that high priced binoculars are sturdier because of better materials and workmanship, and there is also evidence of better quality control. However, if one is willing to familiarize himself with methods for checking lower priced binoculars prior to making a purchase, acceptable binoculars can be obtained at modest prices. Many investigators whose binoculars necessarily undergo rigorous use prefer the less expensive models rather than subjecting a high priced instrument to such treatment. However, this is simply one school of thought, for there are also many investigators who favor higher priced instruments because they are better made and thus better able to withstand rigorous use. *Consumer Reports*,[1] which is available at most public libraries, provides a good, objective discussion of binoculars.

## Binoculars versus Field Glasses

The primary difference between field glasses and binoculars is use of prisms. Binoculars, as illustrated in Figure 56, employ a lens and prism system which causes the light passing through to travel a distance greater than the physical length of the instrument. The result is an optically strong (high degree of magnification) instrument in a relatively small package. Because field and opera glasses employ no prisms, they are not competitive with binoculars insofar as magnifying power and physical size is concerned. Field and opera glasses have a magnification power of only two to five times. Furthermore, the field of view offered by field glasses is comparatively narrow.

## Magnifying Power

When examining binoculars, one will note that there are two numbers printed on the instrument which are separated by an "×." On many binoculars, one will see the numbers 7×35, for example, a very popular binocular for general use. The number

---

1. *Consumer Reports*, November 1971.

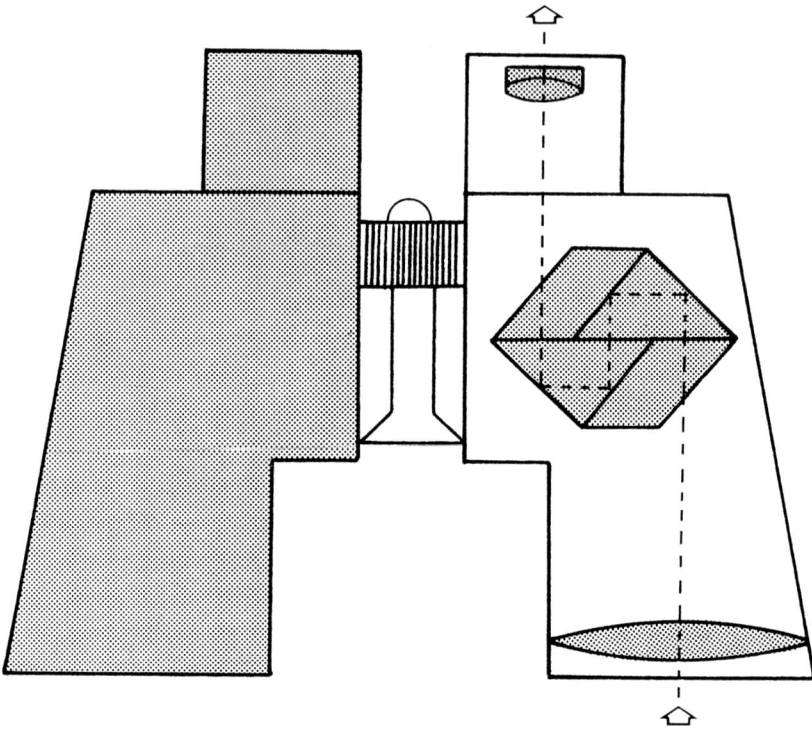

Figure 56. Observe how the prism in binoculars folds the light path, thus reducing the physical size of the instrument.

seven, which precedes the "×," indicates the magnifying power of the instrument. The second number, thirty-five in this case, designates the diameter of the objective lens measured in millimeters. An object viewed through a *seven* power binocular will appear seven times larger than when viewed with the naked eye, or conversely, it will be seen by the observer as though it were only one-seventh the actual distance from the observer's position. Similarly, an eight power binocular will magnify objects eight times, while a ten power binocular will magnify objects ten times.

A binocular whose magnifying power exceeds seven or eight times will prove to be difficult for many people to hand hold effectively, with the degree of difficulty logically increasing as the magnifying power of the instrument is increased. Therefore, a magnifying power greater than seven or eight times will not necessarily provide the viewer with better detail unless the instrument has been properly secured by some means such as a tripod or window mount. The greater the magnifying power of an instrument, the more susceptible it will be to small movement and vibrations that will be amplified to increasingly greater degrees as the power of the instrument is increased. This fact holds true not only for binoculars, but also for telescopes and cameras equipped with telephoto lenses. For this reason, if one anticipates hand holding binoculars, a power not greater than seven or eight times should be selected, reserving the stronger instruments for specialized applications.

To experience the difference that actually exists between binoculars when hand held or mounted securely, select a parked vehicle that is far enough away so that the registration numbers can be read only with a considerable degree of difficulty while hand holding the binoculars. After this has been done, secure the binoculars in a manner that will ensure that they remain perfectly still and note the clarity with which the registration can then be read. This difference becomes increasingly pronounced with greater magnifying powers. Even a $7 \times 50$ binocular, which is acceptable for hand held use, will respond to this simple test.

When considering magnifying power, it should also be recognized that greater magnifying power normally means an increasingly narrow field of view. The cruciality of this point will depend primarily upon the intended use of the instrument and upon the personal preference of the user.

### Field of View

The field of view refers to the width of the area that can be seen through a binocular. While field of view is sometimes expressed in degrees, it is more often expressed by the width in feet that can be seen at a distance of 1,000 yards. A normal field binocular of seven power, for example, will generally have a field of view that falls roughly between 350 and 375 feet at 1,000 yards. A wide field seven power binocular will have a field of view in the 550 to 575 foot vicinity at 1,000 yards. While a wide angle field of view would, without a doubt, be a desirable feature in many instances, it must be recognized that some of the less expensive brands offering a wide field of view lack sharpness around the outer edges, thus defeating the purpose of a wide angle binocular. Therefore, if one is contemplating the purchase of a lower priced wide angle binocular, it would be desirable to check it for this fault by focusing on some straight-line pattern. If the binocular is found to be faulty in this respect, it should be rejected.

Worth noting at this point is the possibility of the subject's being observed at night while he is in the shadows near a bright light. A wide angle binocular can cause problems by including the light in the field of view, thus making it difficult to effectively observe the subject and discern details.

When considering the field of view of a binocular, one should understand that the diameter of the objective lens has nothing to do with the field of view, since this is determined by other factors such as the focal length of the objective and the diameter of the ocular (eye piece lens). Because the ocular of a wide angle binocular is more complex and thus costlier to manufacture than the ocular of a normal field binocular, wide angle binoculars are more expensive. Whether the added expense is justified is something each individual must decide for himself.

## Objective Lens Diameter

In the example of the 7×35 binocular, it was stated that the seven designated the magnification power of the instrument while the thirty-five designated the diameter of the objective lens in *millimeters*. The objective lens is the large lens at the front of the instrument that faces the subject or object being viewed. Most binocular objective lenses range in size from approximately 20mm to 60mm. While there are binoculars that have objective lenses ranging in size from 80mm to 150mm, they are less common.

The primary advantage of a large diameter objective lens lies in the fact that the larger the objective lens the greater will be its light gathering capability. For example, a 7×35 binocular has the same magnifying power as a 7×50 binocular, but the 7×50 is capable of gathering approximately twice as much light as the former. The 7×50 binocular would therefore be the logical choice between the two for low light level work such as at dusk or during nighttime hours.

Whether one should choose a binocular with a large or small objective lens will depend upon a number of factors. As stated, if one will be doing a considerable degree of low light level work, large aperture binoculars will be the logical choice. It must be remembered, however, that the larger the objective lens, the greater will be the weight and bulk of the instrument. For normal daytime use, it is rarely necessary that the diameter of the objective lens be more than five times the magnifying rating of the instrument in order to achieve satisfactory performance. Furthermore, for daytime use, man's eye cannot normally make use of all the light gathered by a larger objective lens. This being the case, large objectives on a binocular that will be used primarily during daytime hours would mean carrying unnecessary bulk and weight, a factor that in many situations could prove to be an inconvenience.

## Exit Pupil Diameter

The diameter of the exit pupil, or in other words, the diameter of the image of the objective lens that is formed by the eyepiece lens, is determined by dividing the objective lens diameter by the magnifying power of the instrument. The quotient is the size of the exit pupil. If one were to hold a pair of binoculars about a foot from his eyes while directing the objective lenses towards the sky (not at the sun) he could see the exit pupils, which would appear as small circles of light in each eyepiece. The small circles of light are images of the objective lenses. An easy method by which one can measure the diameter of the exit pupil of binoculars if it is unknown is to direct the objective towards the sky or some other broad and sufficiently bright light source and then place a piece of paper a short distance from the ocular. By varying the distance between the ocular and the paper, one will observe that at a certain point the circle of light that is formed is at its smallest size and is sharply defined. The diameter of the circular image, which is an image of the objective lens, is the diameter of the exit pupil. Upon obtaining a sharp image of the exit pupil, if one increases or decreases the distance between the paper and the eyepiece lens, the image will become larger, fuzzier, and decrease in intensity. It is for this reason that eye relief (distance between the eyepiece lens and the viewer's eye) is important. This is especially true if working under low light conditions.

When examining the exit pupils, one should note whether they are perfectly delineated and evenly illuminated. If they are not, it is an indication that not *all* of the light entering the objective lenses is passing through the instrument and being emitted by the eyepiece lens. The result will be a loss in the intensity of the light emitted by the eyepiece lens, a factor that can be important if the instrument is intended for use under low light conditions.

When examining the exit pupil, it will be observed that many low priced instruments that use lower cost crown glass in the construction of prisms rather than a better quality and higher cost glass show a somewhat squared exit pupil rather than one that is perfectly clear throughout.

The two most popular binoculars presently on the market are 7×35's and 7×50's. The exit pupil of a 7×35 binocular is about 5mm in diameter (35 ÷ 7 = 5). The exit pupil of a 7×50 binocular is about 7mm in diameter (50 ÷ 7 = 7.14). If the diameter of the exit pupil is greater than the diameter of the opening of the observer's eye, the eye will fail to utilize all of the light that is gathered by the objective lens. The diameter of the human eye when fully contracted is approximately 2mm and when fully dilated about 7mm. Binoculars designed and intended to be used under normal daylight conditions generally feature an exit pupil of between 3 and 5mm in diameter because it has been found that an exit pupil of that size will accommodate the human eye quite well under such conditions. However, when binoculars are intended to be used under nighttime conditions or at dusk, it is desirable to utilize binoculars whose exit pupil measures about 7mm in diameter, which is the case with 7×50 binoculars. Because one's eyes will dilate to about 7mm when in the dark, the eye can then utilize all the light provided by such an instrument.

**Individual Eyepiece Focusing versus Center Focusing**

The most frequently encountered binoculars on the market are the models featuring a center focusing wheel which enables the user to focus both eyepieces simultaneously by turning the center focusing wheel. Binoculars featuring eyepieces that focus independently of each other are not as common; however, it must not be assumed that they are the least desirable of the two types for investigative purposes. In fact, the contrary will generally prove to be the case.

For people who have a frequent need to observe subject matter that is quite close, bird watchers for example, binoculars which feature center focusing will generally prove to be more convenient to use because they can readily be focused to a very short viewing distance by simply turning the center focusing wheel. However, the surveillant will rarely find it necessary to use binoculars for purposes of short range viewing (fifty feet or less); therefore, a binocular's minimum focus is of little concern to him. A drawback of center focusing binoculars is a relatively loose fit of the ocular tubes, which must of necessity have a rather large tolerance to prevent binding when the instrument is focused. As a result of this loose fit, these binoculars are susceptible to moisture, which will have a tendency to fog the interior optical surfaces, and to dirt, which will cause a gradual deterioration of the optical performance of the instrument. The degree to which this is true will naturally depend upon the quality of the instrument.

For one engaged in physical surveillance, binoculars featuring individually focusing eyepieces are worth consideration as they are generally sturdier than center focusing models and once they have been focused on a distant object, no further focusing adjustment is required (providing that no close objects are to be viewed). Furthermore, the design of these binoculars allows them to be well sealed, thus making them a good choice when the instrument is to be used in areas or under conditions where they will be exposed to dirt, dust, and moisture.

## Binocular Alignment

Good binocular performance depends not only on quality optics, but also on proper alignment (collimation) of the two lens barrels. As was previously pointed out, binoculars are merely two telescope type instruments mounted parallel to each other to provide the viewer with both an enlarged and a stereoscopic view of some object. Naturally, it is important that the two lens barrels be correctly aligned so that each eye will see the same view as the other. If the instrument is not correctly aligned, each eye will see a slightly different view and eye strain will result because of their effort to fuse the two images into one. The result of eye strain is a notable degree of eye discomfort and possibly a headache after prolonged use of the defective instrument. If the degree of misalignment is severe, the viewer will actually see two different images, or, more correctly, a double image. *Binoculars that are correctly aligned will cause no eye strain whatever.*

Misalignment is the most common fault encountered in binoculars, especially when dealing with low priced instruments, and it is for this reason that one should be aware of ways to detect such errors. Although it is necessary to have a quality collimator to detect slight errors in alignment, more severe alignment errors can be detected with the eye after a bit of practice. The degree of misalignment that can be tolerated will depend upon the nature of the error and upon the individual using the instrument.

There are three types of alignment errors that can occur in binoculars. They are:

1. Vertical misalignment.
2. Horizontal misalignment.
3. Rotational misalignment.

The first, *vertical misalignment,* results in the view in one eyepiece being higher than the other (see Figure 57A). Vertical misalignment causes severe eye strain even if the degree of error is slight.

The second type of alignment error is *horizontal misalignment*

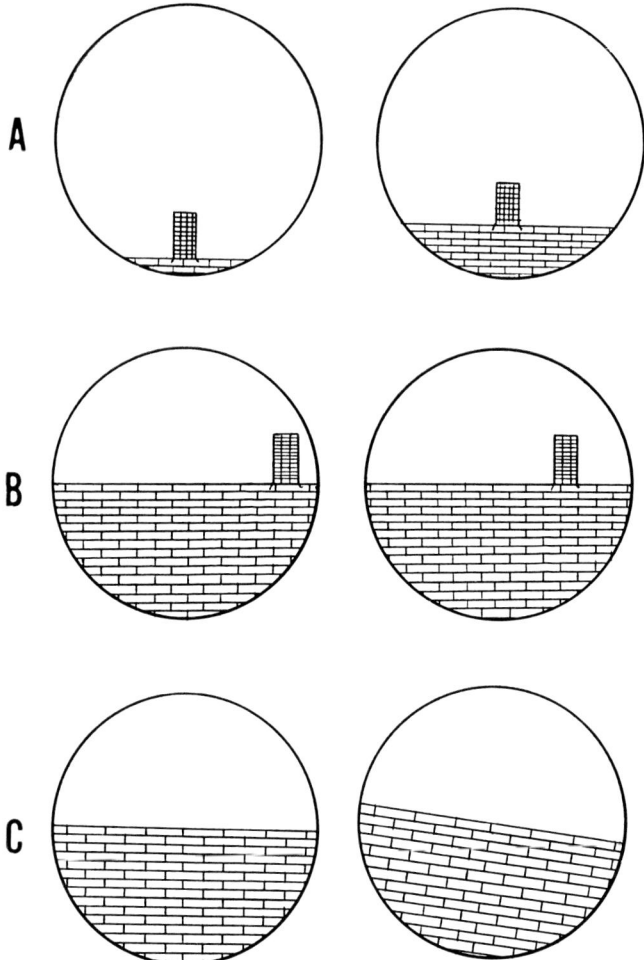

Figure 57. Three common types of binocular misalignment are (A) Vertical, (B) Horizontal and (C) Rotational.

(see Figure 57B). The degree of error that can be tolerated with this type of error will depend upon whether the eyes must attempt to diverge or converge in order to fuse the image. It is not natural for one's eyes to assume a cock-eyed position and to do so will quickly result in a notable amount of eye discomfort and possibly a headache after a short period of time. For the eyes to assume a somewhat cross-eyed state, however, is much easier; consequently, a greater degree of horizontal misalignment requiring a convergence rather than a divergence of the eyes can be tolerated.

The third kind of alignment error that may be encountered is *rotational misalignment,* a condition that is characterized by one image being rotated with respect to the other (see Figure 57C). There is nothing that the eyes can do to correct for this condition.

There are a number of ways by which one can check a binocular for alignment errors, provided, of course, that the errors are sufficiently pronounced. The tests will work best if the binocular can be mounted on a tripod by means of a binocular clamp; however, the first test that will be discussed can be accomplished without tripod mounting the instrument, although not as well.

The first alignment test involves adjusting the eye width distance and then focusing the binoculars on some straight lined object such as a roof top. After the instrument has been focused on the top edge of the roof, slowly move the binoculars away from the eyes, keeping the eyes rigid so that the left eye continues to look into the left eyepiece lens and the right eye continues looking into the right eyepiece lens. When the instrument is about ten inches from the eyes, one should be able to see two separate images that can be compared. It is important that the binoculars be kept perfectly level so that one eyepiece is not higher than the other. Now study the two images and note if the roof is higher in one eyepiece than in the other (Figure 57A) or if one half is different from the other insofar as rotation is concerned, i.e. appears tilted (Figure 57C).

The second alignment test involves focusing the binocular on some distant object that is fairly small, well defined, and has good contrast between itself and the background against which it will be viewed. A chimney and roof top works well. The binoculars must be tripod mounted or secured in some other fashion that permits them to be held perfectly still. After focusing and adjusting the binoculars for proper eye width, back off and give the eyes a chance to rest for a bit. After resting the eyes, look at the object through the binoculars with one objective lens covered. After looking for a brief period at the object, quickly uncover the second objective lens and see if two images appear for a brief moment before the eyes have had a chance to fuse them. If two images are observed, the instrument is out of alignment.

The third alignment test also requires that the binoculars be firmly secured, preferably on a tripod. As before, adjust the binoculars for proper eye width and then focus them upon some object such as a chimney on a house. Next the object is centered left to right within the field of view, with the binoculars then being tilted back so that the object is not only centered left to right, but rests at the bottom of the field of view (six o'clock position). When conducting this test, it is extremely important that the binoculars not be tilted, even slightly, either right or left, so that one eyepiece is higher than the other. After these things have been properly adjusted, look first into one eyepiece and then the other to see if each image is positioned exactly the same as the other insofar as height is concerned. If one is higher than the other, the instrument is out of *vertical alignment* (Figure 57A). Next the binoculars should be repositioned so that the object being viewed is centered halfway between the top and bottom of the field of view and is at either the right or left side of the field (three or nine o'clock position). Again look through each eyepiece one at a time and see if both objects are just as close to the edge of the field of view. If they are not, the instrument is out of *horizontal alignment* (Figure 57B). Finally, position the binoculars so that some straight line such as a roof top is centered midway across the field of view. When looking through each eyepiece independently, note whether both views are perfectly horizontal or if one appears to be rotated with respect to the other. If one is rotated, the binocular is out of *rotational alignment* (Figure 57C).

When one uses any of these methods for checking a binocular for misalignment, it must be remembered that these tests will only disclose problems that are reasonably severe. Detecting small alignment errors requires a quality collimator and a trained technician. One should also understand that not only one but any combination of these alignment errors can exist to varying degrees in any one binocular. It is entirely possible that one binocular could exhibit all three alignment errors. It is also possible for a binocular to be in correct alignment at some particular eye width setting, but be incorrect when set for some other eye width.

In the event that one has a binocular that is out of alignment, the instrument should be taken to a reputable repair shop for service by a qualified repairman rather than attempting to correct the error one's self.

### Proper Use of Binoculars

When using binoculars, it is important that they be used properly if the user is to benefit fully from the instrument's capabilities. It is easy to overlook small and seemingly unimportant considerations because binoculars are, as they appear to be, simple tools that are easy to use. Unfortunately we have a tendency to raise the instrument to our eyes, adjust the distance between the eyepiece lenses to where they feel somewhat comfortable and then focus. While this is not necessarily incorrect, there are a few points worth examining that may prove to be helpful.

Naturally, one should endeavor to become familiar with the binocular so that its use is automatic, requiring no special attention or effort on the part of the investigator. This is important because the investigator has the more important task of observing activity and cannot afford to be hindered by the very tool that is intended to assist him in making his observations.

The barrels of the binocular should be set at the widest distance that will afford a clear circular field of view. After this has been accomplished, note the numerical reading on the center dial and commit it to memory. If the binocular must be focused by adjusting each individual eyepiece, turn both eyepieces out as far as they will go and then focus by viewing some distant object. When focusing on a distant object, one should view the object first with the left eye, focusing until it is in sharp focus, and then repeat the process for the right eye. Unless a need arises to view something from a very close distance, the focus should then be set for life as the binocular should be in correct focus for objects from fifty feet to infinity. If someone else will be using the binocular, however, it will be necessary for them to refocus the instrument to suit their own eyes. After focusing the binocular, note the numerical reading of each eyepiece. If the binocular is one of the more common types that features a mechanism for focusing both eyepieces simultaneously, and one eyepiece (usually the right) that focuses independently for the purpose of making slight corrections in variations between one's eyes, note the diopter reading of the one eyepiece once focusing on a distant object has been accomplished.

A procedure which has proven to work well for focusing this type of binocular consists of turning a center wheel until the bridge supporting the two eyepieces is out as far as it will go. After this has been done, the one eyepiece which focuses independently is turned out as far as it will go. A distant object should then be viewed using only the left eye (provided that the right eyepiece can be adjusted independently) while the center wheel is turned until the object is in sharp focus. Next, the object is viewed with the right eye while the right eyepiece is turned in until the object is in sharp focus. At that point, try viewing the object using both eyes to see if it is in satisfactory focus; if it is not, the process should be repeated. After focusing, note the diopter reading on the right eyepiece and commit it to memory. If no one else will be using the binocular, consider using tape to secure it in that position as it need not be refocused when focusing with the center wheel for near or distant objects.

When using a powerful binocular, ten power or more, it is common to experience some degree of difficulty finding the subject through the binocular. One possible solution involves sighting in the subject by looking over the center bar and then shifting the eyes to the eyepiece lenses without moving the binoculars. The subject should be within the field of view.

When one uses binoculars, it is important that the eyepiece lenses be positioned the correct distance from the eyes. If too great a distance is maintained, one will not see the full field of view. Normally, when the flange around the eyepiece lens is held against the eyebrow, the full field of view will be seen. A person wearing sunglasses or corrective lenses may experience some degree of difficulty, however, and not see the full field of view when attempting to use some binoculars. As a possible solution, one may purchase binoculars that have retractable rubber eyecups. When the binocular is used by someone not wearing glasses, the cups are extended, thus ensuring the correct lens-to-eye distance; when an eyeglass wearer is using the binocular, the rubber eyecups are folded back, thus allowing the binocular eyepiece lens to be positioned very close to the lens of the glasses. In this way, one can maintain nearly the same lens-to-eye distance that existed when the cups were extended for the person not wearing eyeglasses. When an eyeglass wearer is contemplating the purchase of a binocular that features retractable eyecups, it is recommended that he try the instrument first without his glasses with the eyecups extended, and again while wearing his glasses with the eyecups retracted. He should see the same field of view in both cases. If an eyeglass wearer presently owns a pair of binoculars that does not feature retractable eyecups and is experiencing difficulties because of it, he may try removing the eyecups. If it is found that this is an acceptable solution for the problem, the cups can be left off or ground down and then replaced.

Normally, when someone who wears eyeglasses uses binoculars, they can effectively be used without the glasses because the optics of the binoculars will correct for visual deficiencies such as near- and far-sightedness. Binoculars will not, however, correct for other visual defects such as astigmatism. On a stake-out, one will often observe an area with the naked eye until activity is detected, at which time the binoculars are brought into use for a closer examination. It is not uncommon to alternate frequently between the naked eye and binoculars. To remove and replace eyeglasses frequently under such circumstances is inconvenient. When a person will be using binoculars while wearing eyeglasses, it is recommended that the eyeglass lenses be made of glass rather than plastic because the former have proven to be much more resistant to scratches that can result from the binoculars being placed against them. This consideration is especially important if one is using binoculars whose eyecups have been removed as opposed to a binocular that has soft rubber eyecups that can be folded back.

In the event that binoculars are to be used from a boat, moving automobile, or any unsteady surface, a binocular with a wide exit pupil (large shaft of light emitted by the ocular) will prove to be advantageous as it is easier to keep such a binocular positioned so that the shaft of light emitted by the eyepiece lens constantly projects into the opening of the eye. Binoculars have exit pupils that range from just over 3mm to slightly over 7mm. The opening of the human eye at its maximum is approximately 7mm.

Binoculars will often yield better results if some means is taken to prevent bright extraneous daylight from shining into one's eyes from above and from the sides. One's eyes will constrict increasingly as the intensity of the light is increased; consequently, subject matter that is in shadowed areas will not be observed as brightly as would be possible were the eyes shaded in some manner. One may shade the eyes with a hat that can be pulled low over the eyes or by positioning one's hands so that they prevent extraneous light from reaching the eyes from above and from the sides. If one chooses not to wear a hat but rather elects to shade the eyes with the hands, it must be remembered that it will take the eyes a reasonable period of time to readjust themselves to the changing illumination level once the hands have been so positioned.

Binoculars, being precision optical instruments, must be treated as such if they are to remain in good working order. They should be kept clean and cased when not in use. When moving about areas such as on roof tops or through fields and woods, it is advisable to take some measure to prevent the binoculars from being knocked around. If they are being carried on a strap around one's neck, consider the merits of buttoning or zipping one's shirt or jacket around the instrument, or try placing an arm through the long strap so that the binocular is positioned under the arm or possibly just shortening the strap. In inclement weather, some means should be taken to protect the instrument.

Should moisture find its way into the binocular, one can anticipate that the interior optical surfaces will become fogged and the instrument will be of little or no use until the surfaces have cleared themselves.

Sometimes it is necessary to surveil large open areas to detect such things as intruders, or perhaps to simply be aware of any activity that may occur in the area. When large areas are being surveilled, whether they consist of land or bodies of water, one can often use binoculars to good advantage. When using binoculars for such applications, one should not *sweep* the area, but rather, examine the area in sections that equal the viewing angle of the binocular being used. For example, if a binocular with a viewing angle of six degrees is being used, the total area should be systematically studied in six-degree segments. When the entire area has been examined, the process is repeated from the beginning.

### Binoculars for Low Light Level Work

While binoculars are an indispensible tool for many surveillance applications, they have proven to be especially useful for surveillance activity at dusk or during nighttime hours when the level of illumination is less than ideal, provided, or course, that the binocular selected has a *brightness index* suitable for low light level work. Generally speaking, a brightness index of about twenty-five is sufficient for daytime work while an index of fifty or more is recommended for satisfactory low light performance. Table I lists a variety of binoculars and their respective brightness index.

In the section where the diameter of a binocular's objective lens was discussed, it was stated that the greater the diameter of the objective lens, the greater would be the instrument's light gathering capability. At night, using a binocular that has a sufficiently large objective lens, one will observe that it appears to actually increase the existing level of illumination. This results from the fact that the objective lenses, being sufficiently large, are capable of gathering a greater amount of light than is the unaided human eye. Consider for example, that a 7×50 binocular, which is recommended for night work, is capable of gather-

## TABLE I
### BRIGHTNESS INDEX* FOR VARIOUS BINOCULARS

| Binocular Size | Brightness Index |
|---|---|
| 6 × 18 | 9.00 |
| 6 × 20 | 11.10 |
| 6 × 25 | 17.30 |
| 7 × 21 | 9.00 |
| 7 × 35 | 25.00 |
| 7 × 50 | 51.00 |
| 8 × 20 | 6.25 |
| 8 × 24 | 9.00 |
| 8 × 30 | 14.00 |
| 8 × 40 | 25.00 |
| 8 × 56 | 49.00 |
| 9 × 35 | 15.10 |
| 9 × 65 | 52.15 |
| 10 × 20 | 4.00 |
| 10 × 25 | 6.25 |
| 10 × 40 | 16.00 |
| 10 × 50 | 25.00 |
| 10 × 70 | 49.00 |
| 11 × 80 | 52.90 |
| 15 × 60 | 16.00 |
| 20 × 50 | 6.25 |
| 20 × 80 | 16.00 |
| 20 × 120 | 36.00 |
| 30 × 80 | 7.10 |

* Determined by dividing the diameter of the objective by the magnification and squaring the quotient.

ing approximately fifty times more light than the unaided human eye, which has a maximum opening of about one-fourth inch in diameter. A 7×50 binocular will also gather over twice as much light as a 7×35 binocular, because the surface area of a 50mm objective is more than twice that of a 35mm objective.

If one were to compare two binoculars that had the same magnification power but different size objective lenses, it would be found that the binocular with the larger objective would be more efficient for low light level work. If the magnification power of any binocular is increased, it is necessary also to increase the diameter of the objective lens in order to maintain the same low light level performance. Perhaps this can best be illustrated by comparing the *brightness index* of a 7×50, a 10×50, and an 11×80 binocular. The brightness index is derived by dividing the diameter of the objective by the magnification and squaring the quotient. The brightness index for a 7×50 binocular, therefore, is 51. By increasing the magnification power from seven to ten, but not changing the size of the objective, as is the case with the 10×50 binocular, one finds he has a brightness index of only 25, which is not ideal for night work. An 11×80 binocular, which has a magnification power just slightly stronger than a ten power binocular, but an objective that is considerably larger, has a brightness index of 52.9, which places one back into the category of a 7×50 binocular (slightly better) insofar as light gathering capability is concerned. It is evident, therefore, that when increasing the magnification power of a binocular, it is also necessary to increase the size of the objective lens if the instrument's light gathering capability is to be maintained.

One will find that while 7×50 binoculars are ideal tools for night surveillance work, the merits of *high powered, large aperture* binoculars are most noteworthy. The author has worked

Figure 58. 11×80 binocular by Novatron. This instrument is ideally suited for surveillance applications, especially under conditions of poor lighting.

Figure 59. High powered binoculars should be firmly secured to eliminate movement. A tripod works well. Note that the instrument has been mounted in the reverse position so that the handle does not interfere with the observer.

with such binoculars* at night and has found that their usefulness cannot be slighted by anyone who is at all active in stationary surveillance work (see Figure 58). Because of the relatively large physical size of these instruments, it is important that they be secured to a tripod or window mount during a surveillance assignment or optimum results will not be realized (see Figures 59 and 60).

Just as the size of the objective is an important factor that influences a binoculars' desirability for low light level work, so is proper coating of the optical surfaces. If the optical surfaces of a binocular (there are between ten and sixteen, depending on the binocular) have not been coated with an antireflection coating, up to 50 percent of the light entering the objective can be

---

\* Available from Novatron, P.O. Box 718, Big Bear City, California 92314. This company also offers a variety of other large aperture binoculars.

158  Fundamentals of Physical Surveillance

Figure 60. Window mounts also work well for securing high powered binoculars.

lost. One will also observe a hazy appearance within such an instrument that will have a tendency to reduce image contrast and wash out detail. Proper coating of the optical surfaces can reduce the loss of light by half, permitting the utilization of a full 75 percent of the light entering the instrument. The added 25 percent will make a significant difference. It is also important that the lens surfaces be kept clean.

**TELESCOPES**

**General Considerations**

While there is no doubt that binoculars serve as a very useful tool for those engaged in physical surveillance activity, there are often circumstances under which one must make visual observations at distances that exceed the effectiveness of *most* binoculars. When such is the case, the possibility of accomplishing the task using a telescope should be considered.

With telescopes, magnifying powers ranging anywhere from

twenty times to several hundred times are possible; however, for surveillance applications, it will be found that the most useful magnifying range lies somewhere between about twenty and one hundred times, depending upon such things as atmospheric haze, heat waves, and viewer-to-subject distance. Magnifying powers in excess of one hundred times will normally provide useful results only in exceptional cases. The following are some typical problems that will be encountered when using telescopes with high magnifying powers.

1. A high magnifying power results in an increase in problems caused by minute vibrations of the instrument. Adequate support of the telescope is essential.

2. A high magnifying power will result in problems caused by the atmosphere such as heat waves, dust particles, and moisture. The result will be a loss of image detail.

3. High magnifying powers will cause a decrease in the brightness of the image. This may or may not be a problem, depending upon the time of day and the subject's location.

4. High magnifying powers result in an increasingly narrow field of view. Actually, effective use of any high powered telescope (in the vicinity of sixty power or more) requires a fair amount of experience.

Bear in mind, however, that a lot can be accomplished in many instances by using nothing more than a twenty power spotting scope. With such a telescope and favorable conditions, vehicle license plate numbers can be read at distances approaching one-half mile.

Although extremely high powered telescopes have a somewhat limited application for most surveillance operations, one should recognize that some operations will favor such a telescope. If one is working under conditions where there is very little in the way of atmospheric haze and heat waves, remarkable detail can be realized at tremendous distances.

## Telescope Types

Although there are many types of telescopes, it will be found that they all operate on one of two basic principles. The first are *refracting* telescopes that use a refractive lens to gather and

160  Fundamentals of Physical Surveillance

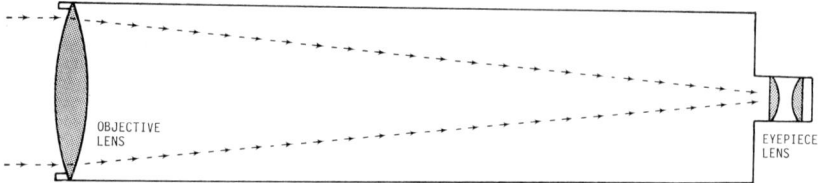

Figure 61. Refractive telescopes use a refractive lens to gather and focus light. The eyepiece lens then magnifies the image formed by the objective.

focus light as shown in Figure 61. An eyepiece lens is then used to magnify the image formed by the objective. The second types are *reflecting* telescopes that employ mirrored surfaces to gather and focus light as illustrated in Figure 62. With reflecting telescopes, as is the case with refracting telescopes, an eyepiece lens is used to magnify the image that has been formed.

When considering reflecting telescopes, one will very likely encounter what is referred to as *catadioptric* lenses. These are optical devices that use a combination of mirrors and refractive lenses to control the light gathered by the instrument. Catadioptric lenses, although they employ both mirrors and refractive

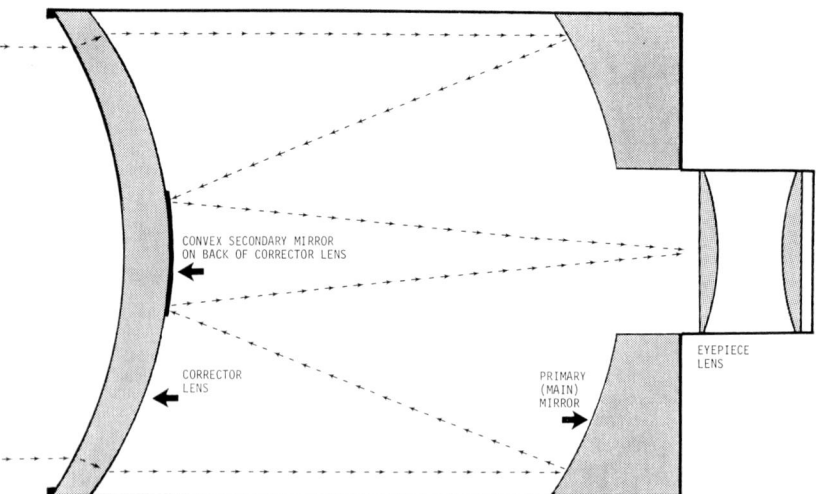

Figure 62. Reflective telescopes use mirrored surfaces to gather and focus light. The eyepiece lens then magnifies the image formed by the mirrors.

lenses, are reflecting instruments. It is simply a case of refracting elements having been introduced to the system to control certain optical aberrations. Reflex mirror lenses designed for photographic applications are also of this design.

### Magnifying Power

The magnifying power of a telescope is determined by dividing the focal length of the objective lens or primary mirror by the focal length of the eyepiece lens. The quotient is the instrument's magnifying power. For example, if a telescope whose objective lens or primary mirror has a focal length of twenty inches is being used with an eyepiece lens whose focal length is one-half inch, the magnifying power will be forty times. If the one-half inch eyepiece lens were to be replaced with one whose focal length were one inch, the instrument would have a magnifying power of twenty times. However, the maximum useful magnification of a telescope is limited by the diameter of the objective lens or mirror.

As stated, with any telescope one can obtain increasingly great magnifying powers by using eyepiece lenses of increasingly short focal lengths; however, a point is reached when an increase in magnifying power will result in a larger image, but not in additional detail. When this point is reached, nothing will be gained by seeking additional magnification. A general rule of thumb is that one can effectively obtain a magnifying power of about fifty times the diameter of the objective. To exceed this will result in an increase only in image size, not in detail.

There have been many telescopes on the market advertised as having very high magnifying powers, yet the diameter of their objective tended to suggest that the purchaser would be getting an instrument whose useful magnifying power was not actually what it was advertised to be. However, the individual who works with a telescope for surveillance purposes will, as was stated, be using relatively low magnifying powers, not several hundred times as do amateur astronomers, and therefore will not normally find this to be a problem. Again, for surveillance purposes, a maximum magnification of between sixty and one hundred times is very real.

## Prismatic Telescopes (Spotting Scopes)

Prismatic telescopes, most commonly referred to as spotting scopes, are used to a considerable degree by sportsmen for such applications as spotting targets when sighting in firearms and for spotting game while hunting. These telescopes have proven to be especially useful for physical surveillance applications because of their compact size, a result of prisms which fold the optical path (as shown in Figure 63), and because the magnifying range of these instruments will fulfill the needs of most surveillance operations that require the use of a telescope.

It will be found that spotting scopes available from various manufacturers offer a variety of features such as fixed magnifying powers that cannot be changed, models featuring interchangeable eyepieces that permit changing the magnifying power in that manner, models featuring several eyepieces on a turret and finally, scopes whose power can be zoomed through the entire magnifying range. Naturally, one will find a significant price difference between various makes.

Spotting scopes, not unlike binoculars, have objective lenses of varying sizes (diameter). The size of the objective will prove to be an important consideration if one will be working with relatively high magnifying powers or under questionable light conditions or both.

It is important that spotting scopes, just as is the case with any

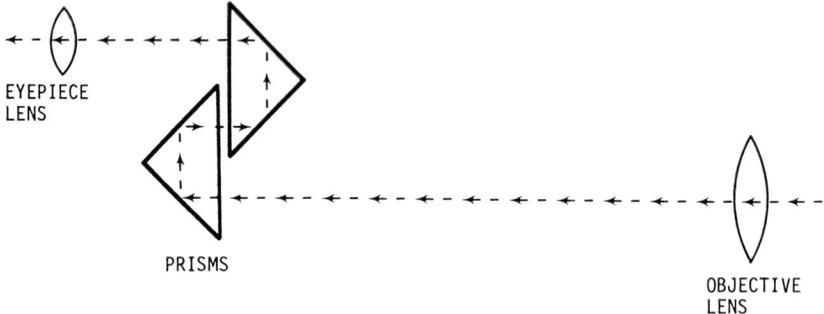

Figure 63. Spotting scopes (prismatic telescopes) are useful for surveillance applications because of their compactness, a result of prisms which shortens the instrument's physical length as shown.

telescope, be mounted in a manner sufficient to prevent all unnecessary movement and vibrations. This becomes increasingly important as the magnifying power of the instrument is increased. If one were to mount a telescope on a tripod or a window mount and then tap lightly on the end of the scope while looking through it, the problems caused by small vibrations would be apparent.

## Using Telescopes in the Field

As indicated earlier, when using a telescope it is essential that the instrument be mounted in a manner that prevents unwanted vibrations and movement. This results from the fact that telescopes will magnify not only the size of the image, but also any vibrations that may be present. A good sturdy tripod is one of the most effective means for accomplishing this task. It will also be found that when working from an automobile, window mounts are very handy items (refer to Figure 60). When such an item is being used, it is important that the engine of the vehicle

Figure 64. Mini-pod is useful in situations where a full size tripod would be too cumbersome.

164  *Fundamentals of Physical Surveillance*

not be running as it will cause severe vibrations. It will also be found that if it is a very windy day, enough movement of the vehicle can result to make viewing difficult. This is especially true if one is using a fairly high magnifying power.

While tripods and window mounts are useful, surveillants are not always working from an automobile nor under conditions whereby a tripod will be anything but cumbersome. When such is the case, other methods must be employed to ensure stability of the scope. Figures 64 through 67 should serve to provide some ideas for possible alternatives.

When using a telescope to observe a subject under low light conditions or in a normally lit building, every effort should be made to keep bright lights out of the field of view. If this is not done, observation of the subject will prove to be difficult. If the lighting arrangement is such that shifting the area of coverage

Figure 65. Mini-pod can sometimes be used to brace a scope against an upright object as illustrated.

Figure 66. Scope being stabilized with a stick in much the same fashion as it would with a mono-pod.

a bit will not eliminate the problem, it may be possible to eliminate the lights from the field of view by using a higher magnifying power.

When using a telescope, it is sometimes advantageous to use a pair of binoculars in conjunction with the telescope. By so doing, one can make general observations of the scene using binoculars and then switch to the telescope for making closer examinations

Figure 67. Scope resting in the crotch of a tree branch provides reasonable stability.

Optical and Related Aids for Vision Extension 167

Figure 68. Mounting a binocular and telescope together permits one to use the binoculars for making general observations of an area and then switching to the telescope for detailed examinations.

when so desired. This can be accomplished by mounting the telescope to a tripod or a window mount, and hand holding the binoculars, or by mounting both instruments as illustrated in Figure 68. Another advantage for making general observations with binoculars and using the telescope only for closer examination is the fact that one's eyes can become tired rather quickly when looking through a telescope. It is easier to look through binoculars for extended periods because one can use both eyes in a manner that is somewhat more natural and, therefore, fatigue sets in much less quickly.

Another advantage for mounting both instruments is that it will leave one's hands free for more important things such as note taking. Furthermore, even seven power binoculars will provide better image detail if they have been securely mounted.

When using a telescope on a hot day, the observer will quickly become aware of air turbulence, often referred to as heat waves. Air turbulence results from the fact that the sun heats the surface of the earth, causing the air near the ground to expand, get lighter, and then rise, being replaced with cooler air from adjoining areas. As a result, the density of the air is not uniform, thus causing light rays traveling from the subject to the observer to refract or bend, resulting in an unsharp and somewhat distorted image. Once realizing and understanding this phenomenon, one can do a number of things to minimize its undesirable effects. While it is true that there will often be a limited selection when choosing a vantage point, one should take advantage of all factors working in his favor.

Air turbulence is not too severe in the early morning hours before the sun has had a chance to heat the earth's surface, so if it is possible, one should consider making necessary observations at that time. If there is more than one prospective vantage point from which to choose, there are a number of factors one should take into consideration. If one selects a fairly high point, such as on a hill or building, much of the air turbulence that is almost always present close to the ground, even on cool days, can be avoided. The amount of air turbulence over a field will be much less severe than over a surface such as a parking lot; the amount of air turbulence over water is even less than will be found over a field.

When selecting a vantage point from which to use a telescope, one should also consider the direction from which the sun will be shining during the period of time that the surveillance is to be conducted. It will be found that back lighting should be avoided because it tends to silhouette the subject, making it difficult to discern details.

Finally, one should not use a magnifying power greater than that which is necessary to provide the desired details. To use an unnecessarily strong magnifying power will mean added problems such as vibrations, air turbulence, and narrower field of view.

## NIGHT VISION DEVICES
### General Considerations

When examining night vision devices, one will find that such equipment generally operates on one of two basic principles. The first type are infrared viewers, which are referred to as *active* devices because they project an infrared beam (invisible to the unaided eye) that illuminates the subject so that it may be viewed with the appropriate equipment. The second is electronic light intensification equipment, which is referred to as being *passive* rather than active inasmuch as such equipment projects no infrared radiation, but simply amplifies the existing light by several thousand times.

After study of the two types of equipment, it will be found that neither can be said to make the other obsolete, but that each offers certain features not present in the other. Generally, although the instruments operating on the principle of light intensification (passive devices) were much more recently invented and in many ways more versatile than infrared viewers, they are also much more expensive.

After a brief discussion of each type of equipment, it will become apparent that the equipment best suited for one's needs will depend upon many factors, not the least of which is price.

### Infrared Viewers

Infrared viewers have been in existence since their introduction during the Second World War. In Figure 69 is a simple drawing of such a scope and in Figure 70 is a photograph of a

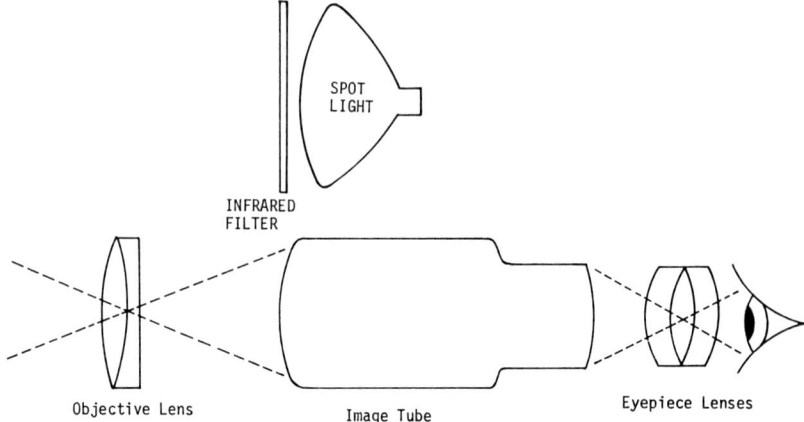

Figure 69. Simple drawing of an infrared viewer. Note that a light source and an infrared filter are necessary to illuminate the subject. The image tube then converts the infrared image to a visible image.

war surplus scope.* By studying these two illustrations, one will observe that there is a spotlight which is covered with an infrared filter. The filter is opaque to visible light but allows the infrared portion to pass through. As a result of the filter, the radiation source is not visible to the unaided eye. The infrared radiation emitted by the radiation source travels to, and is reflected from, the subject. The radiation that is reflected back to the instrument is focused onto the front surface of the image tube by the instrument's objective lens. The rear surface of the image tube then forms a visible image which is viewed through the eyepiece lens and appears as a greenish white.

Since the invention of the Sniperscope, there have been similar but much more modern infrared viewers introduced on the market for a variety of uses including surveillance applications (see Figure 71†). The primary advantage of the modern scopes over the surplus scopes is mainly that of compactness and a notably

---

* Available from Edmund Scientific Company, 620 Edscorp Building, Barrington, New Jersey 08007.

† Available from FJW Industries, 215 East Prospect Avenue, Mt. Prospect, Illinois 60056.

*Optical and Related Aids for Vision Extension* 171

Figure 70. Photograph of the famous WWII Sniperscope.

sharper image. Surplus scopes require not only a battery pack as do the modern scopes, but they also possess a transformer that is quite large and heavy. The transformer in the modern scopes is about the size of a pack of gum and rests in the handle. Additionally, when comparing the length of the two scopes, it will be

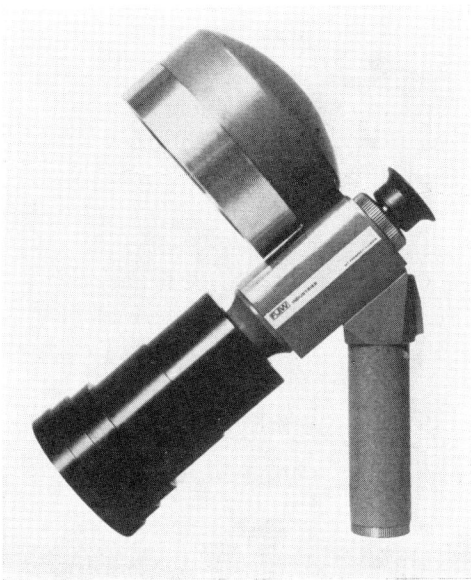

Figure 71. Illustrated is a modern infrared viewer (*Courtesy of* FJW Industries).

found that the war surplus scopes are almost twice as long as the modern scopes. While surplus scopes can be obtained for less than half the price of a modern scope, one must consider the availability of replacement parts. With surplus equipment this could be a problem.

An interesting phenomenon that occurs with infrared equipment is that a subject's clothing is often not observed as being light or dark as it in fact is. For example, a subject who is wearing very dark clothing can appear, when viewed through an infrared viewer, to be wearing clothing that is almost white. This may or may not present a problem, depending upon one's needs and the particulars of a specific case.

The effective range of infrared viewers is dependent upon the strength of the radiation source and upon the focal length of the instrument's objective lens. Generally, a distance of about one hundred yards is very real. While it will not be possible to identify a subject at that distance, the scope will certainly allow one to detect the presence of a person and in many cases determine what he is doing at that distance.

Provided that one's needs are such that a scope operating within these limitations is sufficient, an infrared viewer should prove to be useful. In deciding between an infrared viewer and a passive device (light intensification equipment), which is considerably more expensive, a point to consider is the fact that two, three, or even four infrared viewers can be purchased for the price of one intermediately priced passive device. This being the case, if a large department felt they had need for four night vision devices, it may be worth considering the purchase of three active (infrared) devices and one passive device. The advantage of a passive device is interchangeability of lenses and better suitability for photographic applications.

## Electronic Light Intensifiers

The most recent development in night vision is *passive devices* (NVDs) which were initially used by American forces in Korea. Unlike infrared viewers, passive night vision devices do not require any type of radiation source but simply takes available photons provided by various sources such as stars and streetlights and increases their energy, thus relying on the principle of light intensification. Contrary to popular belief, however, NVDs *will not* operate in total darkness. When it becomes necessary to work under conditions that are so dark that the instrument is rendered ineffective, such as could be the case on a heavily overcast night, an auxiliary infrared radiation source can effectively be employed because these instruments respond to infrared radiation as well as they do to visible light.

The actual gain realized with passive devices will be found to vary depending upon the make of the instrument, but a gain from 35,000 to over 65,000 times is very real. In basic terms, this is accomplished by changing light energy to electrical energy, amplifying it, and then changing it back to light energy. With a first generation system, so termed because they were the first systems to go into production (Figure 72), the photons pass through the objective lens and strike the surface of the photocathode of the intensifier tube. When enough photons have struck the surface of the photocathode, an electron is knocked loose, captured by the voltage of several thousand volts, and greatly accelerated toward the phosphor screen at the rear of the tube. The electron, which is traveling at a tremendous velocity, strikes the phosphor screen at the opposite end of the intensifier tube, creating a glow where it strikes. The intensity of the glow

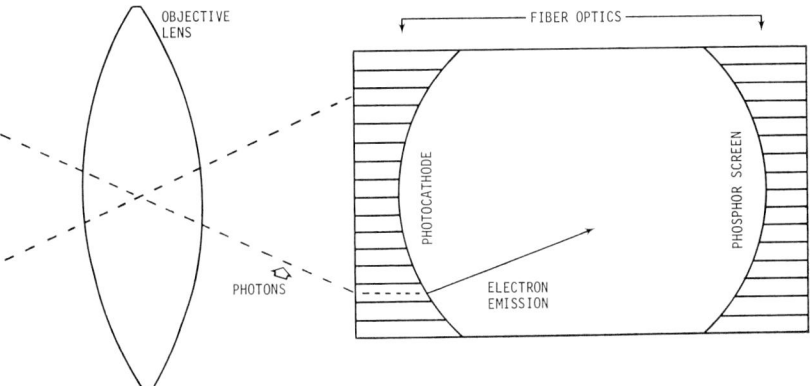

Figure 72. Simple drawing of *one* stage of a *first generation* system. Typically, three such stages are mounted in a series.

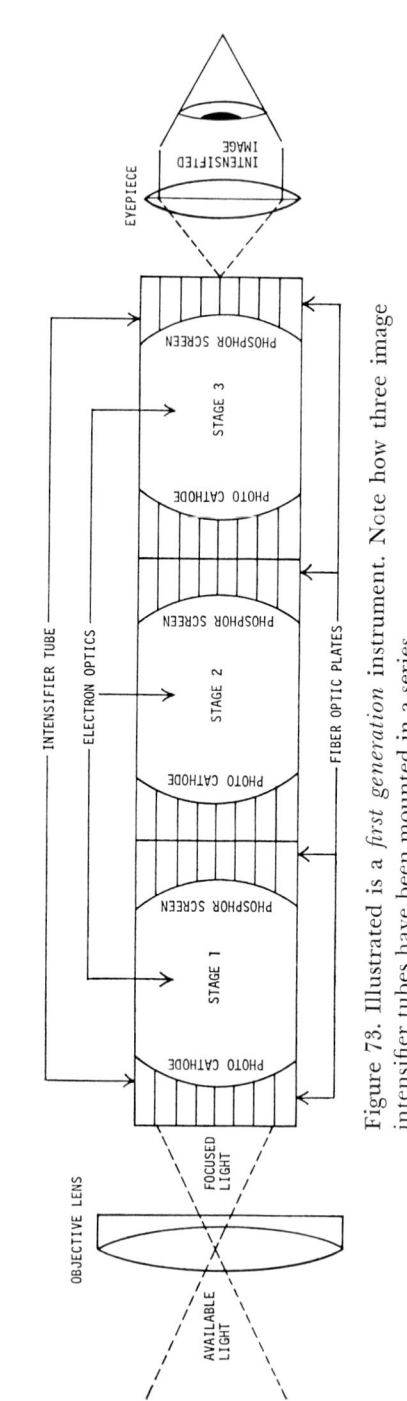

Figure 73. Illustrated is a *first generation* instrument. Note how three image intensifier tubes have been mounted in a series.

# Optical and Related Aids for Vision Extension 175

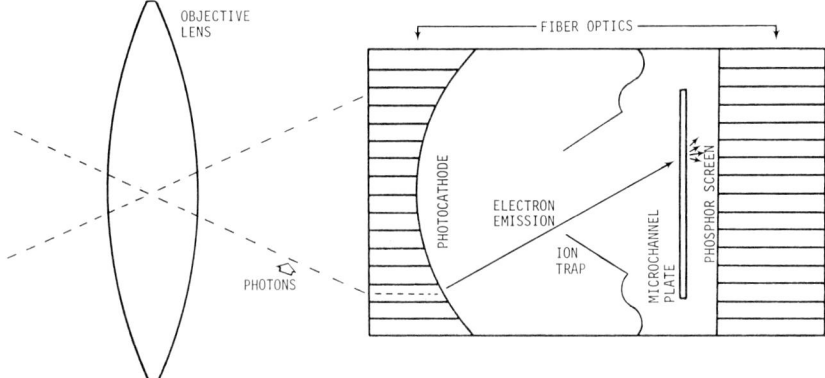

Figure 74. Simple drawing of a *second generation* system. Unlike the first generation systems, these image tubes are not mounted in a series.

is approximately forty times greater than was the intensity of the photons that originally struck the photocathode; thus, one has realized a light gain of about forty times.

To obtain a gain that is even greater, it is possible to mount intensifier tubes in a series as shown in Figure 73. If three such tubes are mounted together, each amplifying the level of illumination reaching it by forty times, the ultimate gain in the level of illumination will be about 64,000 times (40 × 40 × 40 = 64,000).

*Second generation* systems, so called because they were invented after the first generation systems, operate in a manner that is very similar to the first generation systems (refer to Figure 74). With second generation systems, photons pass through the objective lens and are focused on the photocathode. Again, when enough photons strike this surface, an electron will be knocked loose, be captured by the high voltage, and travel at a high velocity towards the microchannel plate. When the electron strikes the microchannel plate, it knocks a *large quantity of secondary electrons* loose, thus obtaining a gain similar to that which was achieved by bonding three intensifier tubes together as is done with first generation systems. Figure 75 illustrates a second generation passive night viewing device.

176     *Fundamentals of Physical Surveillance*

Figure 75. Smith & Wesson Star-tron® Model 303-A with 135mm, f/1.6 objective lens (*Courtesy of* Smith & Wesson).

The primary advantage of a second generation system over a first generation system is a scope that is more compact, suffering only about one-fifth the distortion characteristic of the first generation systems. However, the ultimate resolution of these systems is not quite as good as with first generation systems.

The reader who is contemplating the purchase of such a system is strongly encouraged to secure the promotional literature from the various companies offering such products. It would also be desirable to talk with people who have used such systems.

Almost all manufacturers of light intensifiers offer accessories by which one may couple the instruments to various types of photographic equipment such as still cameras, motion picture cameras, and closed circuit television. It is also possible to obtain a variety of telephoto lenses for these instruments, and in some cases, an adapter that will permit one to use the lens system of a 35mm single lens reflex camera.

## Lenzar Optics

For the purpose of long range surveillance at night, Lenzar Optics Corporation* offers a most remarkable variety of ultra high speed, extreme telephoto catadioptric lenses (reflex-mirror). These lenses are intended primarily for use with low light level television cameras, although they may also be used for direct viewing purposes. At the time of this writing, the following lenses are available on a special order basis: 1000mm f2.8; 700mm f2.0; 500mm f2.8. Figure 76 illustrates a 700mm f2.0

---

*Lenzar Optics Corporation, 210 Brant Road, Lake Park, Florida 33403.

Figure 76. 700mm f/2.0 catadioptric lens equipped with a second generation image intensifier. Lens as illustrated is set up for direct viewing (*Courtesy of* Lenzar Optics Corporation).

Figure 77. 700mm f/2.0 catadioptric lens equipped with a low light level television camera. This lens measures about 1.5 feet in diameter, about 5 feet in length and weighs in the vicinity of 160 pounds (*Courtesy of* Lenzar Optics Corporation).

Figure 78. Photograph taken of the image appearing on the monitor screen when the lens in Figure 77 was focused on a radio tower that was about 2.5 miles away. Taken late at night; it was raining (*Courtesy of* Lenzar Optics Corporation).

lens equipped with a second generation light intensifier which provides a light gain of about 60,000 times. This lens as illustrated is set up for direct viewing. In Figure 77, the 700mm f2.0 lens is equipped with a low light level television camera which also provides a light gain of about 60,000 times. In Figure 78 is a photograph of the image that appeared on the screen of the monitor when this lens (Figure 77) was focused on a radio tower that was about 2.5 miles away. This photograph was taken late at night; there was no artificial illumination in the vicinity of the tower and it was raining, a factor that would naturally have an adverse effect on the resolution of the image.

This lens and camera assembly measures approximately 1.5 feet in diameter, about five feet in length and weighs in the vicinity of 160 pounds. The angle of acceptance is 1° and the focusing range extends from about thirty feet to infinity.

## CHAPTER 11

# Surveillance Photography

### GENERAL CONSIDERATIONS

**B**ECAUSE OF THE FREQUENCY with which photographic equipment is utilized in conjunction with surveillance operations, investigators and enforcement officers should be familiar with the rudiments of photography as it applies to this usage. It is not necessary that one be a specialist in this area, but he should have an understanding of what type of photographic equipment will fill his particular needs under various circumstances and be capable of correctly operating such equipment when in the field. *Never should an investigator embark on a case with a camera he has not familiarized himself with to the point where he is comfortable with it and its proper operation.*

This chapter on surveillance photography, while offering the highlights of this unique application of photography, is not intended to offer more than its general aspects, for this is a very specialized area of photography. For those who wish to make a closer study of this application of photography, there is a how-to book available that deals strictly and specifically with this discipline.[1] This chapter will, nonetheless, serve to make the reader aware of the highlights concerning surveillance photography.

As would be expected, to be effective as a surveillance photographer one must also be effective at the art of physical surveillance. In most instances, this will involve selecting a good vantage point at which to set up the necessary equipment. Occasionally, however, the investigator will find himself using a camera while on a moving surveillance.

### CAMERA TYPES USED FOR SURVEILLANCE PHOTOGRAPHY

As a general rule, it will be found that the cameras best suited for surveillance photography are 35mm single lens reflex cam-

---

1. Siljander, Raymond P.: *Applied Surveillance Photography.* Springfield, Thomas, 1975.

Figure 79. Minolta 16II subminiature camera. This camera accepts a special cassette containing 16mm film and is quite versatile featuring a wide range of shutter speeds and aperture settings. The pen has been included for size comparison.

eras, Super 8, and 16mm motion picture cameras, and in some unique situations, the subminiature cameras that are about the size of a pack of cigarettes or smaller (see Figure 79).

The value of subminiature cameras lies primarily in their small size and easy concealment. The most notable advantage of 35mm SLR cameras and 16mm motion picture cameras is their fast lenses and the wide variety of film types available for them. Super 8 motion picture cameras are preferred by many private

Figure 80. The Nicnon is a 7×50 binocular with a built-in half frame 35mm motor drive camera capable of taking photographs at a rate of about one exposure per second.

investigators because of their ease of operation, the rapid replacement of exposed film (possible because film is supplied in cassette form), and the comparatively low cost and availability of film when on out-of-town assignments. Recognize, however, that there is a limited selection of film types available for Super 8 cameras. This can present a problem when working under low light conditions where push-processing of the film may be necessary.

In addition to the cameras most commonly used for surveillance photography are special purpose cameras, one of which is the Nicnon®* (see Figure 80). The Nicnon is a 7×50 binocular with a built-in half frame 35mm motor drive camera featuring a vertical picture format. Because the camera is a half frame (24.0 × 17.2mm), a twenty exposure roll of film will record forty exposures. Similarly, a thirty-six exposure roll of film will record seventy-two exposures. Each winding of the drive mechanism will provide about twenty exposures at a rate of about one exposure per second.

The Nicnon features three shutter speeds ($\frac{1}{60}$, $\frac{1}{125}$, and $\frac{1}{250}$ seconds) from which to choose and the aperture range extends from f/3.5 through f/11. The focal length of the objective lenses is 165mm, which provides an image magnification on the film that is 3.3 times greater than that of a 35mm camera's normal lens of 50mm (see Figure 81).

When the Nicnon is hand held, it is desirable to select the fastest shutter speed ($\frac{1}{250}$ second) to avoid image blur which can result from camera movement. In the event that it becomes necessary to use a slower shutter speed, it is advisable to brace the instrument against something solid or secure it with a window mount or tripod.

## TELEPHOTOGRAPHY

Because of the extreme importance of telephoto lenses to those engaged in the covert photographing of people, investigators should be familiar with them and their proper use.

Except for some distinct problems that are quite characteristic

---

* Available from Walcam Enterprises, Inc., 412 West 6th Street, Los Angeles, California 90014.

of telephotography, much of the art of telephotography is simply that of taking pictures. A telephoto lens working at f/16 is very much like any other lens working at f/16 insofar as exposure is concerned, the only exception being mirror lenses which employ a system of mirrors to shorten the optical (light) path; with such lenses, there is a light loss of about two thirds of an f/stop which results because of a mirror's inability to reflect 100 percent of the light striking its surface.

The only distinguishing feature of a telephoto picture is a flat, long perspective. *This, however, is a result of the long camera-to-subject distance and has nothing to do with the lens system being used.*

Because telephoto lenses tend to amplify any vibrations that may be present, firm support of the camera and lens assembly is essential. Figures 82 through 87 show some of the more common methods of ensuring camera and lens stability. In addition, the photographer should exploit the advantages offered by a cable release.

In dealing with telephoto lenses, there are two basic types one will encounter: refractive lenses and reflex mirror (catadioptric) lenses. The former are much larger physically than are mirror lenses that have a system of mirrors and lenses to fold up the optical path causing the light passing through the instrument to do so in a *zig-zag* fashion, thus greatly reducing the physical length of the unit. Naturally, for surveillance applications, the compactness of mirror lenses is an attractive feature.

An *extremely compact* mirror lens that was recently introduced by Vivitar® will, because of its small size, have a definite application for surveillance photography. The lens being referred to is a 600 mm f/8 lens that measures only 3 5/16 inches long physically, depicted lifesize in Figure 88. In the near future, Vivitar will offer both an 800mm and a 1200mm lens of this design.

Figure 81. (A) Subject vehicle photographed using a 35mm camera with a normal (50mm) lens. (B) Subject vehicle photographed from the same position using the Nicnon.

Figure 82. When hand holding a telephoto lens, both elbows should be firm against the body for support.

Figure 83. Gun stock mount is very effective when working with telephoto lenses. Here it is being used with a 500mm f/8 reflex-mirror lens.

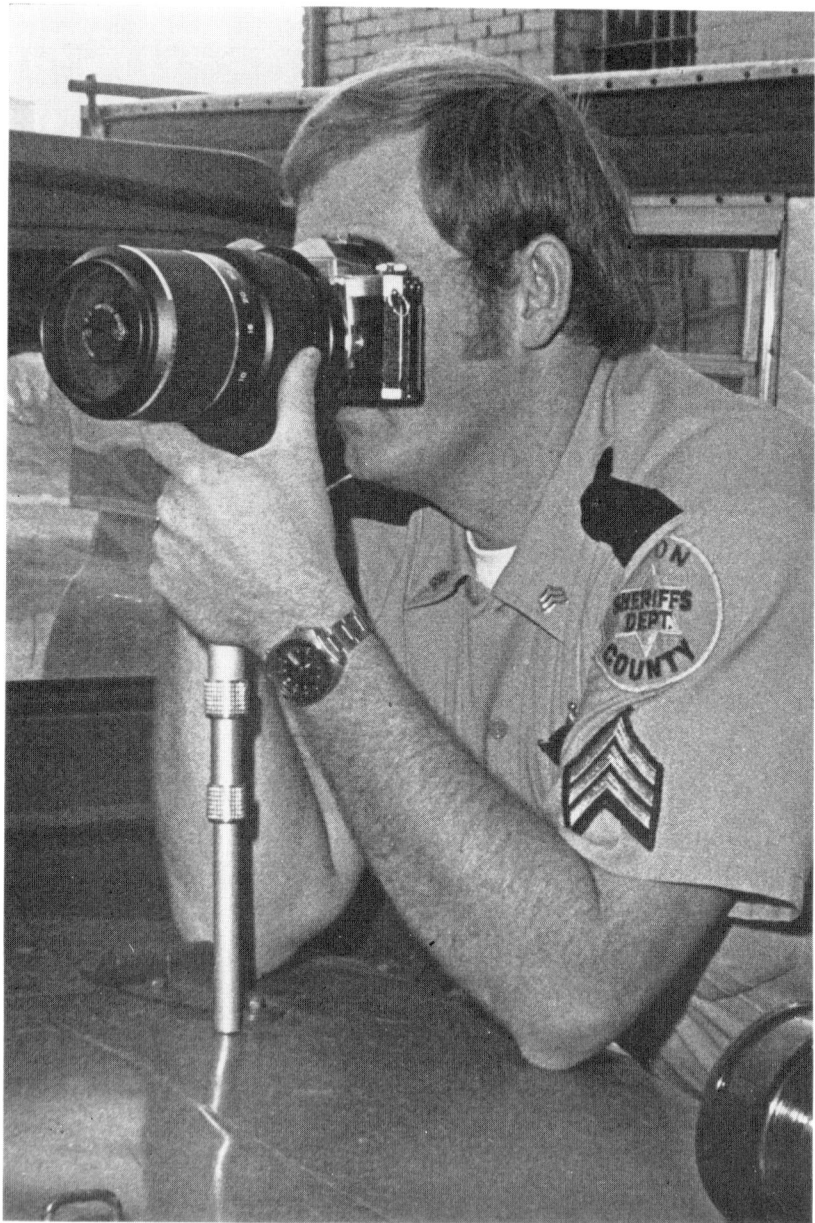

Figure 84. Belt pod being used as a mono-pod, a technique that often works well with long lenses.

## Surveillance Photography

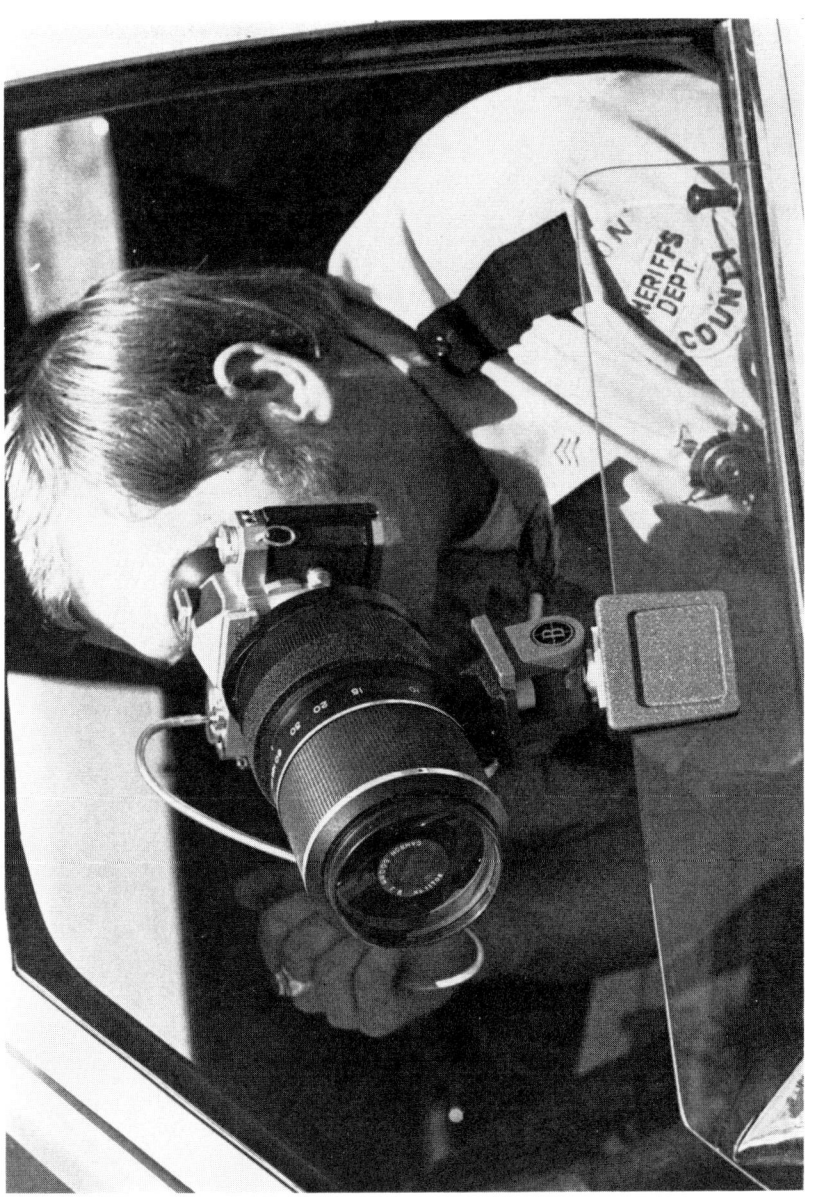

Figure 85. Window mounts are very useful when working from an automobile. Be sure to shut the engine off as its vibrations will have a devastating effect on sharpness.

188  *Fundamentals of Physical Surveillance*

Figure 86. Belt pod is a useful aid when working with short to moderate telephoto lenses, still or motion pictures.

## Surveillance Photography

Figure 87. Utilizing two tripods is often helpful in extreme telephoto work. A cable release is also desirable. Shown is an 800mm f/8 Vivitar lens.

Generally, a focal length of 500mm or more (on a 35mm camera) will place the lens into the *extreme telephoto* category. In an urban setting where effective camera-to-subject distances do not generally exceed 500 feet, a focal length of 400mm to 500mm is the maximum that will generally be needed. However, for the investigator working under a unique set of circumstances or in a rural area where greater distances are encountered, 500mm will often not provide the results needed and one will find that focal lengths in the 1000mm to 3000mm range will be needed.

For extreme telephoto work, one may make a lens by purchasing the optical elements and constructing the housing himself,[2] he may purchase an extreme telephoto lens manufactured by a camera manufacturer, or he may purchase an astronomical telescope along with the appropriate camera adapter. All avenues will provide good results.

In Figure 89 is illustrated a 2000mm f/11 Reflex Mirror Lens manufactured by Nikon®. In Figure 90 is illustrated a 1300mm f/14.4 Questar® with a 35mm camera body attached to it. This lens is their Field Model which has been designed for observation and photography. Questar also offers a larger astronomical telescope that is suitable for photographic applications and has, when coupled with a 35mm camera body, an effective focal length of 2800mm and an f/16 aperture. In Figures 91 and 92 are photographs that were taken with such a lens under *very favorable atmospheric conditions*. Recognize that such ideal conditions do not normally exist during a surveillance assignment;

---

2. Discussed in Siljander, Raymond P.: *Applied Surveillance Photography*. Springfield, Thomas, 1975.

---

Figure 88. Shown at its actual size is the Vivitar 600mm f/8 Catadioptric lens. The merit of this lens's unusual compactness lies both in its easy concealment and the fact that the short physical length reduces the horizontal and vertical travel of the front end of the lens in relation to the film plane, thereby increasing the sharpness of hand-held shots (*Courtesy of* Ponder & Best, Inc.).

# Vivitar Series 1
# 600 f/8 Solid Catadioptric Telephoto Lens

3 5/16 inches (8.4 cm)

192    *Fundamentals of Physical Surveillance*

however, these two illustrations do serve to illustrate the kind of results that are possible given good equipment and the proper conditions under which to work. The individual who took the photograph of the vehicles in Figure 92 stated that when using the same lens as a telescope he was able to read the name of the state on the vehicle's registration plates. However, this is not surprising inasmuch as it is generally possible to discern greater detail when looking into a telescope than when photographing through it.

In Figure 93 is illustrated a Celestron 8® astronomical telescope coupled to a Nikkormat® body by means of the appropri-

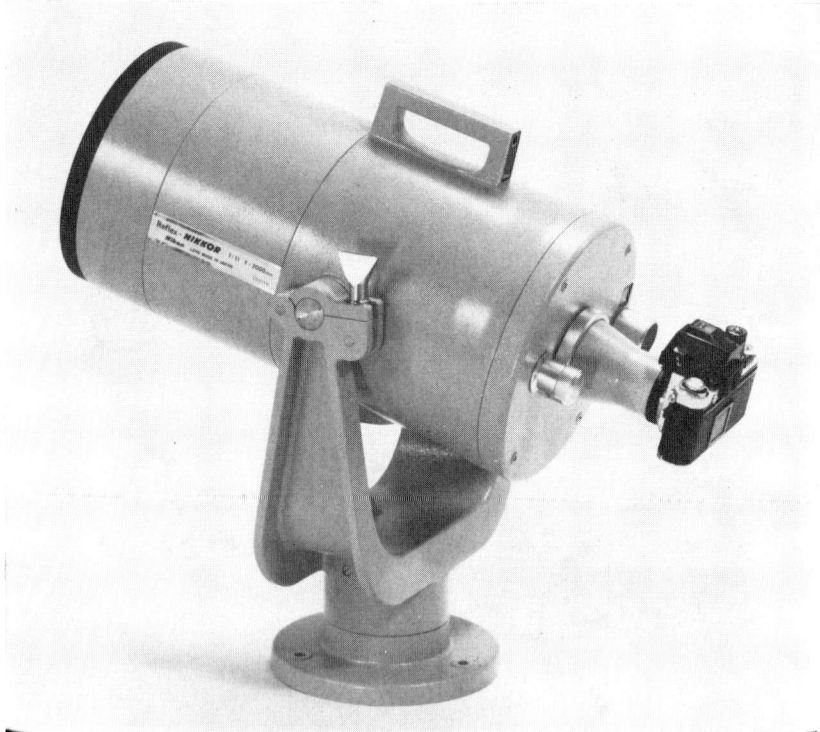

Figure 89. Nikon F2S Photomic® mounted on a 2,000mm f/11 Reflex-Nikkor® with mounting yoke. While this lens is 80 inches (2,000mm) long optically, it is only 23 $7/16$ inches long physically because of its optical design (*Courtesy of* Ehrenreich Photo-Optical Industries, Inc.).

## Surveillance Photography

Figure 90. The Field Model QUESTAR, designed expressly for observation and photography of terrestrial objects (*Courtesy of* Questar Corporation).

ate adapter. In Figure 94A is a cover photo showing the lens mounted to a tripod with an arrow indicating a vehicle that is approximately one-fifth mile from the camera position. In Figure 94B is illustrated a photograph of the vehicle that was taken using the camera and lens assembly shown in Figure 94A. This photograph is a bit more typical of the results one can expect to obtain when using such lenses under field conditions. The results do not compare with those taken with the Questar only because the conditions under which the photographs were taken are not as favorable. In Figure 95 is an aerial view showing both the camera and the subject position when Figures 94A and 94B were recorded. This illustration should also serve to emphasize that

Figure 91. Visitors at Yellowstone National Park taken from a distance of about 2,000 feet using a Questar Seven® lens (*Courtesy of Questar Corporation*).

## Surveillance Photography

Figure 92. View of vehicles across Elliott Bay in Seattle, a distance of 2.2 miles, taken with a Questar Seven. Note the clarity of the vehicles' registration numbers (*Courtesy of* Questar Corporation).

Figure 93. Celestron 8 astronomical telescope (2,000mm) coupled to a Nikkormat camera body.

when topographical conditions prevent selecting a vantage point that is reasonably close to the subject's position, it is sometimes possible to work from a considerable distance using the appropriate optical equipment and do a very effective job of it.

Naturally, astronomical telescopes are not the most compact instruments with which to work; however, when using them, one is generally working under conditions whereby a vantage point offering good cover is selected, the equipment is set up, and then the waiting begins. Compactness under such circumstances is not normally a priority. Furthermore, when working with focal lengths in the 1000mm to 3000mm range, one is most often working at such great camera-to-subject distances that the distance itself provides a considerable degree of cover for the rather large size of the lens.

Many spotting scopes and monoculars can also be used as photographic lenses (telephoto). One will most likely recall having read advertisements regarding spotting scopes and monoculars that may also be used as telephoto lenses for photographic applications by simply utilizing the appropriate camera adapter. Such advertisements are correct from the standpoint that it is possible to obtain a variety of magnifying powers, some extremely powerful, by this method and yet have a reasonably compact and inexpensive unit. The drawback arises from the fact that, in extremely high magnifying powers, the effective aperture of such lenses is generally comparatively small, meaning that while the lens may perform reasonably well under normal daylight conditions, exposure problems may be experienced at dusk. Each individual must assess his own needs in this respect.

One of the factors that tends to appeal to some investigators is knowing that they are investing in an instrument that will serve a dual purpose. With the spotting scope (monocular) and adapter, they may use the instrument as a telescope and as a telephoto lens, depending upon their immediate needs. In Figure 96 is illustrated a very compact 10×30 monocular that can be coupled to almost any 35mm format camera.* Available also for

---

* Manufactured and marketed by Walcam Enterprises, Inc., 412 West 6th Street, Los Angeles, California 90014 .

Figure 94. (A) View taken of the Celestron 8 with camera adapted showing the subject vehicle in the distance (see arrow). The camera-to-subject distance is about ⅕ mile. (B) View of the subject vehicle taken with the camera and lens assembly positioned as shown in (A).

Figure 94 *(continued)*

Figure 95. In this aerial view is indicated the camera position (A) and the vehicle position (B) that was illustrated in Figure 94.

Figure 96. Ten power monocular coupled to a 35mm SLR camera by means of an adapter.

this instrument are a number of extension rings that enable one to select a variety of magnifying powers all the way to an effective focal length of 1000mm. Figure 97 illustrates a cover photo taken with a normal lens and a photo that was taken with the monocular.

**SURVEILLANCE PHOTOGRAPHY AT NIGHT USING ULTRAHIGH SPEED FILM**

It will very often be found that the needs for surveillance photography arise at night. When this is the case, the surveillance photographer or investigator must decide between using ultrahigh speed film and working with available light, using infrared materials, or using a night viewing device (NVD).

When working with ultrahigh speed film and available light, there is no easy way to ensure proper exposure. One can, nonetheless, be assured of a very good percentage of success by doing some experimental work taking photographs of a person under various conditions so as to form an understanding of how to best

Figure 97. (A) Photograph taken with a 35mm camera and a normal (50mm) lens. (B) Photograph taken from the same position using the monocular and camera illustrated in Figure 96.

A

B

202  *Fundamentals of Physical Surveillance*

Figure 98. Night photograph of a subject in a normally lit building. Subject was photographed from about 150 feet using a 500mm f/6.3 lens and an exposure duration of 1/30 second. Tri-X film rated at E.I. 4,000 was used.

approach various situations. Try photographing a subject standing under a streetlight or in a normally lit building from outside as shown in Figure 98. One may also wish to attempt photographing a subject as the lights of a passing automobile pass over him briefly. Be sure, however, that any light source is a little bit in front of the subject so as to avoid a silhouette that will have little or no value for identification purposes.

Finally, when working at night with ultrahigh speed film, it will often be necessary to use as large an f/setting as possible and as slow a shutter speed as conditions will permit to avoid underexposure. The large f/setting will limit depth of field, and accurate focus is essential. Consider using an eyepiece magnifier; it will help assure good focus. Because the shutter speed will be quite slow, proper support of the camera and lens is essential or there will be image blur.

## PUSH-PROCESSING PHOTOGRAPHIC FILM

As stated previously, the fast films and lenses of the 35mm still and the 16mm motion picture cameras are useful to the surveillance photographer. Unfortunately, these alone are often not enough and it will be found that the speed of the fastest film available, even when used with a very fast lens, is not sufficient to produce an acceptable negative under the particular set of circumstances. The photographer can, in such cases, pretend the film is of an ASA rating much higher than it actually is and later compensate for the resultant underexposure by overdeveloping the film. For example, Tri-X film, which is actually 400 ASA, may be exposed as if it were really 1600 ASA. This film will naturally be underexposed as a result, and the photographer, realizing that fact, will compensate by overdeveloping the film. This is accomplished by increasing the development time, the development temperature, or both. This is called *push-processing*. Although the quality of a negative that has been so processed will suffer from increased grain and contrast, the slight loss should prove to be inconsequential when one considers that the push-processing enabled him to obtain a printable negative under conditions that would otherwise not have permitted it. Recognize also that the use of a flash unit is out of the question in surveillance photography.

In Table II is a list of films and the recommended developing formulas for push-processing the films to various ASA ratings. The reader should recognize that these development formulas are only recommended starting points, and the photographer should experiment a bit, as he may wish to adjust the times and temper-

## TABLE II
### FORMULAS FOR PUSH-PROCESSING PHOTOGRAPHIC FILMS*

Kodak Tri-X Film.
Agitate at 60-second intervals.

| | | |
|---|---|---|
| | 400 ASA | Normal development. |
| E.I. | 800 ASA | D-76, 12 minutes at 68°F. |
| E.I. | 1200 ASA | D-76, 9¾ minutes at 75°F or HC-110 (dil. A), 6½ minutes at 68°F or Acufine® developer, 5¼ minutes at 68° |
| E.I. | 1600 ASA | D-76, 13 minutes at 75°F or HC-110 (dil. A), 8 minutes at 68°F. |
| E.I. | 2400 ASA | Diafine®, two-step development process, see instructions on package. |
| E.I. | 4000 ASA | HC-110 replenisher, 1:15 (one-part replenisher to 15-parts water). Develop for 8 minutes at 75°F. Agitate at 3 and 6 minutes. Discard at 8 minutes. EXPERIMENT, AS YOU MAY WISH TO ALTER THE LENGTH OF DEVELOPMENT TIME AND THE AGITATION INTERVALS TO SUIT YOU BEST. |

Kodak 2475 High-Speed Recording Film.

| | | |
|---|---|---|
| E.I. | 4000 ASA | DK-50, 9 minutes at 68°. |
| E.I. | 6400 ASA | Diafine; mix solutions A & B at 70°F. Develop in solution A for 3 minutes and then in solution B for 3 minutes; rinse well in running water for 1 minute at about 70°F and redevelop 2 minutes in both solutions A & B respectively. Rinse, fix and dry. |

Kodak High-Speed Ektachrome Film.
Follow instructions provided with E-4 Chemicals.
Extend first development times only.

| | (Daylight) | (Tungsten) |
|---|---|---|
| Normal Development | 160 ASA | 125 ASA |
| Normal plus 35% increase | E.I. 320 ASA | E.I. 250 ASA |
| Normal plus 75% increase | E.I. 640 ASA | E.I. 500 ASA |

Kodak Ektachrome-X Film.
Follow instructions provided with E-4 Chemicals.
Extend first development times only.

| | |
|---|---|
| Normal Development | 64 ASA |
| Normal plus 35% increase | E.I. 125 ASA |
| Normal plus 75% increase | E.I. 250 ASA |

*These are general guides and may be altered to better suit individual needs and techniques. This is true especially for tri-X rated at E.I. 4000 ASA.

atures to best suit him and his specific needs. This is especially true when pushing Tri-X film to 4000 ASA.

## INFRARED SURVEILLANCE PHOTOGRAPHY

### The Light Spectrum

The visible light spectrum is made up of various wavelengths of electromagnetic radiation. The spectrum is made up of violet light on one end with a wavelength of about 400 millimicrons, and as the wavelengths get longer, one gets into blue, then green, yellow, orange, and finally deep red, which is about 700 millimicrons. Beyond the two extremes is electromagnetic radiation, which continues to get shorter in wavelength on the violet and longer on the red end. Infrared photography takes place in the region just beyond the red end of the spectrum between about 700 and 900 millimicrons. This region of the spectrum is not visible to the human eye. Although the spectrum does continue far beyond 900 millimicrons, it has nothing to do with infrared surveillance photography.

### Basic Technique

Basically, all one needs to take an infrared photograph surreptitiously of someone in the dark is any 35mm camera, a roll of Kodak High Speed Infrared film, a gelatin Kodak Wratten Filter Number 87, and an electronic strobe unit. The higher the BCPS (candlepower) rating of the strobe the better. The film is a special film that is sensitive to a range of electromagnetic radiation between 700 and 900 millimicrons. Unfortunately, this film is also sensitive to the visible region of the spectrum.

To utilize the equipment that has just been outlined, one need only place the film into the camera. This must be done in total darkness because the cassette will not block the infrared radiation as it does the visible light. A change bag is handy for this purpose. Next, place the infrared filter over the strobe unit. Electrician's tape and a small square of glass will work well for this purpose. It has been stated that infrared film is sensitive and will respond to visible light just as it will to infrared radiation. There is no need to place a filter over the lens, however, because the

206  *Fundamentals of Physical Surveillance*

Figure 99. Subject photographed at 100 feet in total visual darkness using infrared materials and a 500mm f/6.3 lens.

photographing will take place in darkness. Lights in the vicinity such as streetlights will present no problem. The filter over the strobe unit is necessary so that the subject does not detect the flash when he is photographed.

Once the camera assembly has been made ready, it will be necessary to establish a guide number so that proper exposure can be determined for various camera-to-subject distances. This is easily accomplished by taking a subject at a known distance (twenty feet, for example) and photographing that subject at all f/settings. After being developed, the film is examined and the f/setting which gave the best exposure is multiplied by the camera-to-subject distance. For example, if the camera-to-subject distance was twenty feet and it is found that f/4 gave the most correct exposure, eighty is the guide number to be used with that film type, strobe, and filter ($4 \times 20 = 80$). In the future, determine the correct exposure by dividing eighty by the camera-to-subject distance, and the quotient will be the proper f/setting to use.

In infrared photography, it is necessary to make an adjustment in focus because the lens, when properly focused for a visual image, will not be properly focused for an infrared image. This correction is made by extending the lens from the film plane by 0.25 percent of the focal length of the lens being used. Most lenses made for 35mm cameras have an indicator mark on the lens to aid the photographer in this respect.

The technique that has been discussed will offer a camera-to-subject distance of about fifty feet. There is a method of using a fresnel lens to make a telephoto strobe out of a normal strobe unit that will make it possible to photograph subjects in detail in the 200-foot range. This is discussed in detail in *Applied Surveillance Photography*. Also discussed in that book is infrared motion picture photography.

In Figure 99 is a subject that was photographed in *total* darkness using infrared materials.

## HONEYWELL PENTAX NOCTA

The Honeywell Pentax Nocta® (Figure 100) is a special infrared camera designed specifically for photographic surveil-

Figure 100. Honeywell Pentax Nocta. This infrared camera is equipped with a 300mm f/3.3 lens, an image converter tube, and an instantaneous radiation source for film exposures and a continuous radiation source for subject viewing (*Courtesy of* Honeywell Pentax).

lance. The Nocta is equipped with a 300mm f3.3 telephoto lens, an image converter system similar to that in the WWII Snooperscope, a filtered spotlight for viewing, and an instantaneous radiation source (filtered flash bulbs) for exposing the film.

### PHOTOGRAPHY AT NIGHT USING PASSIVE NIGHT VISION EQUIPMENT

Passive Night Vision Devices (NVD's) are a modern and more sophisticated version of the famous WWII snooperscopes. Passive NVD's differ from snooperscopes mainly in that they operate on the principle of light intensification rather than on infrared radiation, which is the case with infrared snooperscopes. Generally, one star will provide sufficient illumination for pas-

Figure 101. 35mm single lens reflex camera coupled, by means of a relay lens, to a Smith & Wesson Star-tron MK 222 with an 85mm, f/1.8 lens (*Courtesy of* Smith & Wesson).

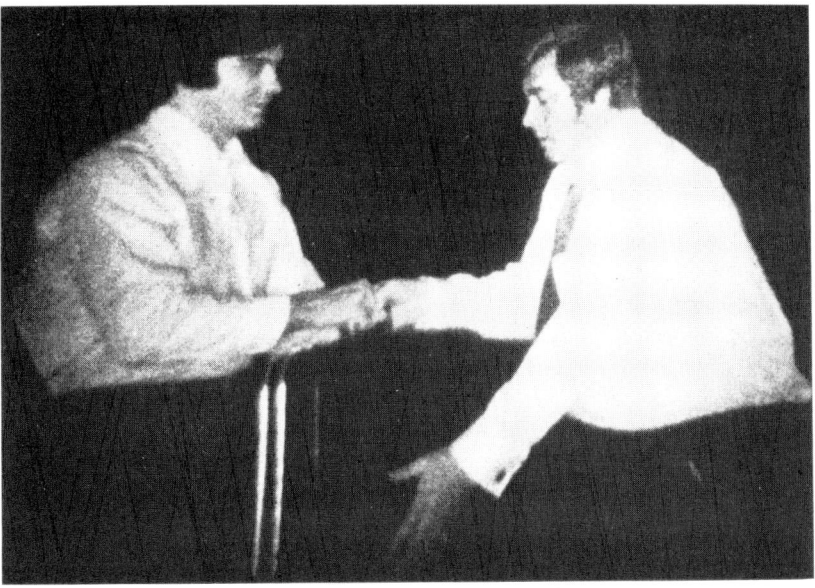

Figure 102. Subjects were photographed through a Star-tron at a distance of about 80 feet using Kodak 2475 high speed recording film rated at E.I. 1,000 ASA. Exposure was 1/20 second with an illumination level approximating normal starlight conditions (*Courtesy of* Smith & Wesson).

sive NVD's to function satisfactorily. Basically, the light intensification is accomplished by taking light energy, changing it to electrical energy, amplifying it, and then changing it back to light energy. The image produced is a greenish white.

Most manufacturers and distributors of such equipment offer adapters by which cameras may be attached to their unit for night photography (see Figures 101 and 102). Among the cameras that may successfully be adapted to NVD's are most 35mm SLR's, motion picture cameras, and video cameras.

**CLOSED CIRCUIT TELEVISION**

There are a number of attractive features offered by closed circuit television equipment for surveillance applications aside from their extensive use in the field of industrial security.

Unlike conventional motion picture film, a video tape offers instant replay because no chemical development is necessary. Video tapes may also be erased and reused when no longer needed, thus resulting in a significant saving insofar as cost is concerned. An-

Figure 103. Video camera coupled with an 800mm telephoto lens by means of a "C" mount adapter.

Figure 104. Photograph of the monitor screen when the camera and lens assembly illustrated in Figure 103 was focused on a subject slightly over one city block away.

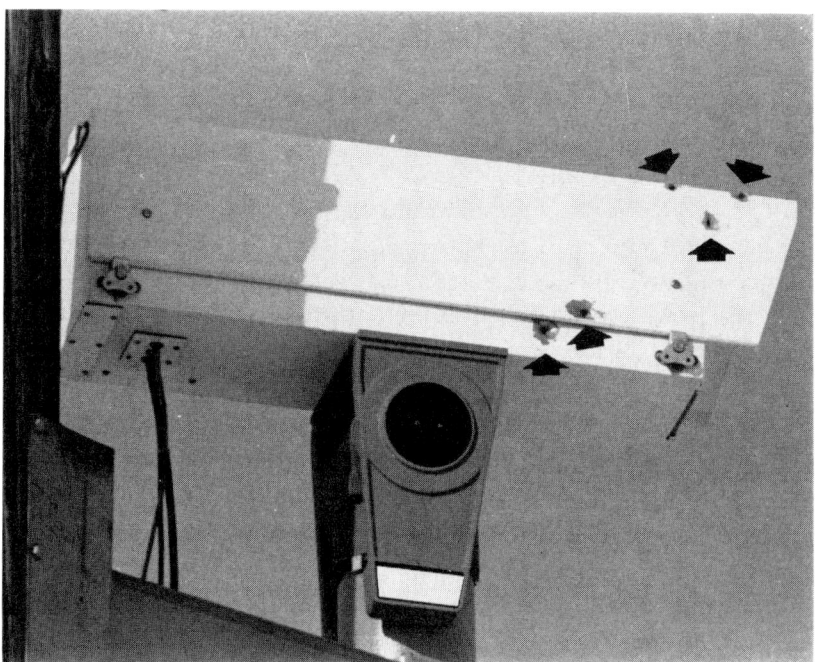

Figure 105. Remote control CCTV cameras in remote locations are subject to sabotage. Note the arrows indicating the many bullet holes which resulted during a labor disturbance.

other attractive feature is the fact that *one* video tape can be used to record activity that would require several hundred feet of conventional motion picture film. Naturally, this would result in a further savings.

Video cameras, just as almost any professional quality camera, may be used with telephoto lenses. In Figure 103 is a video camera that has been coupled to an 800mm f8 lens by means of a "C" mount adapter. A "C" mount adapter is a simple device that enables one to mount the lenses of a 35mm camera system to a video camera or a 16mm motion picture camera. Figure 104 is a photograph of the monitor screen when using the camera and lens assembly shown in Figure 103. The subject is slightly over one city block from the camera position. The door behind the subject is approximately 1½ blocks from the camera.

Closed circuit television (CCTV) and video camera systems may also prove useful in situations where it is not possible or practical for a man to surveil an area directly. By using a CCTV system, it is often possible to secrete a camera and someone can then surveil the area by observing a monitor some distance away. A setup such as described would also enable one individual to surveil several areas at one time. It is possible also to obtain CCTV cameras equipped for low light level situations (LLLTV).

Low light level television cameras function by changing light energy to electrical energy, amplifying it, and then changing it back to light energy. This is the same basic principle upon which passive night vision devices operate.

When considering the placement of a CCTV camera in a remote location, recognize that, unless they are protected or concealed in some manner, they are vulnerable to sabotage (see Figure 105).

Figure 106. (A) Night photograph taken from the low light level television monitor with the camera's zoom lens at its widest coverage. Note window indicated by the arrow. (B) Camera has zoomed in to examine the window indicated by the arrow. Note that although the only illumination in the room is that provided from outside, the presence of the pictures on the interior wall is evident (*Courtesy of* Photo Security Systems).

A

B

There has been some interesting experimental work done in recent years regarding the use of low light level television cameras for police surveillance of high crime areas in urban settings. Such a program would permit law enforcement agencies to mount a camera inside an environmental housing (protective casing) which would then be placed at some strategic point, perhaps on a telephone pole. The camera would then enable the department's personnel to monitor activity in the given area from the police station. Such cameras should naturally feature a pan and tilt control allowing the observer to manipulate the position of the camera from the station. Another ideal feature is a zoom lens which would also be controlled from the station. This feature allows the observer to surveil the general area and then zoom in for a closer examination of any suspicious activity that may occur.

Photographs taken of the monitor screen when such an experiment was conducted in an urban setting at about 1:00 AM using a LLLTV camera are shown in Figure 106. In Figure 106A, the camera's lens was set for its widest coverage. In Figure 106B, the lens was zoomed in so as to examine the darkened interior of the room that is designated by the arrow in the center of Figure 106A. Note that although the only illumination within the room is that small amount provided by the streetlights outside, the presence of the pictures on the wall is quite evident. The potential of such equipment for certain surveillance applications should be apparent.

### PASSIVE PHOTOGRAPHIC SURVEILLANCE SYSTEMS

In situations where it would be impossible or impractical to observe directly the area of interest, it is often possible to conceal a closed circuit television camera, a motion picture camera, or a camera that will begin taking a sequence of *still* photographs when activated.

There are a number of cameras available that will take sequence still photographs in a variety of formats ranging from 8mm to 35mm. Naturally, the larger formats will enable one to obtain the same area of coverage while using a longer focal

Figure 107. Speaker housing to conceal surveillance camera (*Courtesy of* Merrill Hughes).

length lens, thus obtaining a larger image and, consequently, better subject identification.

Such cameras can, in many instances, be concealed with little difficulty, and there are many ways in which they can be activated. One method of activation might be a pressure switch that will respond when an intruder steps on a mat. Another possible method may be a switch that will activate the camera when a weight is removed from it, such as certain merchandise or bills in a cash register drawer. Alarm systems (ultra-sonic, proximity, etc.) may also be coupled to such a photographic system so that they activate the camera either independently or in conjunction with an alarm of some type.

A Hennepin County (Minnesota) Sheriff's Deputy developed such a camera system using a reasonably inexpensive 35mm format camera featuring a spring-wound motor-driven system. The camera features a 35mm (moderately wide angle) f2.8 lens, and is encased in a 13 × 14½ inch speaker cabinet (see Figure 107). In Figure 108 is a simulated service station hold-up photographed with this system. It is interesting to note how little effect the grill of the speaker housing actually has upon the quality of the photograph.

The camera system illustrated here, and others similar to it, may be modified to photograph using infrared materials rather than simply using available light in conjunction with high speed film such as Tri-X (400 ASA).

## THERMOVISION

A remarkable instrument that has proven to possess unique possibilities for certain surveillance applications is a product that is being marketed in Sweden called the AGA 750 Infrared Camera. This instrument is very portable and can easily be carried upon one's person, as illustrated in Figure 109, or mounted and used from a helicopter.

The uniqueness of this instrument lies in the fact that it *does not* detect or register light as does conventional photographic equipment, but rather, it detects an infrared temperature differential of as little as .2 degrees Centigrade that is emitted by various objects. Although this instrument responds to heat rather than to light, its most useful surveillance application is that of detecting or locating someone at night when other (conventional) visual aids cease to be as effective as during daylight hours.

A system such as this can be adjusted so that it responds to the temperature of a person's body, and when so adjusted, it tends

Figure 108. Photograph taken by a 35mm surveillance camera concealed in the speaker housing shown in Figure 107 (*Courtesy of* Merrill Hughes).

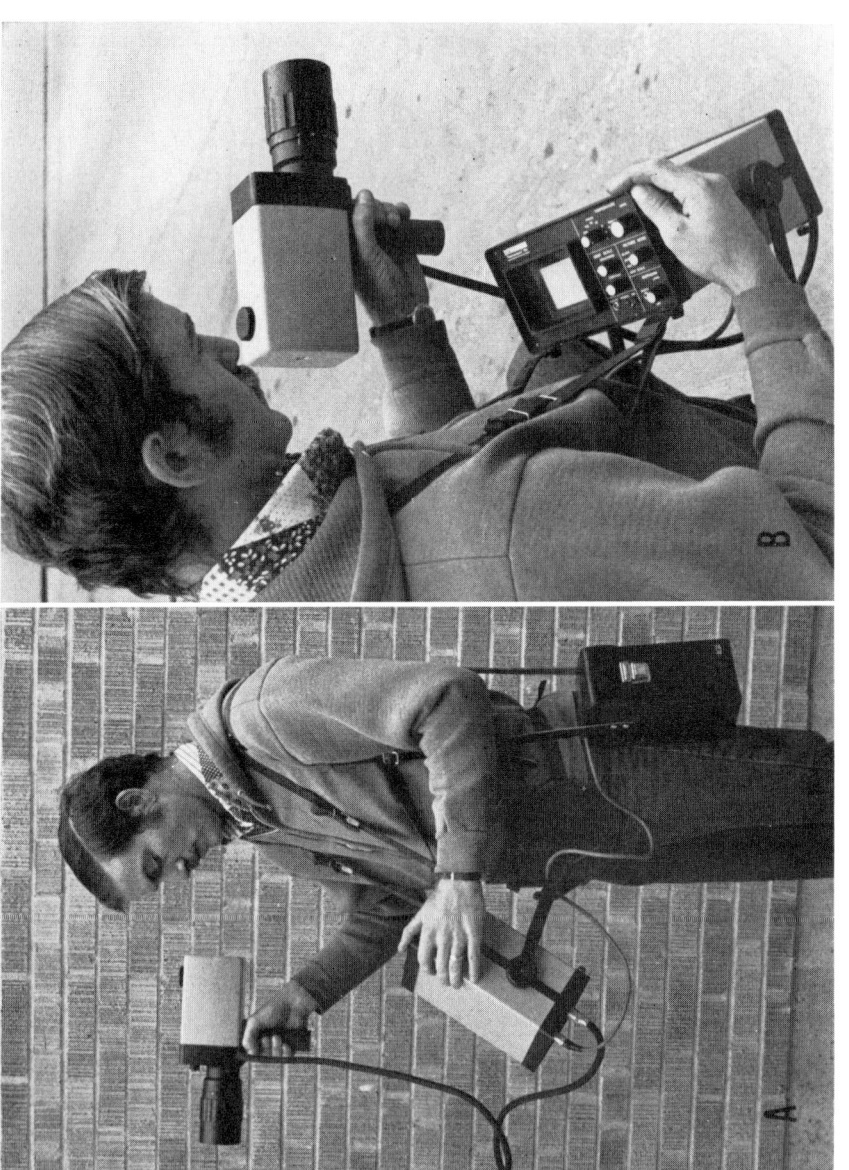

Figure 109 A & B. The AGA 750® Infrared Camera is very portable. This camera does not respond to light, but rather, discerns an infrared temperature differential of as little as .2 degrees Centigrade.

Figure 110. Polaroid® photograph of the AGA 750 monitor screen showing how a person can be expected to appear (*Courtesy of* Energy Conservation Consultants, Inc.).

to discriminate between a person and other objects in a given area, thus making for ready detection of people. This instrument should prove to be highly effective for such applications as border surveillance. It has proven in the past to be useful for the detection of fugitives from a helicopter when they have taken to fields and wooded areas at night.

In Figure 110 is an example of how a person appears on the monitor's screen. Naturally, the size of the image depends upon the focal length of the system's objective lens (lenses are interchangeable) and upon the distance between the subject and the system. A very distant subject will often appear as only a white dot, which would be the case when operating at the maximum range of about 1000 meters.

Some have found that when using such a system from a helicopter to locate a fugitive in a rural area, it is best, in many instances, to continue on and appear to be continuing the search even after the fugitive's position has been determined. In this way, the fugitive is more likely to continue on his intended course rather than taking evasive action, thus complicating the apprehension. Specific circumstances, however, will determine the merit of such a tactic.

Should the reader desire further information regarding this product, he is encouraged to contact Energy Conservation Consultants, Inc., 9001 East Bloomington Freeway, Bloomington, Minnesota 55420.

## PHOTOGRAPHY DURING A LABOR DISTURBANCE
### Introduction

The remaining pages of this chapter will discuss the use of photography during labor disputes. This section has been prepared by Mr. John E. Waaraniemi, former business associate of the author, and was prepared for the benefit of those readers involved in industrial security and investigations who may, in some way, become involved with a firm during a labor dispute. Mr. Waaraniemi has had considerable experience in this area of photography.

While it will be noted that there is some discussion regarding photography as a means of documenting property damage caused by strikers, the greatest portion of this discussion emphasizes the importance of *surveillance photography* during labor disputes and what can realistically be accomplished by employing such an operation. It is for this reason that this section is presented.

While it may be considered an unfair labor practice to photograph the legal and peaceful activities of pickets, it must be recognized that the role of the surveillance photographer in such instances is not to harass pickets, but rather to document any illegal activity that may occur. This cannot be said to be a violation and certainly does not constitute questionable ethics. Any company whose employees go on strike certainly has both a right and an obligation to protect itself against the illegal and damaging activities so often associated with a labor dispute.

### General Considerations

While studying this section, the reader will observe that there are four critical areas in which photography will perform an important function in the protection of a client's property and per-

sonnel during the period of disagreement. These four areas consist of:
1. Documentation of illegal activity.
2. Documentation of damage to property or injury to personnel.
3. Agitator identification.
4. Deterrent effect.

These areas are interrelated and will overlap to some extent.

## Documentation of Illegal Activity

There are two areas of activity that the photographer will be able to record. The first area is illegal picket activity. The picket line is where the most violence will generally occur. This is where targets with the easiest accessibility exist. These targets will be in the form of personnel and equipment entering and leaving the client's property. The photographer will be able to record any acts of violence or sabotage directed at these targets.

The second area of activity is the sabotage of company property in areas away from the picket line. These targets will generally be in isolated areas. One may pick the most likely targets in advance by studying the past activities of the union during labor disputes, by determining where they can do the most damage with the least likelihood of being discovered, and by accessibility.

Easy access to isolated installations or machinery will make these the most likely targets. In a situation such as this, the photographer would secrete himself in a position that affords maximum visibility of the installation. He is then in a position to document sabotage as it takes place. It should be pointed out that acts against these areas can often be predicted by any change in the client/union relationship that would be viewed by the union members as a threat to their security. An example might be when normal production resumes following a walkout, with management taking over the worker functions. When negotiations stall or break off, vandalism will often be used to apply pressure; however, the most critical period will most likely be shortly after the walkout itself takes place.

Documentation that is obtained during a labor dispute can then be used at the client's discretion. Arrests may be made, in which case the photographs may be used as evidence, or they may be used at arbitration hearings which may result from a company desire to discipline offending employees. In any case, concrete evidence will be available in the photographs.

### Documentation of Damage

This area does not need a great deal of elaboration; it is for the most part self-explanatory. However, there are a few points that should be noted. The results of vandalism should always be documented. The courts will require proof of damage in any case of vandalism brought to trial. Documentation will also be useful at injunction hearings and with insurance companies in the settlement of claims. Arbitrators may also require documented evidence in arbitration hearings after the strike has been settled.

### Agitator Identification

Past experience shows that there always are a number of men, depending on the size of the work force, who by their actions propel others to acts of violence. It is extremely important to identify these persons immediately. A photographer will become rapidly aware of the person or persons involved in this activity. A series of photographs should be prepared showing this individual to be continually involved in illegal activity. The client may then go to court or to the NLRB and obtain an injunction prohibiting the individual from being around client property for the duration of the strike. By identifying and isolating the trouble makers, one will greatly decrease the number of violent acts which take place in a situation of this type. Additionally, this will benefit the client in that persons likely to cause problems on the job will also be identified.

### Deterrent Effect

The presence of a photographer will serve effectively in keeping illegal picket line activity at a tolerable level. People become reluctant to involve themselves in illegal activity when they realize that their actions will be recorded. Again, past experience shows that illegal picket activity will drop off drastically when a photographer is present. The effect is even greater once photographs have been used in prosecuting an offender.

## CHAPTER 12

# Report Writing

### GENERAL CONSIDERATIONS

WHILE IT HAS BEEN SAID that an investigator is only as good as the reports which he writes, many otherwise capable investigators experience a considerable degree of difficulty with this most necessary function. If an investigator does an outstanding job of developing information while in the field but is unable to convey his findings in a written report that is clear and concise, he will prove to be of little value to a client or employer. For such an individual to be of any real value, it would be necessary for someone to write, or at least rewrite, his reports for him. It should be readily apparent why this cannot be: One supervisor, faced with the task of writing reports for several investigators working under his direction, would have little time for other responsibilities.

When preparing a report, it is desirable to avoid terminology that is characteristic of the investigative profession unless the recipient of the report is an investigator himself.

The actual format of investigative reports is not important so long as they are neat and organized in a manner that makes for easy reading. It should also be understood that *investigative reports must contain facts, not opinions.* When it is deemed desirable for some reason to include an opinion, it must be presented as such.

Investigative reports must, as was stated, be factual documents reflecting all information that is pertinent to a matter under investigation and address the following questions: (1) Who? (2) What? (3) When? (4) Where? (5) Why? (6) How?

It will be found that well prepared reports are useful in a number of ways, some of which are the following:
1. Keep an employer or client informed of case developments.
2. Enable other investigators to take up efficiently where the first investigator left off.

3. Enable other investigators to study the case and thereby assist with the investigation.
4. Assist an attorney in preparing a case for court.
5. Enable one to go back and review the case from the beginning. This is useful for purposes of refreshing one's memory, to determine if patterns exist, or perhaps to show the existence of inconsistencies regarding various allegations.

### DESCRIPTIONS OF PERSONS AND VEHICLES

When preparing a report, it is important that descriptions of persons and vehicles be complete. Such descriptions should also be presented in the generally accepted format which is as follows:

Descriptions of persons:
1. Sex
2. Color
3. Age
4. Height
5. Weight
6. Build
7. Complexion
8. Hair
9. Eyes
10. Peculiarities
11. Dress

Descriptions of vehicles:
1. Year
2. Color (top to bottom)
3. Make
4. Model
5. Year of registration
6. State of registration
7. Registration number

Examples of descriptions presented in this manner are provided in the sample surveillance report.

### SURVEILLANCE REPORTS

The actual format of surveillance reports will be found to differ somewhat depending upon the requirements of the agency for which the investigator is employed; however, it will be found that, in all but the most exceptional cases, surveillance reports are *time caption narrative reports.*

Surveillance reports, just as is the case with any investigative report, must provide factual information regarding the matter in question. Again, the questions *who, what, when, where, why, and how* must be taken into consideration when conducting the surveillance and when preparing the written report. In a surveillance report, the time, as well as descriptions, is very important.

The following is a brief example of a *time caption narrative surveillance report*. Consider that, in this example, the investigator is following an individual when he leaves his home in the morning to determine where he is employed. This example is very general and is provided simply to provide the reader with an idea of how such a report may appear. Naturally, exactly what information is included in any report will be determined by the needs of the case. In this example, all that was desired was information regarding the subject's place of employment. However, were the nature of the case different and the exact route taken by the subject deemed to be of importance, a time log would have been maintained reflecting when and where each turn was made.

REPORT PREPARED FOR: ABC Manufacturing Firm   Date: 8-10-76
FILE NUMBER: 0-000                            INVESTIGATOR: DAR

*Commenced:* 4:00 AM    I arrived in the vicinity of 426 James Avenue, Minneapolis, Minnesota, residence of Arnold Mathew Jones.

A position was taken on the next block that afforded an unobstructed view of the subject's residence, his drive, and his vehicle, which is described as:

> 1976, white over blue, Chevrolet, Impala, two-door sedan, 1976 Minnesota registration number HC 9158

7:10 AM    The subject, Arnold Mathew Jones, described as:

> Male, Caucasian, 37 years, 5'10", 180 lbs., heavy build, medium complexion, brown hair, blue eyes, heavy sideburns, normal walk, tan work trousers, long sleeved tan work shirt, and black work boots.

left his residence carrying a lunch pail, got into his vehicle, and drove north on James Avenue.

7:19 AM     The subject arrived at 152 West Freemont Avenue where he picked up a passenger described as:

> Male, Caucasian, about 45 years, 6'1", 175 lbs., light build, ruddy complexion, black hair with hint of graying, short sideburns, normal walk, tan work trousers, long sleeved tan work shirt, black socks, and black shoes.

These two individuals appeared to know each other well and were observed talking quite a lot during the remainder of the surveillance.

7:30 AM     The subject and his passenger arrived at Arnold's Radiator Repair Shop at 546 George Avenue where they parked in the rear of the shop, left the vehicle, and unlocked the shop's front door.

8:00 AM     The subject and his passenger were observed opening the business and beginning work.

## FINAL
### EXPENSES

Whether expenses should be itemized on a separate report form or placed at the end of the main report will depend upon the organization by whom the investigator is employed.

Expense items should be listed in a simple but complete manner.

### UNDERCOVER REPORTS

The specific considerations regarding what is or is not to be included in an undercover report will depend upon the nature of the operation and specifically what type of information is desired or needed. The following discussion is slanted towards *industrial and commercial undercover operations* because, excluding federal governmental operations, most undercover work is done by and for large business and industry, with most investigators being employed by private companies and then assigned to a client's firm for a fee.

There are different schools of thought regarding reporting techniques for undercover operations. Some companies allow their undercover investigators to write reports in the first person while others require reports to be written in the third person for purposes of security. When preparing a report in this manner, the investigator will include himself in it as if someone else were writing the report. A technique or method such as this has considerable merit, since if an unauthorized person should happen to read the report he would not be able to identify the investigator. To teach an investigator to write reports in the third person takes time, but the one time a report ends up in the wrong hands makes the effort worthwhile. It is also recommended that reports be sent to a location other than the client's place of business.

Along the lines of secrecy, the investigator should use a number or other identifying trademark, but never his real name when signing the reports. This is especially true if the reports are being written in the third person, for to do otherwise would defeat the purpose of writing in the third person. It is also important that the investigator never refer to the client company by its name in his reports. The client's facilities should be referred to simply as *the company* or the *client's facility*. All persons involved who have a *need to know* will be aware of the identity of *the company*. No other person should possess this information. When the reports go into the mail, they should be sent to an address other than the client's place of business, and there should be no return address upon the envelopes. These precautions are necessary as a safeguard against unauthorized persons reading the reports and identifying the investigator and the client facility. Someone from outside the company who does not recognize the subjects' names will have no idea as to which company the reports pertain. Should a report turn up missing in the mail, it will be a simple matter to have a copy from the investigator's file reproduced. All these precautions and safeguards may appear, on the surface, to be a bit clandestine or, if you prefer, *cloak-and-daggerish,* but they could save an investigator and his client a considerable amount of embarrassment should a report be lost, not to mention the continued success of the operation. Besides, once having gotten into the habit of operating in this fashion, it requires very little extra time, effort, and expense to add these small measures of security.

The following is an example of a third person commercial undercover report. In this fictitious example, assume that the investigator's name is Andrew Strands. Note, however, that by the way the report has been written, the identity of the agent is not apparent.

*Monday, August 1, 1976*

The agent reported to the company for work at about 11:45 PM on this date.

Work began as usual and continued until about 2:00 AM when all employees except Robert Carson of maintenance were observed in the lunchroom. At about 2:15 AM Robert Carson appeared in the lunchroom and went to sit with Jim Little, a friend. They were observed talking in low tones for a couple of minutes before joining the others in general conversation. Activity of this nature has been observed on several occasions.

Later during the shift, Andrew Strands asked Robert Carson in the presence of Jim Little if he had by chance forgotten it was time for the 2:00 AM break, whereupon Robert hesitated, then stated he had gone to the men's room. Andrew Strands appeared satisfied with that explanation.

Andrew Strands, Samuel Van Dale, and Albert Waren engaged in conversation in the incinerator room from about 3:30 AM to about 4:00 AM. It was learned that during this conversation Albert Waren stated he had recently stolen a motorcycle helmet from the company that was valued at $39.95 by passing it out of the building through a gap by one of the receiving dock doors and retrieving it as soon as he got off work in the morning before the day crew arrived.

The agent reports that nothing else of an unusual nature was observed or learned on this date.

# CHAPTER 13

# Legal Aspects of Surveillance

## GENERAL SURVEILLANCE WITH AND WITHOUT OPTICAL AIDS

WHEN ENGAGED in surveillance activity, one is sometimes seeking nothing more than investigative leads or perhaps gathering intelligence data that is not intended to be used as evidence in court. In other instances, however, one is seeking evidence that will be used in court, and when this is the case, it is important that the task be accomplished in a manner that ensures the court's acceptance of the evidence thus obtained.

During surveillance activity, one must exercise care not to violate the subject's fourth amendment rights, for if the defense can show in court that a violation of these rights has in fact occurred, the evidence thus obtained will most likely be ruled inadmissible under the *exclusionary rule*.[1] This of course, would defeat the purpose of the investigation.

The fourth amendment provides: *The right of the people to be secure in their persons, houses, papers, and effects, against unreasonable searches and seizures, shall not be violated, and no Warrants shall issue, but upon probable cause, supported by Oath or affirmation, and particularly describing the place to be searched, and the persons or things to be seized.* The protection provided by the fourth amendment against *unreasonable searches* protects one against such searches by governmental agents. It does not protect against unreasonable searches by civilians.

The question to be considered when engaged in surveillance activity is "Could my actions in any way be considered to be violating the subject's reasonable expectation of privacy?" If the answer is clearly negative, one is most likely all right. However,

---

1. The exclusionary rule bars the use of evidence obtained through an unreasonable search and seizure. See Mapp v. Ohio, 367 U.S. 643.

if such is not the case, one would do well to reexamine the situation. It may be desirable at that point, if time permits, to consult the city or county attorney or the department's legal advisor if one is available.

When questioning whether a subject has a reasonable expectation of privacy under various circumstances, an understanding of a few pertinent cases and good judgment are all that will generally be required. For example, when a subject is in the public's view, such as in his yard, on the street, or in a public building, he cannot, under most circumstances, reasonably expect that his actions are secret. Similarly, if the subject is in his home with the drapes open, he has no *reasonable expectation of privacy* so long as others in the area can simply look in and see him. To view the subject under such circumstances does not constitute a violation of his fourth amendment rights. Should the subject pull his drapes, however, thus making it necessary to approach the window and peek through the gap in the drapes to see inside, one will be violating the subject's *reasonable expectation of privacy* because while in such a setting, he does in fact have an expectation of privacy that society would most likely recognize as being *reasonable*.

It was stated that the fourth amendment protects against *unreasonable searches* by the government, not by private citizens. Private security personnel and private investigative personnel will fall into the classification of private citizens and are not bound by search and seizure laws as are governmental agents. Consequently, unlike police officers, private citizens can conduct an illegal search or violate a person's reasonable expectation of privacy and still succeed in having the evidence thus obtained admitted into evidence in court. However, should the actions of the citizen be directed by a police officer, the court will find that the citizen was acting as the *officer's agent* and the evidence will become inadmissible as a result, just as though the officer himself had obtained the evidence by way of an illegal search.

Another point that one should consider is the possibility of a civil suit being filed against the investigator in the event that it can be shown that he has violated the subject's right to privacy as provided under the fourth amendment. The laws regarding privacy will vary among states and one should be familiar with the laws of his area. Recognize also that while states cannot enact a law that is more liberal than the corresponding federal law, they can be stricter.

When conducting a physical surveillance operation in a manner that does not leave one open to reproach, the fact that one is using binoculars, a telescope, or photographic equipment will not, under normal circumstances, be a determining factor regarding whether one's actions constitute a violation of a subject's fourth amendment rights.

To better understand the position of the courts on these matters, it would serve well to examine briefly a few cases of significance. In some of these, officers have used optical equipment, only to have the defense claim that the use of such equipment served to violate their fourth amendment rights. Another objection sometimes presented by the defense is that because of the officers' vantage point, i.e. officers on the defendant's property, the search was unreasonable.

In *Coppola v. Minnesota,* which was decided on August 31, 1976, a neighbor of Coppola complained to the police in Eagle Lake, Blue Earth County, Minnesota, that the defendant was growing marijuana on his premises. The officers from the street outside the residence observed what appeared to be marijuana growing in containers sitting in the defendant's second story window. Closer observation through a telescopic device confirmed the officers' suspicions that the observed growth was, in fact, marijuana. The Eagle Lake officers, in conjunction with a Blue Earth County Deputy Sheriff, obtained a warrant to search the defendant's house based upon the above observation and upon the officers' sworn testimony that they were trained in the identification of marijuana. A valid search of the defendant's home revealed large quantities of marijuana and related paraphernalia. Defendant was subsequently charged under Minnesota Statute Section 152.09, Subdivision 1 (2).

The defendant filed a motion to dismiss charges based upon a number of contentions, one of which was that the investigating officer's use of a telescope device constituted an unreasonable and unconstitutional search. In response to the argument regarding the use of optics the court stated:

> Defendant's claim that the investigating officer's use of a telescopic device constituted an unreasonable search is without merit. Defendant chose to grow his marijuana in a window. Any passer-by could see it and if trained in the identification of marijuana would know what it was. Objects placed in "plain view" cannot, absent other circumstances, be the subject of a search. In *State v. Huffstutler*,[2] the court said: "To see that which is in plain view is not a search." See also *Coolidge v. New Hampshire*,[3] *State v. Clifford*,[4] *State v. Shevchuk*.[5] That the officers here used a telescope to aid their identification does not detract from the "plain view" doctrine despite anything said in *Katz v. U.S.*,[6] where it was held one can have a justifiable right to privacy in a public place, a public telephone booth, since defendant could hardly place justifiable reliance on the privacy of objects he placed in his window for all the world to see. Cf. *U.S. v. Minton*,[7] *Fullbright v. U.S.*[8]

In its decision, the Court brought to light a number of cases regarding *search and seizure* and the *plain view doctrine*. Two of the cases are particularly interesting inasmuch as the use of optical equipment by law enforcement officers was objected to by the defendant as constituting an unreasonable search.

In the case *U.S. v. Minton,* federal agents had received a tip from a reliable informant that a whisky delivery was to be made at the defendant's premises between 6:00 and 7:00 PM. On that date and in response to that tip, they positioned themselves on a twelve-to-fourteen-foot embankment looking down onto the defendant's building from a distance of eighty to ninety feet. A van was observed arriving shortly after 6:00 PM and, by use of binoculars, they were able to observe one-gallon plastic containers being unloaded from the vehicle. They also detected the odor of illicit whisky. Officers then entered the premises and ap-

---

2. 269 Minn. 153, 130 N.W.2d 347 (1964).
3. 403 U.S. 443, 91 S.Ct. 2022, 29 L.Ed.2d 564.
4. 273 Minn. 249, 141 N.W.2d 124 (1966).
5. 291 Minn. 375, 191 N.W.2d 557 (1971).
6. 389 U.S. 347, 88 S.Ct. 507, 19 L.Ed.2d 576 (1967).
7. 488 F.2d 37 (4th CA), *cert. den.,* 417 U.S. 936.
8. 392 F.2d 432 (10th Cir. 1968), *cert. den.,* 401 U.S. 914.

proached the van while the defendant was unloading it, and while so doing, they again saw the one-gallon containers and smelled what they had reason to believe was illicit whisky. They arrested the defendant and seized the whisky and van.

Minton was tried and convicted before the United States District Court for the Middle District of North Carolina, of possession, transportation, and removal of illicit liquor, and he appealed. The Court of Appeals held that:

> Officers' viewing of defendant's premises through binoculars did not constitute an extension of their persons so as to put them within the curtilage,* that considering the time of day and all the surrounding circumstances *there was no reason for expectation of privacy* and that a search warrant was not required since seizure of the illicit whisky was *incident to a lawful arrest*. The officers, when they entered upon the defendant's premises and approached the van, had reason to believe that a felony was being committed in their presence. It is not clear that the embankment from which the officers made their observations belonged to the defendant, but even if it did, such a location at such a distance is probably not within the curtilage.

The Court further stated that: "The seizure of the illicit whisky in the van and in the building may be justified as within the *plain view* doctrine. It may further be justified as incident to a lawful arrest."

In another case, *Fullbright v. U.S.*, which occurred on the night of April 6, 1967, federal investigators for the Alcohol Tax Unit of the Internal Revenue Service, acting upon information received from an unnamed informant, whom they stated was a *reliable* source of information, went upon the farm of one Marzett, codefendant of the appellant, and took up positions for observation of a house and shed from a distance. With the aid of binoculars, they observed through an open door the three defendants operating a still inside the shed, the appellant in particular being recognized. They also watched the defendants load bottles of distilled spirits from the shed into a 1957 Ford automobile and then saw the Ford leave the premises followed by a

---

* Curtilage is defined in Blacks Law Dictionary as: The enclosed space of ground and buildings immediately surrounding a dwelling-house.

1965 Chevrolet driven by appellant. The investigators followed the two cars for several miles, never losing sight of them, and then stopped and searched the cars and arrested the occupants. During the search, seventy-four gallons of non-tax paid distilled spirits were found in the Ford. Thereafter, the investigators secured a warrant for search of the Marzett premises, which search took place that same night and revealed two distilleries, 1,400 gallons of mash, other miscellaneous distilling apparatus, and eighteen gallons of non-tax paid distilled spirits.

The appellant argued that the arrests and the search of the automobiles were based upon information gained by the agents through an illegal search while they were trespassers upon the Marzett premises, and with this being the case, the evidence should be ruled inadmissible under the *poisoned tree doctrine*.\*

In response to this argument, the Court found that:

> When the investigators made their initial observation, the door to the shed was open and its light was sufficient to reveal what was going on. The extent of the investigators' action at the time was to look. *The use of binoculars did not change the character or admissibility of the evidence or information gained.* It has been consistently held that open fields are not protected by the fourth amendment. The investigator here did not make a *search* of any papers, house, persons, or effects in the usual sense but rather made distant observations of a house and shed, and the direct search of which we shall assume would have been constitutionally prohibited without a warrant as being within the *curtilage*. If the investigators had physically breached the curtilage there would be little doubt that any observations made therein would have been proscribed. *But observations from outside the curtilage of activities within are not generally interdicted by the Constitution. Indeed, to so hold might require passing officers to close their eyes to the commission of felonies on front door steps.* The observations from the field sustained in *Hester v. U.S.*[9] penetrated the immediate vicinity of the home where the plaintiff in error lived. By this we do not mean to say that surveillance from outside the curtilage

---

\* Under the "Fruit of the poisonous tree" doctrine, an incriminating statement made by an accused after law enforcement officers have unlawfully entered his home or unlawfully arrested him would be inadmissible as the "fruit" of the unlawful conduct. Moreover, if the tainted statement leads to the discovery of physical evidence, the latter evidence would also be ruled inadmissible. See Wong Sun v. United States, 371 U.S. 471.

9. 265 U.S. 57, 44 S.Ct. 445, 68 L.Ed. 898.

under no circumstances could constitute an illegal search in view of the teachings of *Katz v. U.S.* It is our opinion, however, that on the record before us in light of Hester the observations in question may not be deemed an unreasonable search if they were made from outside the curtilage of the Marzett farm.

In the case *Hester v. United States,* Hester was convicted of concealing distilled spirits. This situation involved revenue officers who went toward the house of Hester's father, where plaintiff in error lived, and as they approached saw one Henderson drive near to the house. They concealed themselves from 50 to 100 yards away and saw Hester come out and hand Henderson a quart bottle. An alarm was given. Hester went to a car standing near, took a gallon jug from it, and he and Henderson ran. One of the officers pursued and fired a pistol. Hester dropped his jug, which broke but kept about a quart of its contents. Henderson threw away his bottle also. The jug and bottle both contained what the officers, being experts, recognized as moonshine whisky, that is, whisky illicitly distilled, said to be easily recognizable. The other officer entered the house, but being told there was no whisky there left it. He found outside a jar that had been thrown out and broken that also contained whisky. The officers had no warrant for search or arrest, and it was contended that this made their evidence inadmissible, it being assumed, on the strength of the pursuing officer's saying that he supposed they were on Hester's land, that such was the fact. It is obvious that even if there had been a trespass, the above testimony was not obtained by illegal search or seizure. The defendant's own acts and those of his associates disclosed the jug, the jar, and the bottle, and there was no seizure in the sense of the law when the officers examined the contents of each *after it had been abandoned.* This evidence was not obtained by the entry into the house and it is immaterial to discuss that. The suggestion that the defendant was compelled to give evidence against himself does not require an answer. The only shadow of a ground for bringing up the case is drawn from the hypothesis that the examination of the vessels took place upon Hester's father's land. As to that, it is enough to say that, apart from the justification, the special protection accorded by the fourth amendment to the people in their *persons, houses, papers, and effects* is not extended to the open fields.

Referring back at this time to *Coppola v. Minnesota,* take note that the court stated: "Objects placed in *plain view* cannot, *absent other circumstances,* be the subject of a search." It is interesting that the court stated *absent other circumstances,* which would indicate that there are possible exceptions to the rule. The court further stated: "That the officers here used a telescopic device to aid their identification does not detract from the *plain view* doctrine despite anything said in *Katz v. U.S.,* where it was held one can have a justifiable right to privacy in a public place, a public telephone booth, since defendant could hardly place justifiable reliance on the privacy of objects he placed in his window for all the world to see."

Essentially what the court is saying in this instance is that while objects placed in plain view cannot, under normal circumstances, be the subject of a search, there are exceptions. One such exception is illustrated in *Katz v. U.S.,* whereby the Court found that under certain circumstances a person can have a *reasonable expectation of privacy* in a public place. To better understand the Court's position on this matter, it would serve well to examine briefly the case of *Katz v. U.S.*

In *Katz v. U.S.,* FBI agents had reason to believe that a certain public telephone booth was being used on a regular basis by one Charles Katz to place wagering information in Miami and Boston from Los Angeles. As a result, agents monitored and recorded the conversations of Katz by placing an electronic monitoring and recording device on top of the phone booth. Katz was, as a result of the information thus obtained, tried and found guilty of a federal violation. Katz appealed to the California Supreme Court who affirmed his conviction. He then appealed to the United States Supreme Court and the decision was overturned.

In appealing, Katz contended that the information obtained by federal agents was a result of an illegal *search and seizure* inasmuch as the public telephone booth was a constitutionally protected area and agents, when monitoring his conversations therein, violated his reasonable expectation of privacy as protected under the fourth amendment.

The government maintained that their actions did not constitute a search and seizure because *no physical penetration of the booth occurred*. The government further argued that because the phone booth was constructed partly of glass, thus making it possible to observe visually anyone using the booth, *Katz had no reasonable expectation of privacy* while using the telephone in question.

The U.S. Supreme Court held that "government's activities in electronically listening to and recording defendant's words spoken into telephone receiver in public telephone booth violated the privacy upon which defendant justifiably relied while using the telephone booth and thus constituted a *search and seizure* within the meaning of the fourth amendment, and the fact that the electronic device employed to achieve that end did not happen to penetrate the wall of the booth could have no constitutional significance." The Court further stated:

> The Government stresses the fact that the telephone booth from which the petitioner made his calls was constructed partly of glass, so that he was as visible after he entered it as he would have been if he had remained outside. But what he sought to exclude when he entered the booth was not the intruding eye; it was the uninvited ear. He did not shed his right to do so simply because he made his calls from a place where he might be seen. No less than an individual in a business office, in a friend's apartment, or in a taxicab, a person in a telephone booth may rely upon the protection of the fourth amendment. One who occupies it, shuts the door behind him, and pays the toll that permits him to place a call is surely entitled to assume that the words he utters into the mouthpiece will not be broadcast to the world.

In viewing the cases thus far examined, one can see that the primary test to which one's actions will be put is whether he has violated another's *reasonable expectation of privacy* as protected by the fourth amendment. Whether viewing *Katz v. U.S., U.S. v. Minton,* or *Fullbright v. U.S.,* one will note that the courts consistently consider the question of whether that observed was in *plain view,* whether the person in question had a *reasonable expectation of privacy,* and of *location* (such as in a public place, open fields, and also curtilage).

Referring again to the case of *Katz v. U.S.,* the Court expressed the opinion that:

*The fourth amendment protects people, not places.* The question, however, is what protection it affords to those people. Generally, as here, the answer to that question requires reference to a *place.* My understanding of the rule that has emerged from prior decisions is that there is a twofold requirement, first that a person have exhibited an actual (subjective) expectation of privacy and, second, that the expectation be one that society is prepared to recognize as *reasonable.* Thus a man's home is, for most purposes, a place where he expects privacy, but objects, activities, or statements that he exposes to the *plain view* of outsiders are not *protected* because no intention to keep them to himself has been exhibited. On the other hand, conversations in the open would not be protected against being overheard, for the expectation of privacy under the circumstances would be *unreasonable.*

This discussion thus far has examined a number of cases addressing the use of optical related aids by investigators and why the use of such equipment without a warrant, has been deemed justifiable by the courts. It would appear, however, by studying *United States v. Kim,*[10] that the courts may be beginning to shift somewhat in their views regarding the use of such equipment without first obtaining a warrant.

In *United States v. Kim,* agents of the Federal Bureau of Investigation used a telescope to observe activity occurring in the apartment of Kim. This surveillance was accomplished from another building a quarter of a mile from Kim's building. There were no buildings in the line of sight closer to Kim than that being used for a vantage point.

By using a telescope, agents were able to observe Kim and other defendants, both on Kim's balcony and within the apartment. Additionally, they observed Kim making numerous telephone calls while reading what the telescope revealed to be *J.K. Sports Journal.* The latter was allegedly used in connection with Kim's operation of the "telephone spot" for a major gambling operation.

From a second vantage point on the opposite side of the building, a second group of agents used $7 \times 35$ binoculars to surveil an

---

10. Cr. Nos. 75-0154, 75-0155, and 76-0005. United States District Court, D. Hawaii, June 9, 1976.

outdoor terrace which connected the apartment building elevator in Kim's building with the entrance to his apartment. The purpose of this position was to determine who frequented Kim's apartment.

The information acquired during the surveillance of Kim's apartment was used both to establish probable cause for court approval of a wiretap on Kim's telephone and to demonstrate that the wiretap was necessary since the surveillance and other "normal" investigative procedures could not produce enough evidence to convict the suspected gamblers.

Kim and the other defendants contended that using artificial viewing aids constituted a search and because of the fact that no warrant had been obtained, the search was unreasonable. On these grounds the defense moved that all evidence obtained as a result of the search (surveillance) be ruled inadmissible.

The government argued that the activity in and around Kim's apartment was in *plain view* and also that the agents had a right to be where they were at the time they made their observations. The contention was that with this being the case, no *search* could have taken place and consequently no warrant would have been required.

The primary question facing the court in this case is whether the agents' conduct did or did not constitute a search within the meaning of the fourth amendment. In deciding this case, the court decided that while under many circumstances investigators may legitimately employ optical aids of some type without first obtaining a warrant, *using such aids to look into another's home* can constitute a search within the meaning of the fourth amendment.

The court said:

> Not all surveillances with visual aids constitute invasions of privacy. There are cases upholding police surveillance with telescopes or binoculars of non-private places. These cases do not answer the question of whether using artificial aids to observe activities within an individual's home intrudes on that individual's privacy and therefore constitutes a search.
>
> We are not concerned here with police observations into a home

which were made unaided by a telescope or binoculars. Nor are we deciding the extent to which an agent may *crane his neck, or bend over, or squat,* . . . so long as what he saw would have been visible to any curious passerby. . . . It is inconceivable that the government can intrude so far into an individual's home that it can detect the material he is reading and still not be considered to have engaged in a search.

In response to the government's claim that the activity occurring in and around Kim's apartment was in *plain view* and therefore not the subject of a search, the court stated: "A 'plain' view of Kim's apartment was impossible; only an aided view could penetrate. In view of the powerful technology used by law enforcement agents in this case, the 'plain' in plain view must be interpreted as permitting only an unaided view." The government further argued that Kim had no *subjective expectation of privacy* because he failed to draw his curtains *and* because he himself used binoculars from his own window, allegedly to determine if he was under surveillance. In regard to Kim's failure to draw his curtains, the court found, as already noted, *a plain view of Kim's apartment was impossible.* As for his use of binoculars to detect a surveillance, the court stated: "Were Kim's actions interpreted as a renunciation of his expectation of privacy, the result might be that anyone taking steps to protect his privacy would run the risk of being considered to have forsaken it."

Another argument posed by the government was that because of recent newspaper articles describing the increased use of optical instruments by civilians to look into the windows of high-rise apartments and condominiums, Kim had no reasonable expectation of privacy. In response to this the court stated:

> These articles, even if true, can have no bearing on whether Kim's activities were in plain view and therefore not private. The fact that Peeping Toms abound does not license the government to follow suit. In the particular context of this case, lack of concern about intrusions from private sources has little to do with an expectation of freedom from systematic governmental surveillance. Government agents occasionally engage in surveillance with more zeal and for different purposes than private citizens.

The court expressed the feeling that had the agents' observations been limited to the balcony alone, their observations may not have invaded Kim's privacy and therefore would likely not have constituted a search within the meaning of the fourth amendment. However, the agents observed activity occurring not only on the balcony but *in* the apartment as well. As for the second surveillance being conducted on the opposite side of the building for the purpose of determining who frequented Kim's apartment, the court stated: "There is no reason to suppress the fruits of the surveillance of the terrace leading from the elevator to Kim's apartment. The terrace is a shared walkway, similar in many respects to a hallway. It does not belong to any of the defendants and no defendant could have had a legitimate expectation that his comings and goings via the terrace were not being observed." Note again the court's regard to the subject's *reasonable expectation of privacy*.

This case of *U.S. v. Kim* occurred in Federal District Court and evidences the possibility of a shift in the court's view as to what may and may not constitute a search when law enforcement officers use optically related aids to view a subject. Fortunately, the court's only real objection in this case was that agents used optical aids (without a warrant) to look into a subject's home under conditions where an unaided view *could not* have penetrated. It will be interesting to see what the full impact of this case will be on similar cases in the future in other judicial districts.

An interesting comment the court made regarding the future conduct of police personnel when using optical aids was as follows: "There is welcome room for legislation or perhaps enlightened internal regulations by the law enforcement agencies themselves in working out the procedures governing the issuance, execution and return of search warrants for visually aided searches." In light of this statement, it is interesting to note that some of the larger metropolitan departments have already, at the time of this writing, developed a written policy regarding surveillance activities in general. If more departments would define a policy regarding surveillance and intelligence-gathering operations, it would perhaps serve to soften the blow when and if there is legislation in this area. The following are a few excerpts from the policy of one such department and should serve to illuminate what kind of a policy may be in order for other departments.

*Physical Surveillance*

Surveillances shall not be conducted by members of the Division in any matter not related to the active investigations of criminal offenses as provided by these guidelines.

Physical surveillances may be conducted upon individuals or premises in the course of active criminal investigations when they are known or suspected to be centrally involved in criminal activity and such surveillance would prove or disprove their connection.

Surveillances shall be authorized by officials of the Investigative Services Division as follows:

(1) A surveillance for less than eight hours may be authorized and initiated by the official then in charge of the unit.

(2) A surveillance for more than eight hours shall be authorized by the Branch Head Captain or Lieutenant.

(3) Extended surveillances shall be authorized by the Director.

Whenever a surveillance is initiated at any of the above noted levels, the authorizing official shall report to the Director the reason and commitment.

*Photographic Surveillance*

Cameras and photographic equipment may be used by members of the Division in accordance with the following provisions.

a. Criminal Investigations.

Investigators conducting criminal investigations may use camera equipment to make films or photos which will:

(1) Assist in the identification of persons or property sought in the investigative objective, or

(2) Establish a necessary element for successful case prosecution in the Courts of ———.

Investigators requiring the use of camera equipment shall make such request to their supervising official, who, if he approves such use, will log the data in a book established for that purpose within his Branch.

All films or photos, after processing, will be forwarded by the supervising official to the Director for his filing approval.

b. Non-Criminal Photography

No member of the Division shall use camera equipment for any non-criminal activities, except from the explicit authority of the Assistant Chief, Inspectional Services Bureau.

## USE OF BUMPER BEEPER SYSTEMS

At the time of this writing there have been a couple of federal court decisions regarding the use of beepers for physical surveillance applications. It is now necessary in some jurisdictions to obtain a warrant for the use of a beeper if the owner of the vehicle has not consented to the beeper's placement upon that vehicle. The recent decisions provide that a person is protected under the fourth amendment against unreasonable searches and has a right to expect that his property (vehicle in this case) is free from the trespass necessary to install a beeper.[11] This right to privacy, according to the courts, extends to one's freedom to travel about without unreasonable government monitoring. In *United States v. Martyniuk*,[12] the court found that, in installing a beeper, investigators were *looking for* evidence and instrumentalities of crime which would incriminate the person in possession of the property to which the beeper was attached, thus constituting a search under the fourth amendment. For this reason, the court stated that the placement of a beeper constituted a search under the fourth amendment. The court stated that the placement of the beeper was in violation of the subject's right to privacy as it served to monitor his movements and location, both of which may be legitimately private.

What these decisions essentially mean is that if a private investigator's client desires to have, for example, his delivery trucks surveilled, and consents to the placement of a beeper on vehicles owned or controlled by him, it is perfectly proper for an investigator to engage in such activity. However, law enforcement officers will not normally find a subject willing to consent to the placement of a beeper upon his vehicle for obvious reasons and, consequently, a warrant should first be secured.

## BODY TRANSMITTERS AND TAPE RECORDERS

It is not uncommon for an undercover investigator to conceal upon his person a miniature tape recorder for the purpose of re-

---

11. *United States v. Holmes*, No. 74-2419, October 8, 1975.
12. 395 F. Supp. 42, decided May 19, 1975.

cording conversations that may occur between himself and a suspect. Equally common are miniature radio transmitters that will transmit the conversations to a nearby recording device or to another agent who has a receiver. When considering the legality of using such equipment, one will find that he is dealing with regulations of the Federal Communications Act and a subject's fourth amendment rights.

Basically, the question that will arise is whether the investigator carrying the recorder or transmitter is a party to the conversation or, in the event that he is not, one individual who is a party to the conversation must have prior knowledge of the monitoring and have consented to same. If one of the above conditions exist and the monitoring is for lawful purposes, it is legal. The following excerpts from Public Law 90-351, Section 2511 "Interception and disclosure of wire or oral communications prohibited" should serve to clarify precisely what the law is in these regards.

> 2 (c) It shall not be unlawful under this chapter for a person acting under color of law to intercept a wire or oral communication, where such person is a party to the communication or one of the parties to the communication has given prior consent to such interception. (d) It shall not be unlawful under this chapter for a person not acting under color of law to intercept a wire or oral communication where such person is a party to the communication or where one of the parties to the communication has given prior consent to such interception unless such communication is intercepted for the purpose of committing any criminal or tortious act in violation of the Constitution or laws of the United States or of any State or for the purpose of committing any other injurious act.

An interesting and enlightening case regarding a government agent who did use a means of recording a conversation between himself and another is *Lopez v. United States*.[13] In this case, a federal investigator was in the office of Lopez investigating possible evasion of excise taxes on cabarets; while there, Lopez attempted to bribe him by making an offer of money and a free weekend at the Inn for him and his wife as *guests* of Lopez.

---

13. 373 U.S. 427, 83 S.Ct. 1381.

## Legal Aspects of Surveillance 245

The agent, after being strongly persuaded by Lopez, took the money and then reported the incident to his supervisor. The next time the agent went to the office of Lopez, he carried a miniature tape recorder and a radio transmitter. Unfortunately the transmitter failed to operate. Again Lopez attempted to bribe the agent and was subsequently charged and tried for the offense, found guilty, and he appealed.

Lopez's defense addressed the recording of the conversation, which he claimed was obtained in violation of his rights under the fourth amendment. His theory was that, in view of the agent's alleged falsification of his mission, he gained access to his office by misrepresentation and all evidence obtained in the office, i.e. his conversations with him, was illegally *seized*.

In response to this the court stated:

> We need not be long detained by the belated claim that the agent should not have been permitted to testify about the conversation of October 24 (with Lopez). The agent was not guilty of an unlawful invasion of petitioner's office simply because his apparent willingness to accept a bribe was not real. He was in the office with petitioner's consent, and while there he did not violate the privacy of the office by seizing something surreptitiously without petitioner's knowledge. The only evidence obtained consisted of statements made by Lopez to the agent, statements which Lopez knew full well could be used against him by the agent if he wished. We decline to hold that whenever an offer of a bribe is made in private, and the offeree does not intend to accept, that offer is a constitutionally protected communication.
> 
> Once it is plain that the agent could properly testify about his conversation with Lopez, the constitutional claim relating to the recording of that conversation emerges in proper perspective. The Court has in the past sustained instances of *electronic eavesdropping* against constitutional challenge, when devices have been used to enable government agents to overhear conversations which would have been beyond the reach of the human ear. It has been insisted only that the electronic device not be planted by an unlawful physical invasion of a constitutionally protected area. The validity of these decisions is not in question here. Indeed this case involves no *eavesdropping* whatever in any proper sense of that term. The Government did not use an electronic device to listen in on conversations it could not otherwise have heard. Instead, the device was used only to obtain the most reliable evidence possible of a conversation in which the Government's own

agent was a participant and which that agent was fully entitled to disclose. The device was not planted by means of an unlawful physical invasion of petitioner's premises under circumstances which would violate the Fourth Amendment. It was carried in and out by an agent who was there with petitioner's assent, and it neither saw nor heard more than the agent himself.

Stripped to its essentials, petitioner's arguments amounts to saying that he has a constitutional right to rely on possible flaws in the agent's memory, or to challenge the agent's credibility without being beset by corroborating evidence that is not susceptible of impeachment. For no other argument can justify excluding an accurate version of a conversation that the agent could testify to from memory. We think the risk that petitioner took in offering a bribe to the agent fairly included the risk that the offer would be accurately reproduced in court, whether by faultless memory or mechanical recording.

The function of a criminal trial is to seek out and determine the truth or falsity of the charges brought against the defendant. Proper fulfillment of this function requires that, constitutional limitations aside, all relevant, competent evidence be admissible, unless the manner in which it has been obtained—for example by violating some statute or rule of procedure—compels the formulation of a rule excluding its introduction in a federal court.

When we look for the overriding considerations that might require the exclusion of the highly useful evidence involved here, we find nothing. There has been no invasion of constitutionally protected rights, and no violation of federal law or rules of procedure. Indeed, there has not even been any electronic eavesdropping on a private conversation which government agents could not otherwise have overheard. There has, in short, been no act of any kind which could justify the creation of an exclusionary rule. We therefore conclude that the judgment of the Court of Appeals must be affirmed.

## LEGAL ASPECTS OF SURVEILLANCE PHOTOGRAPHS

When engaged in a surveillance operation in a manner that does not serve to violate the laws regarding search and seizure and trespass, one may generally take photographs and introduce them into evidence with little difficulty. Generally speaking, anything that is legally observed by an officer or investigator may legally be documented photographically. However, whether the photographs may be introduced into evidence will depend upon a number of considerations.

Generally, the rules of evidence as they apply to the collection, handling, and introduction of any kind of physical evidence, as well as crime scene photographs, will apply also to surveillance photographs. The most important consideration is a solid chain of custody showing that the history of the evidence can be accurately accounted for. It is also essential that the photographs be relevant to the case and in no way misleading. Photographs that are to be used as evidence must be a true representation of that which was photographed and must be free from any distortions. The photographer must be in a position to verify that the films or prints are a true resemblance of that which he observed and photographed inasmuch as evidential photographs will not stand alone on their own merits but must be authenticated by someone who personally observed that which the photographs are intended to portray.

It was stated that the chain of custody is important. It is for this reason that, when the services of a commercial laboratory are utilized for the processing of photographic materials, it is essential to secure an affidavit showing who received the films, who supervised the processing, and in general, who can account for the materials from the time they were given to the laboratory until the cameraman signed for them and took them with him. If the laboratory service one desires to do business with does not have an affidavit for this purpose, one can make some up himself. The affidavit shown in Figure 111 is the form used by Sly-Fox Films, Inc., located in Minneapolis, Minnesota. When utilizing the services of a commercial laboratory, they should be instructed to keep all motion picture films intact. No part of the film should be cut off regardless of how unimportant it may appear to be. This holds true even if a portion of the film is blank. Similarly, nothing may be added to the film.

After signing for and receiving the processed materials from the laboratory, if one intends to pass them on to someone else, a receipt should be made out and signed to show when and to whom the evidence was given. These are basic rules that apply to evidence in general. They also apply to photographic evidence.

Before attempting to introduce films or photographs as evidence in a court of law, be sure that the films or photographs are

## AFFIDAVIT

STATE OF MINNESOTA }
                    } ss.
COUNTY OF HENNEPIN }

I, .............., having been duly sworn, on oath depose and say that I am the .............. of Sly-Fox Films, Inc., 1025 Currie Avenue, Minneapolis, Minnesota 55403.

That on the .. day of ......, 19.., at ... o'clock ..M. I received from .............. at the office of Sly-Fox Films, Inc., as shown above, ................................................ of film for development or printing.

That the films in the said containers were processed under my supervision and control and they were processed in the normal and customary manner for development of film of the particular type.

That these films were not cut, edited, or changed, negatives were not reversed, superimposed by other film, retouched, over- or under-developed, nor was any other thing done which could alter or change the film in any manner or what the film attempts to portray.

That, after processing, the films and/or prints were returned to .............. at ... o'clock ..M. on the .. day of ......, 19...

..............................
Subscribed and sworn before me this .. day of ......, 19...

..............................

Figure 111. When the services of an outside laboratory are used for the processing of photographic materials, one should obtain an affidavit reflecting when and by whom the materials were received and who supervised the processing and can attest to the treatment to which the materials were subjected (*Courtesy of* Sly-Fox Films, Inc.).

a true and accurate representation of the scene or whatever it is they are intended to portray. Also, anything one can obtain to support photographic evidence will be helpful. One should consider making a sketch showing where the subject was at the time he was photographed, where the camera and photographer were, possibly the position of the sun, as well as anything else that may be pertinent under the circumstances. Some surveillance photographers when shooting motion pictures like to expose a few feet at the beginning of the film showing the front page of that day's newspaper with the date being clearly visible. While this cannot prove that the filming was not done at some later date, it will serve to establish that it was not done prior to that date. If there is anyone besides the photographer who can testify to such things as when, where, and how the photographic evidence was obtained, that is also an advantage.

After securing the desired photographic evidence, it is important that the films, negatives, prints, and so on, be properly filed. Although it is not usually necessary to include all the technical information such as camera settings and other details on the back of each individual print, the file or case number on the back of the prints should direct one to the appropriate record in the file bearing such information. The method of filing will vary with various organizations, and the method chosen is not important so long as it is accurate. It is absolutely essential, however, to have the files under lock and key to avoid having to admit in court that it would not be difficult for someone to get in and tamper with the contents. With photographic evidence, just as with any kind of evidence, if it can be discredited or if enough doubt cast upon it, the photographs will not be allowed in as evidence. Accuracy and security of the files is important.

The following is a basic summary of what has been discussed regarding surveillance photographs:
1. Maintain a solid chain of evidence.
2. Obtain as much evidence as possible to support photographic evidence.
3. Obtain the evidence in a manner that does not leave one open to reproach.

4. Be sure the evidence is pertinent to the case and not just meant to be sensational.
5. Maintain accurate and secure records and files.
6. Do not cut or splice (alter) motion picture films in any manner.

**ENTRAPMENT**

One of the most effective methods by which to obtain evidence and information regarding certain types of irregularities or crimes is to have an investigator establish a rapport with the suspected violater(s) in an undercover capacity. However, undercover investigators, when associating with a suspect for the purpose of determining the nature and extent of his activities, must exercise care not to entrap the individual, or in other words, cause him to commit an act or violation that he would not otherwise commit, for the purpose of prosecuting him.

To bait a trap for a suspected thief, or in other words, provide him with an opportunity to commit an offense, does not constitute entrapment. While entrapment itself is not actually a crime, it can sometimes be used by a defendant as a defense if he can demonstrate that he was in fact the victim of entrapment. The burden of proof does, however, lie with the defendant.

Although the undercover investigator cannot suggest that an offense be committed or take part in the actual planning of same, he can pretend to go along with an idea once it has been suggested by another. One exception does present itself and that is in situations where it can be shown that an individual is consistently engaged in a given type of activity. For example, the undercover narcotics investigator who approaches a drug dealer and expresses a desire to purchase a quantity of narcotics is in fact suggesting that the suspect commit an unlawful act, i.e. sell contraband. However, he is not suggesting that the suspect do something that he would not otherwise do.

The laws regarding entrapment do vary inasmuch as some states fail to recognize entrapment as a defense while others consider that it can be effectuated not only by police officers, but by private investigators and private citizens as well.

Care should be exercised not to confuse the necessary outwitting of an offender (often by acting as a decoy) with the act of inducing another to commit an offense he had neither the desire, intent, nor motivation (save the encouragement of the investigator) to commit.

## UNION ACTIVITIES

When conducting business and industrial undercover operations, one must be sure never to make reports to management regarding union activities or collective bargaining processes of employees. There are federal laws against civil investigators making such reports to management. Anyone intending to engage in this area of undercover work would do well to consider obtaining a copy of the federal statutes pertaining to such activities.

## ELECTRONIC SURVEILLANCE

Inasmuch as this book has concerned itself with *physical surveillance* rather than with *electronic surveillance* (wiretapping and bugging), little discussion will be devoted to the legal ramifications regarding the latter. Rather, certain portions of the 1968 Omnibus Crime Control and Safe Streets Act will be provided for the benefit of those readers who may have occasion to engage in electronic surveillance or who may simply entertain questions regarding the legality of same.

### Title III—Wiretapping and Electronic Surveillance

*Findings*

> SEC. 801. On the basis of its own investigations and of published studies, the Congress makes the following findings:
>
> (a) Wire communications are normally conducted through the use of facilities which form part of an interstate network. The same facilities are used for interstate and intrastate communications. There has been extensive wiretapping carried on without legal sanctions, and without the consent of any of the parties to the conversation. Electronic, mechanical, and other intercepting devices are being used to overhear conversations made in private, without the consent of any of the parties to such communications. The contents of these communications and evidence derived therefrom are being used by public and private parties as evidence in court and administrative proceedings,

and by persons whose activities affect interstate commerce. The possession, manufacture, distribution, advertising, and use of these devices are facilitated by interstate commerce.

(b) In order to protect effectively the privacy of wire and oral communications, to protect the integrity of court and administrative proceedings, and to prevent the obstruction of interstate commerce, it is necessary for Congress to define on a uniform basis the circumstances and conditions under which the interception of wire and oral communications may be authorized, to prohibit any unauthorized interception of such communications, and the use of the contents thereof in evidence in courts and administrative proceedings.

(c) Organized criminals make extensive use of wire and oral communications in their criminal activities. The interception of such communications to obtain evidence of the commission of crimes or to prevent their commission is an indispensable aid to law enforcement and the administration of justice.

(d) To safeguard the privacy of innocent persons, the interception of wire or oral communications where none of the parties to the communication has consented to the interception should be allowed only when authorized by a court of competent jurisdiction and should remain under the control and supervision of the authorizing court. Interception of wire and oral communications should further be limited to certain major types of offenses and specific categories of crime with assurances that the interception is justified and that the information obtained thereby will not be misused.

SEC. 2510. DEFINITIONS. As used in this chapter—

(1) "wire communication" means any communication made in whole or in part through the use of facilities for the transmission of communications by the aid of wire, cable, or other like connection between the point of origin and the point of reception furnished or operated by any person engaged as a common carrier in providing or operating such facilities for the transmission of interstate or foreign communications;

(2) "oral communication" means any oral communication uttered by a person exhibiting an expectation that such communication is not subject to interception under circumstances justifying such expectation;

(3) "State" means any State of the United States, the District of Columbia, the Commonwealth of Puerto Rico, and any territory or possession of the United States;

(4) "intercept" means the aural acquisition of the contents of any wire or oral communication through the use of any electronic, mechanical, or other device.

(5) "electronic, mechanical, or other device" means any device or apparatus which can be used to intercept a wire or oral communication other than—

(a) any telephone or telegraph instrument, equipment or facility, or any component thereof, (i) furnished to the subscriber or user by a communications common carrier in the ordinary course of its business and being used by the subscriber or user in the ordinary course of its business; or (ii) being used by a communications common carrier in the ordinary course of its business, or by an investigative or law enforcement officer in the ordinary course of his duties;

(b) a hearing aid or similar device being used to correct subnormal hearing to not better than normal;

(6) "person" means any employee, or agent of the United States or any State or political subdivision thereof, and any individual, partnership, association, joint stock company, trust, or corporation;

(7) "Investigative or law enforcement officer" means any officer of the United States or of a State or political subdivision thereof, who is empowered by law to conduct investigations of or to make arrests for offenses enumerated in this chapter, and any attorney authorized by law to prosecute or participate in the prosecution of such offenses;

(8) "contents," when used with respect to any wire or oral communication, includes any information concerning the identity of the parties to such communication or the existence, substance, purport, or meaning of that communication;

(9) "Judges of competent jurisdiction" means—

(a) a judge of a United States district court or a United States court of appeals; and

(b) a judge of any court of general criminal jurisdiction of a State who is authorized by a statute of that State to enter orders authorizing interceptions of wire or oral communications;

(10) "communication common carrier" shall have the same meaning which is given the term "common carrier" by section 153 (h) of title 47 of the United States Code; and

(11) "aggrieved person" means a person who was a party to any incepted wire or oral communication or a person against whom the interception was directed.

SEC. 2511. INTERCEPTION AND DISCLOSURE OF WIRE OR ORAL COMMUNICATIONS PROHIBITED.

(1) Except as otherwise specifically provided in this chapter any person who—

(a) willfully intercepts, endeavors to intercept, or procures any other person to intercept or endeavor to intercept, any wire or oral communication;

(b) willfully uses, endeavors to use, or procures any other person to use or endeavor to use any electronic, mechanical, or other device to intercept any oral communication when—

(i) such device if affixed to, or otherwise transmits a signal through, a wire, cable, or other like connection when used in wire communication; or

(ii) such device transmits communications by radio, or interferes with the transmission of such communication; or

(iii) such person knows, or has reason to know, that such device or any component thereof has been sent through the mail or transported in interstate or foreign commerce; or

(iv) such use or endeavor to use (A) takes place on the premises of any business or other commercial establishment the operations of which affect interstate or foreign commerce; or (B) obtains or is for the purpose of obtaining information relating to the operations of any business or other commercial establishment the operations of which affect interstate or foreign commerce; or

(v) such person acts in the District of Columbia, the Commonwealth of Puerto Rico, or any territory or possession of the United States;

(c) willfully discloses, or endeavors to disclose, to any other person the contents of any wire or oral communication, knowing or having reason to know that the information was obtained through the interception of a wire or oral communication in violation of this subsection; or

(d) willfully uses, or endeavors to use, the contents of any wire or oral communication, knowing or having reason to know that the information was obtained through the interception of a wire or oral communication in violation of this subsection;

shall be fined not more than $10,000 or imprisoned not more than five years, or both.

(2) (a) It shall not be unlawful under this chapter for an operator of a switchboard, or an officer, employee, or agent or any communication common carrier, whose facilities are used in the transmission of a wire communication, to intercept, disclose, or use that communication in the normal course of his employment while engaged in any activity which is a necessary incident to the rendition of his service or to the protection of the rights or property of the carrier of such communication: *Provided*, That said communication common carriers shall not utilize service observing or random monitoring except for mechanical or service quality control checks.

(b) It shall not be unlawful under this chapter for an officer, employee, or agent of the Federal Communications Commission, in the normal course of his employment and in discharge of the monitoring responsibilities exercised by the Commission in the enforcement of chapter 5 of title 47 of the United States Code, to intercept a wire communication, or oral communication transmitted by radio, or to disclose or use the information thereby obtained.

(c) It shall not be unlawful under this chapter for a person acting under color of law to intercept a wire or oral communication, where such person is a party to the communication or one of the parties to the communication has given prior consent to such interception.

(d) It shall not be unlawful under this chapter for a person not acting under color of law to intercept a wire or oral communication where such person is a party to the communication or where one of the parties to the communication has given prior consent to such interception unless such communication is intercepted for the purpose of committing any criminal or tortious act in violation of the Constitution or laws of the United States or of any State or for the purpose of committing any other injurious act.

(3) Nothing contained in this chapter or in section 605 of the Communications Act of 1934 (48 Stat. 1143; 47 U.S.C. 605) shall limit the constitutional power of the President to take such measures as he deems necessary to protect the Nation against actual or potential attack or other hostile acts of a foreign power, to obtain foreign intelligence information deemed essential to the security of the United States, or to protect national security information against foreign intelligence activities. Nor shall anything contained in this chapter be deemed to limit the constitutional power of the President to take such measures as he deems necessary to protect the United States against the overthrow of the Government by force or other unlawful means, or against any other clear and present danger to the structure or existence of the Government. The contents of any wire or oral communication intercepted by authority of the President in the exercise of the foregoing powers may be received in evidence in any trial hearing, or other proceeding only where such interception was reasonable, and shall not be otherwise used or disclosed except as is necessary to implement that power.

SEC. 2515. PROHIBITION OF USE AS EVIDENCE OF INTERCEPTED WIRE OR ORAL COMMUNICATIONS.

Whenever any wire or oral communication has been intercepted, no part of the contents of such communication and no evidence derived therefrom may be received in evidence in any trial, hearing, or other proceeding in or before any court, grand jury, department, officer, agency, regulatory body, legislative committee, or other authority of the United States, a State, or a political subdivision thereof if the disclosure of that information would be in violation of this chapter.

SEC. 2516. AUTHORIZATION FOR INTERCEPTION OF WIRE OR ORAL COMMUNICATIONS.

(1) The Attorney General, or any Assistant Attorney General specially designated by the Attorney General, may authorize an application to a Federal judge of competent jurisdiction for, and such judge may grant in conformity with section 2518 of this chapter an order authorizing or approving the interception of wire or oral communications by the Federal Bureau of Investigation, or a Federal agency having responsibility for the investigation of the offense as to which the application is made, when such interception may provide or has provided evidence of—

(a) any offense punishable by death or by imprisonment for more than one year under sections 2274 through 2277 of title 42 of the United States Code (relating to the enforcement of the Atomic Energy Act of 1954), or under the following chapters of this title: chapter 37 (relating to espionage), chapter 105 (relating to sabotage), chapter 115 (relating to treason), or chapter 102 (relating to riots);

(b) a violation of section 186 or section 501 (c) of title 29, United States Code (dealing with restrictions on payments and loans to labor organizations), or any offense which involves murder, kidnapping, robbery, or extortion, and which is punishable under this title;

(c) any offense which is punishable under the following sections of this title: section 201 (bribery of public officials and witnesses), section 224 (bribery in sporting contests), section 1084 (transmission of wagering information), section 1503 (influencing or injuring an officer, juror, or witness generally), section 1510 (obstruction of criminal investigations), section 1751 (Presidential assassinations, kidnapping, and assault), section 1951 (interference with commerce by threats or violence), section 1952 (interstate and foreign travel or transportation in aid of racketeering enterprises), section 1954 (offer, acceptance, or solicitation to influence operations of employee benefit plan), section 659 (theft from interstate shipment), section 664 (embezzlement from pension and welfare funds), or sections 2314 and 2315 (interstate transportation of stolen property);

(d) any offense involving counterfeiting punishable under section 471, 472, or 473 of this title;

(e) any offense involving bankruptcy fraud or the manufacture, importation, receiving, concealment, buying, selling, or otherwise dealing in narcotic drugs, marihuana, or other dangerous drugs, punishable under any law of the United States;

(f) any offense including extortionate credit transactions under sections 892,893, or 894 of this title; or

(g) any conspiracy to commit any of the foregoing offenses.

(2) The principal prosecuting attorney of any State, or the principal prosecuting attorney of any political subdivision thereof, if such attorney is authorized by a statute of that State to make application to a State court judge of competent jurisdiction for an order authorizing or approving the interception of wire or oral communications, may apply to such judge for, and such judge may grant in conformity with section 2518 of this chapter and with the applicable State statute an order authorizing, or approving the interception of wire or oral communications by investigative or law enforcement officers having responsibility for the investigation of the offense as to which the application is made, when such interception may provide or has provided evidence of the commission of the offense of murder, kidnapping, gambling, robbery, bribery, extortion, or dealing in narcotic drugs, marihuana or other dangerous drugs, or other crime dangerous to life, limb, or property, and punishable by imprisonment for more than one year, designated in any applicable State statute authorizing such interception, or any conspiracy to commit any of the foregoing offenses.

SEC. 2517. AUTHORIZATION FOR DISCLOSURE AND USE OF INTERCEPTED WIRE OR ORAL COMMUNICATIONS.

(1) Any investigative or law enforcement officer who, by any means authorized by this chapter, has obtained knowledge of the contents of any wire or oral communication, or evidence derived therefrom, may disclose such contents to another investigative or law enforcement officer to the extent that such disclosure is appropriate to the proper performance of the official duties of the officer making or receiving the disclosure.

(2) Any investigative or law enforcement officer who, by any means authorized by this chapter, has obtained knowledge of the contents of any wire or oral communication or evidence derived therefrom may use such contents to the extent such use is appropriate to the proper performance of his official duties.

(3) Any person who has received, by any means authorized by this chapter, any information concerning a wire or oral communication, or evidence derived therefrom intercepted in accordance with the provisions of this chapter may disclose the contents of that communication or such derivative evidence while giving testimony under oath or affirmation in any criminal proceeding in any court of the United States or of any State or in any Federal or State grand jury proceeding.

(4) No otherwise privileged wire or oral communication intercepted in accordance with, or in violation of, the provisions of this chapter shall lose its privileged character.

(5) When an investigative or law enforcement officer, while engaged in intercepting wire or oral communications in the manner authorized herein, intercepts wire or oral communications relating to offenses other than those specified in the order of authorization or approval, the contents thereof, and evidence derived therefrom, may be disclosed or used as provided in subsections (1) and (2) of this section. Such contents and any evidence derived therefrom may be used under subsection (3) of this section when authorized or approved by a judge of competent jurisdiction where such judge finds on subsequent application that the contents were otherwise intercepted in accordance with the provisions of this chapter. Such application shall be made as soon as practicable.

SEC. 2518. PROCEDURE FOR INTERCEPTION OF WIRE OR ORAL COMMUNICATIONS.

(1) Each application for an order authorizing or approving the interception of a wire or oral communication shall be made in writing upon oath or affirmation to a judge of competent jurisdiction and shall state the applicant's authority to make such application. Each application shall include the following information:

(a) the identity of the investigative or law enforcement officer making the application, and the officer authorizing the application;

(b) a full and complete statement of the facts and circumstances relied upon by the applicant, to justify his belief that an order should be issued, including (i) details as to the particular offense that has been, is being, or is about to be committed, (ii) a particular description of the nature and location of the facilities from which or the place where the communication is to be intercepted, (iii) a particular description of the type of communications sought to be intercepted, (iv) the identity of the person, if known, committing the offense and whose communications are to be intercepted;

(c) a full and complete statement as to whether or not other investigative procedures have been tried and failed or why they reasonably appear to be unlikely to succeed if tried or to be too dangerous;

(d) a statement of the period of time for which the interception is required to be maintained. If the nature of the investigation is such that the authorization for interception should not automatically terminate when the described type of communication has been first obtained, a particular description of facts establishing probable

## Legal Aspects of Surveillance

cause to believe that additional communications of the same type will occur thereafter;

(e) a full and complete statement of the facts concerning all previous applications known to the individual authorizing and making the application, made to any judge for authorization to intercept, or for approval of interceptions of, wire or oral communications involving any of the same persons, facilities or places specified in the application, and the action taken by the judge on each such application; and

(f) where the application is for the extension of an order, a statement setting forth the results thus far obtained from the interception, or a reasonable explanation of the failure to obtain such results.

(2) The judge may require the applicant to furnish additional testimony or documentary evidence in support of the application.

(3) Upon such application the judge may enter an ex parte order, as requested or as modified, authorizing or approving interception of wire or oral communications within the territorial jurisdiction of the court in which the judge is sitting, if the judge determines on the basis of the facts submitted by the applicant that—

(a) there is probable cause for belief that an individual is committing, has committed, or is about to commit a particular offense enumerated in section 2516 of this chapter;

(b) there is probable cause for belief that particular communications concerning that offense will be obtained through such interception;

(c) normal investigative procedures have been tried and have failed or reasonably appear to be unlikely to succeed if tried or to be too dangerous;

(d) there is probable cause for belief that the facilities from which, or the place where, the wire or oral communications are to be intercepted are being used, or are about to be used, in connection with the commission of such offense, or are leased to, listed in the name of, or commonly used by such person.

(4) Each order authorizing or approving the interception of any wire or oral communication shall specify—

(a) the identity of the person, if known, whose communications are to be intercepted;

(b) the nature and location of the communications facilities as to which, or the place where, authority to intercept is granted;

(c) a particular description of the type of communication sought to be intercepted, and a statement of the particular offense to which it relates;

(d) the identity of the agency authorized to intercept the communications, and of the person authorizing the application; and

(e) the period of time during which such interception is authorized, including a statement as to whether or not the interception shall automatically terminate when the described communication has been first obtained.

(5) No order entered under this section may authorize or approve the interception of any wire or oral communication for any period longer than is necessary to achieve the objective of the authorization, nor in any event longer than thirty days. Extensions of an order may be granted, but only upon application for an extension made in accordance with subsection (1) of this section and the court making the findings required by subsection (3) of this section. The period of extension shall be no longer than the authorizing judge deems necessary to achieve the purposes for which it was granted and in no event for longer than thirty days. Every order and extension thereof shall contain a provision that the authorization to intercept shall be executed as soon as practicable, shall be conducted in such a way as to minimize the interception of communications not otherwise subject to interception under this chapter, and must terminate upon attainment of the authorized objective, or in any event in thirty days.

(6) Whenever an order authorizing interception is entered pursuant to this chapter, the order may require reports to be made to the judge who issued the order showing what progress has been made toward achievement of the authorized objective and the need for continued interception. Such reports shall be made at such intervals as the judge may require.

(7) Notwithstanding any other provision of this chapter, any investigative or law enforcement officer, specially designated by the Attorney General or by the principal prosecuting attorney of any State or subdivision thereof acting pursuant to a statute of that State, who reasonably determines that—

(a) an emergency situation exists with respect to conspiratorial activities threatening the national security interest or to conspiratorial activities characteristic of organized crime that requires a wire or oral communication to be intercepted before an order authorizing such interception can with due diligence be obtained, and

(b) there are grounds upon which an order could be entered under this chapter to authorize such interception,

may intercept such wire or oral communication if an application for an order approving the interception is made in accordance with this section within forty-eight hours after the interception has occurred, or begins to occur. In the absence of an order, such interception shall immediately terminate when the communication sought is obtained or when the application for the order is denied, whichever is earlier. In the event such application for approval is denied, or in any other case where the interception is terminated without an order having been issued, the contents of any wire or oral communication intercepted shall be treated as having been obtained in violation of this chapter, and an inventory shall be served as provided for in subsection (d) of this section on the person named in the application.

(8) (a) The contents of any wire or oral communication intercepted by any means authorized by this chapter shall, if possible, be recorded on tape or wire or other comparable device. The recording of the contents of any wire or oral communication under this subsection shall be done in such way as will protect the recording from editing or other alterations. Immediately upon the expiration of the period of the order, or extensions thereof, such recordings shall be made available to the judge issuing such order and sealed under his directions. Custody of the recordings shall be wherever the judge orders. They shall not be destroyed except upon an order of the issuing or denying judge and in any event shall be kept for ten years. Duplicate recordings may be made for use or disclosure pursuant to the provisions of subsections (1) and (2) of section 2517 of this chapter for investigations. The presence of the seal provided for by this subsection, or a satisfactory explanation for the absence thereof, shall be a prerequisite for the use or disclosure of the contents of any wire or oral communication or evidence derived therefrom under subsection (3) of section 2517.

(b) Applications made and orders granted under this chapter shall be sealed by the judge. Custody of the applications and orders shall be wherever the judge directs. Such applications and orders shall be disclosed only upon a showing of good cause before a judge of competent jurisdiction and shall not be destroyed except on order of the issuing or denying judge, and in any event shall be kept for ten years.

(c) Any violation of the provisions of this subsection may be punished as contempt of the issuing or denying judge.

(d) Within a reasonable time but not later than ninety days after the filing of an application for an order of approval under section 2518(7)(b) which is denied or the termination of the period of an order or extensions thereof, the issuing or denying judge shall cause to be served, on the persons named in the order or the application, and such other parties to intercepted communications as the judge may determine in his discretion that is in the interest of justice, an inventory which shall include notice of—

(1) the fact of the entry of the order or the application;

(2) the date of the entry and the period of authorized, approved or disapproved interception, or the denial of the application; and

(3) the fact that during the period wire or oral communications were or were not intercepted.

The judge, upon the filing of a motion, may in his discretion make available to such person or his counsel for inspection such portions of the intercepted communications, applications and orders as the judge determines to be in the interest of justice. On an ex parte showing of good cause to a judge of competent jurisdiction the serving of the inventory required by this subsection may be postponed.

(9) The contents of any intercepted wire or oral communication or evidence derived therefrom shall not be received in evidence or otherwise disclosed in any trial hearing, or other proceeding in a Federal or State court unless each party, not less than ten days before the trial, hearing, or proceeding, has been furnished with a copy of the court order, and accompanying application, under which the interception was authorized or approved. This ten-day period may be waived by the judge if he finds that it was not possible to furnish the party with the above information ten days before the trial, hearing, or proceeding and that the party will not be prejudiced by the delay in receiving such information.

(10) (a) Any aggrieved person in any trial, hearing, or proceeding in or before any court, department, officer, agency, regulatory body, or other authority of the United States, a State, or a political subdivision thereof, may move to suppress the contents of any intercepted wire or oral communication, or evidence derived therefrom, on the grounds that—

(i) the communication was unlawfully intercepted;

(ii) the order of authorization or approval under which it was intercepted is insufficient on its face; or

(iii) the interception was not made in conformity with the order of authorization or approval.

Such motion shall be made before the trial, hearing, or proceeding unless there was no opportunity to make such motion or the person was not aware of the grounds of the motion. If the motion is granted, the contents of the intercepted wire or oral communication, or evidence derived therefrom, shall be treated as having been obtained in violation of this chapter. The judge, upon the filing of such motion by the aggrieved person, may in his discretion make available to the aggrieved person or his counsel for inspection such portions of the intercepted communication or evidence derived therefrom as the judge determines to be in the interests of justice.

(b) In addition to any other right to appeal, the United States shall have the right to appeal from an order granting a motion to suppress made under paragraph (a) of this subsection, or the denial of an application for an order of approval, if the United States attorney shall certify to the judge or other official granting such motion or denying such application that the appeal is not taken for purposes of delay. Such appeal shall be taken within thirty days after the date the order was entered and shall be diligently prosecuted.

SEC. 2519. REPORTS CONCERNING INTERCEPTED WIRE OR ORAL COMMUNICATIONS.

(1) Within thirty days after the expiration of an order (or each extension thereof) entered under section 2518, or the denial of an order approving an interception, the issuing or denying judge shall report to the Administrative Office of the United States Courts—

(a) the fact that an order or extension was applied for;

(b) the kind of order or extension applied for;

(c) the fact that the order or extension was granted as applied for, was modified, or was denied;

(d) the period of interceptions authorized by the order, and the number and duration of any extensions of the order;

(e) the offense specified in the order or application, or extension of an order;

(f) the identity of the applying investigative or law enforcement officer and the agency making the application and the person authorizing the application; and

(g) the nature of the facilities from which or the place where communications were to be intercepted.

(2) In January of each year the Attorney General, an Assistant Attorney General specially designated by the Attorney General, or the principal prosecuting attorney of a State, or the principal prosecuting attorney for any political subdivision of a State, shall report to the Administrative Office of the United States Courts—

(a) the information required by paragraphs (a) through (g) of subsection (1) of this section with respect to each application for an order or extension made during the preceding calendar year;

(b) a general description of the interceptions made under such order or extension, including (i) the approximate nature and frequency of incriminating communications intercepted, (ii) the approximate nature and frequency of other communications intercepted, (iii) the approximate number of persons whose communications were intercepted, and (iv) the approximate nature, amount, and cost of the manpower and other resources used in the interceptions;

(c) the number of arrests resulting from interceptions made under such order or extension, and the offenses for which arrests were made;

(d) the number of trials resulting from such interceptions;

(e) the number of motions to suppress made with respect to such interceptions, and the number granted or denied;

(f) the number of convictions resulting from such interceptions and the offenses for which the convictions were obtained and a general assessment of the importance of the interceptions; and

(g) the information required by paragraphs (b) through (f) of this subsection with respect to orders or extensions obtained in a preceding calendar year.

(3) In April of each year the Director of the Administrative Office of the United States Courts shall transmit to the Congress a full and complete report concerning the number of applications for orders authorizing or approving the interception of wire or oral communications and the number of orders and extensions granted or denied during the preceding calendar year. Such report shall include a summary and analysis of the data required to be filed with the Administrative Office by subsections (1) and (2) of this section. The Director of the Administrative Office of the United States Courts is authorized to issue binding regulations dealing with the content and form of the reports required to be filed by subsections (1) and (2) of this section.

SEC. 2520. RECOVERY OF CIVIL DAMAGES AUTHORIZED.

Any person whose wire or oral communication is intercepted, disclosed, or used in violation of this chapter shall (1) have a civil cause of action against any person who intercepts, discloses, or uses, or procures any other person to intercept, disclose, or use such communications, and (2) be entitled to recover from any such person—

(a) actual damages but not less than liquidated damages computed at the rate of $100 a day for each day of violation or $1,000, whichever is higher;

(b) punitive damages; and

(c) a reasonable attorney's fee and other litigation costs reasonably incurred.

A good faith reliance on a court order or on the provisions of section 2518 (7) of this chapter shall constitute a complete defense to any civil or criminal action brought under this chapter.

# Index

A-B-C, foot surveillance technique, 19-27
Adaptability, quality of surveillant, 5
Affidavit, for photo processing, 247-248
AGA 750, infrared camera, 216, 218-220
Air turbulence (heat waves), 168
Aircraft, for surveillance of vehicles, 117, 120
Attitude, quality of surveillant, 4
Automobile surveillance, 31-75
  binoculars for, 64-65
  blind spots, 36-38
  bumper beepers, 66-75
  cut-out switches, 35-36
  detecting and eluding a tail, 45, 57-60
  disguises, 33, 91
  field of vision, drivers, 37-38
  general considerations, 31-32
  miscellaneous techniques, 42-56
  parallel surveillance, 38-39, 41, 43
  preparing for, 32-34
  progressive surveillance, 40, 43
  reestablishing contact in a broken surveillance, 60-64
  tailing at night without lights, 45
  techniques generally, 34-65
Background information, on subject, 12-14
Belt pod, for camera and lens support, 186, 188
Binoculars
  aircraft surveillance, 120
  alignment of, 146-150
  binoculars versus field glasses, 139
  brightness index, 154-155
  exit pupil diameter, 143-145
  field of view, 141-142
  for low light level work, 154-157
  high powered, large aperture, 156-157
  individual eyepiece focusing versus center focusing, 145-146
  magnifying power, 139-141
  objective lens diameter, 142-143
  proper use of, 150-154
  retractable eyecups, 152
  use by patrol officers, 92
Blackout lights, 100, 112-115
Blind spots
  optic disc, 133
  vehicle driver's, 36-38
Blinds
  for rural areas, 96
  for surveillance trucks, 80
Bloodhound, Wackenhut surveillance system, 71-72
Bumper beeper, 66-75
  bloodhound, 71-72
  null zone, 70-71
  parasitic beepers, 68-69
  reflected radio signals of beeper, 72-73
  triangulation, pinpointing target vehicle, 72-74
"C" mount adapter, 210, 212
Camouflaging techniques, 109-111
Campers, for stationary surveillance, 79
Catadioptric lenses, telescopes, 160-161
Celestron, 192, 196, 198
Closed circuit television, 210-214
Courtesy light, disconnect, 88
Cut-out switches, 35-36, 115
  for courtesy light, 88
Descriptions, of people and vehicles, 224
Detection, of surveillance, 27-29, 57-60
Disguises, 33, 91-92
Driving skill, qualities of surveillant, 8
Driving without lights at night
  patrol officers, 90, 92
  rural surveillance at night, 115-116
Edmund Scientific Company, 170
Energy Conservation Consultants, Inc., 219-220

Entrapment, defense of, 128, 250
Evasion, of surveillant, 27-30, 57-60
Exclusionary rule, of evidence, 229
Eyesight, good vision, 7
Fictitious names, use of, 126-127
Field of vision, 37-38, 134-135
Fixed surveillance, see stationary surveillance
FJW Industries, 170-171
Foot surveillance, 15-30
  general considerations, 15-16
  general techniques, 16-19
  multiple man techniques, 19-27
  tactics for detection and evasion, 27-30
Fovea, of eye, 129-131
Foxholes, for concealment in rural areas, 111
Glass, one-way, 79-80
Good judgment, quality of surveillant, 6
Gun stock mount, for telephoto lens, 185
Hearing, good hearing, 7
Heat waves (air turbulence), 168
High speed film, for night photography, 200, 202-203
Honeywell Pentax, 207-208
Infrared photography, 205-208
Infrared viewers, 169-172
Legal aspects of surveillance, 229-264
  body transmitters and tape recorders, 243-246
  bumper beepers, use of, 243
  Coppola v. Minnesota, 231, 236
  electronic surveillance, 251-264
  entrapment, 128, 250-251
  exclusionary rule, 229
  Fourth Amendment, 229
  Fullbright v. U.S., 233
  Hester v. U.S., 235
  Katz v. U.S., 236
  Lopez v. U.S., 244
  poisoned tree doctrine, 234
  surveillance photographs, 246-250
  union activities, reporting of, 251
  U.S. v. Kim, 238
  U.S. v. Minton, 232
Lenzar Optics Corporation, 116-119, 176-178

Light intensifiers
  night vision, 169, 172-178
  photography, 208-210
Memory, quality of surveillant, 4-5
Mini-pod, for telescope support, 163-164
Mono-pod, for lens support, 186
Multiple man, surveillance technique, 19-27
Nicnon, camera-binocular, 180-181
Nikon, 190, 192
Nocta, infrared camera, 207-208
Novatron, binoculars, 156-157
Null zone, of bumper beeper, 70-71
Nyctalopia, 132
Observation posts, 77-82
Observation, powers of, 4
One-way glass, 79-80
Optic disc (blind spot), 133
Optical aids, for vision extension, 136-178
  binoculars, 137-159. *See also* Binoculars.
  infrared viewers, 169-172
  light intensifiers, 169, 172-178
  telescopes, 158-169. *See also* Telescopes.
Parallel surveillance, 38-39, 41, 43, 90
Parasitic beepers, 68-69
Patience, quality of surveillant, 5
Periscope, for night driving, 116-119
Perseverance, quality of surveillant, 5
Photo security systems, 212
Photography, for surveillance, 179-222
  camera types, 179-181
  CCTV, 210-214
  during labor disturbance, 220-222
  general considerations, 179
  high speed film at night, 200, 202-203
  infrared, 205-208
  light intensification equipment, 208-210
  passive photographic surveillance systems, 214-217
  push-processing film, 203-205
  telephotography, 181-200
  thermovision, infrared, 216, 218-220
Physical condition, quality of surveillant, 7

Powers of observation, quality of surveilant, 4
Preliminary survey, 10-11, 76
Preparing for surveillance, 9-14
  background information on subject, 12-14
  general considerations, 9-10
  preliminary survey, 10-11
  subject identification, 12-14
  when to conduct the surveillance, 11-12
Prismatic telescopes (spotting scopes), 162
Progressive surveillance, 40, 43
Push-processing film (force-processing), 203-205
Qualities of a surveillant, 3-8
  attitude, 4
  average physical size, 7
  competent police officer or investigator, 3-4
  driving skill, 8
  good eyesight, 7
  good hearing, 7
  good judgment, 6
  good physical condition, 7
  patience and perseverance, 5
  personal qualities, 3-6
  physical qualities, 7-8
  powers of observation, 4
  report writing ability, 6
  resourcefulness and adaptability, 5
  self-confidence, 6
  verbal communication, 6-7
Questar, 190, 193-195
Report writing, 6, 223-228
  descriptions of persons & vehicles, 224
  general considerations, 223-224
  surveillance reports, 224-226
  undercover reports, 226-228
Resourcefulness, quality of surveillant, 5
Roping, interview technique, 121-122
Rural surveillance, 93-120
  aircraft for vehicle surveillance, 117, 120
  blackout light, 100, 112-115
  blinds for cover, 96
  camouflaging techniques, 109-111
  cut-out switches for night surveillance, 115
  driving without lights at night, 115-116
  foxholes, for concealment, 111
  general considerations, 93
  moving into the area, 98-109
  periscope for night driving, 116-119
  preliminary survey, 93-94
  skin toning, for camouflaging, 110
  vantage points, 94-98
Self-confidence, quality of surveillant, 6
Skin toning, for camouflaging, 110
Sly-Fox Films, Inc., 247-248
Smith and Wesson, 176, 209
Sneak light. *See* blackout light
Snooperscope, 169-172
Social Security, when using alias, 126-127
Spotting scopes (prismatic telescopes), 162
Stake-out. *See* Stationary surveillance
Stationary surveillance, 76-82
  automobiles, from, 78
  general considerations, 76-77
  observation posts, 77-82
  preliminary survey, 76
  roof tops, from, 81
  rooms in neighboring buildings, 80-81
  uniformed patrol officers, 83-90
  vans and campers, 79-80
Subject identification, 12-14
Sub-rosa, type of undercover work, 122
Sunglasses, for eye protection, 133
Switches, cut-out, 35-36
Telescopes, 158-169
  field use of, 163-169
  general considerations, 158-159
  magnifying power, 161
  types, 159-162
Thermovision, 216, 218-220
Toning, for camouflaging, 110
Triangulation, locating vehicle with beepers, 72-74
Trucks, for surveillance, 79-80
Undercover surveillance, 121-128
  act the part, 123
  entrapment, 128, 250

fictitious names and Social Security, 126-127
industrial and commercial operations, 124-127
initial contact, 122-123
roping, 121
sub-rosa, 122
Undercover techniques, 121-128
stationary surveillance, 82
uniformed patrol officers, 91-92
Uniformed officers
moving techniques, 90, 92
stationary techniques, 83-90
surveillance by, 83-92
undercover techniques, 91-92
Vans for stationary surveillance, 79
Vantage points
rural surveillance, 94-98
stationary surveillance, 77-82

Verbal communication, quality of surveillant, 6
Video systems, 210-214
Vision
blind spot (optic disc), 133
cross section of eye, 131
day and night vision, 129, 131-133
facts about, 129-135
field of, 37-38, 134-135
fovea, 129-131
nyctalopia, 132
sunglasses for eye protection, 133
visual purple, for night vision, 132
Visual Purple, for night vision, 132
Vivitar, mirror lens, 182, 191
Wackenhut Security Systems, bloodhound, 71-72
Walcam Enterprises, 181, 197
Window mounts, 164, 167, 187